ADOBE® PHOTOSHOP® ELEMENTS 8

CLASSROOM IN A BOOK®

The official training workbook from Adobe Systems

www.adobepress.com

Adobe

Adobe Press books are published by Peachpit, a division of Pearson Education located in Berkeley, California. For the latest on Adobe Press books, go to www.adobepress.com. To report errors, please send a note to errata@peachpit.com. For information on getting permission for reprints and excerpts, contact permissions@peachpit.com.

Printed and bound in the United States of America

ISBN-13:   978-0-321-66032-9
ISBN-10:   0-321-66032-3

9 8 7 6 5 4 3 2 1

WHAT'S ON THE DISC

Here is an overview of the contents of the Classroom in a Book disc

Lesson files ... and so much more

The *Adobe Photoshop Elements 8 Classroom in a Book* disc includes the lesson files that you'll need to complete the exercises in this book, as well as other content to help you learn more about Adobe Photoshop Elements 8 and use it with greater efficiency and ease. The diagram below represents the contents of the disc, which should help you locate the files you need.

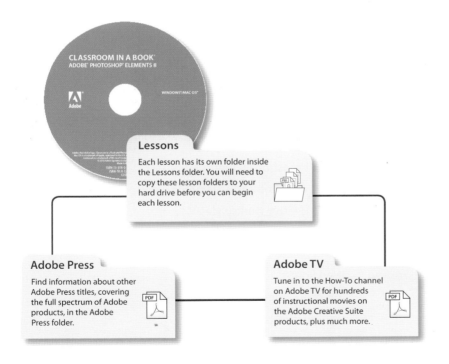

Lessons

Each lesson has its own folder inside the Lessons folder. You will need to copy these lesson folders to your hard drive before you can begin each lesson.

Adobe Press

Find information about other Adobe Press titles, covering the full spectrum of Adobe products, in the Adobe Press folder.

Adobe TV

Tune in to the How-To channel on Adobe TV for hundreds of instructional movies on the Adobe Creative Suite products, plus much more.

CONTENTS

GETTING STARTED

Adobe® Photoshop® Elements 8 delivers image-editing tools that balance power and versatility with ease of use. Whether you're a home user or hobbyist, a professional photographer or a business user, Photoshop Elements 8 makes it easy to produce good-looking pictures, share your stories in sophisticated creations for both print and web, and manage and safeguard your precious photos.

If you've used an earlier version of Photoshop Elements, you'll find that this Classroom in a Book® will teach you advanced skills and covers the many new innovative features that Adobe Systems introduces in this version. If you're new to Adobe Photoshop Elements, you'll learn the fundamental concepts and techniques that will help you master the application.

About Classroom in a Book

Adobe Photoshop Elements 8 Classroom in a Book is part of the official training series for Adobe graphics and publishing software developed by Adobe product experts. Each lesson in this book is made up of a series of self-paced projects that will give you hands-on experience using Photoshop Elements 8.

The *Adobe Photoshop Elements 8 Classroom in a Book* includes a CD attached to the inside back cover. On the CD you'll find all the image files used for the lessons in this book, together with additional learning resources.

Prerequisites

Before you begin the lessons in this book, make sure that you and your computer are ready.

Requirements on your computer

You'll need about 700 MB of free space on your hard disk—around 150 MB for the lesson files and up to 550 MB for the work files that you'll create as you work through the exercises.

Required skills

● **Note:** In this book, the forward slash character (/) is used to separate equivalent terms and commands for Windows / Mac OS, in the order shown here.

The lessons in this book assume that you have a working knowledge of your computer and its operating system. Make sure that you know how to use the mouse and the standard menus and commands, and also how to open, save, and close files. Can you scroll (vertically and horizontally) within a window to see content that may not be visible in the displayed area? Do you know how to use context menus, which open when you right-click (Windows) / Control-click (Mac OS) items? If you need to review these basic and generic computer skills, see the documentation included with your Microsoft® Windows® or Apple® Mac® OS X software.

Installing Adobe Photoshop Elements 8

You must purchase the Adobe Photoshop Elements 8 software separately and install it on a computer running Windows Vista®, Windows® XP, or Mac® OS X. For system requirements and complete instructions on installing the software, see the Photoshop Elements 8 Read Me file on the application disc and the accompanying documentation.

Copying the Classroom in a Book files

● **Note:** The files on the CD are practice files, provided for your personal use in these lessons. You are not authorized to use these files commercially, or to publish or distribute them in any form without written permission from Adobe Systems, Inc. and the individual photographers who took the pictures, or other copyright holders.

The CD attached to the inside back cover of this book includes a Lessons folder containing all the digital files you'll need for the lessons. As you work through the exercises, learning to organize and manage these files is an essential part of many of the projects in this book. Keep the lesson files on your computer until you have completed all the exercises.

Copying the Lessons files from the CD

1   Create a new folder named **PSE8CIB** inside the *username/My Documents* (Windows) or *username/Documents* (Mac OS) folder on your computer.

2   Insert the *Adobe Photoshop Elements 8 Classroom in a Book* CD into your CD-ROM drive. For Windows users: if a message appears asking what you want Windows to do, choose Open Folder To View Files Using Windows Explorer, and then click OK. If no message appears, open My Computer and double-click the CD icon to open it.

3   Locate the Lessons folder on the CD and copy it to the PSE8CIB folder you've just created on your computer.

4   When your computer has finished copying the Lessons folder, remove the CD from your CD-ROM drive and put it away.

Complete the procedures on the following pages before you begin the lessons.

Creating a work folder

Now you need to create a folder for the work files you'll produce as you work through the lessons in this book.

1   In Windows Explorer (Windows) / the Finder (Mac OS) open the Lessons folder that you copied to your new PSE8CIB folder on your hard disk.

2   Choose File > New > Folder (Windows) / File > New Folder (Mac OS). A new folder is created inside the Lessons folder. Type **My CIB Work** as the name for the new folder.

The remainder of this chapter concerns only those using Photoshop Elements on Windows. **Mac OS users can skip ahead to the notes in "Additional resources" on page 7, and then go on to Lesson 3, "Basic Organizing on Mac OS."**

● **Note:** In this book, the forward arrow character (>) is used to denote submenus and commands found in the menu bar at the top of the workspace or in context menus; for example, Menu > Submenu > Command. The forward slash character (/) is used to separate equivalent terms and commands for Windows / Mac OS, in the order shown here.

Creating a catalog file

The first time you launch Photoshop Elements it automatically creates a catalog file on your hard disk. This catalog file is used to store information about the images that you bring into the application from your digital camera or your hard disk.

You'll now create a new catalog to manage the image files that you'll use for the lessons in this book. This will allow you to leave the default catalog untouched while you're working through the lessons, and help you to keep your lesson files grouped together so that they'll be easily accessible.

1   Start Adobe Photoshop Elements 8. Click the Organize button in the Welcome screen to launch the Photoshop Elements Organizer module.

WELCOME TO
ADOBE® PHOTOSHOP® ELEMENTS 8

ORGANIZE

EDIT

Create an Adobe ID to register your software and enable your backup and sharing services.

Create Adobe ID

Already have an Adobe ID? Sign in below.   Learn more

Sign In With Your Adobe ID :
Adobe ID
Password
Sign in

Don't have an Adobe ID ?
Create New Adobe ID   Learn More...
Adobe Privacy Policy...

Benefits of an Adobe ID...
Help and Support...

● **Note:** If this is the first time you have started the Organizer, an alert message may appear asking if you would like to specify the location of photos. If this alert message appears, click No. Don't be concerned about the prompt to create an Adobe ID; this topic is covered in Lesson 1.

2   When the Organizer has opened, choose File > Catalog.

3 In the Catalog Manager dialog box, click New. Don't change the location setting, which specifies where the Catalog file is stored.

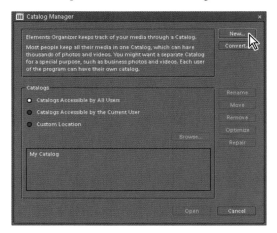

4 In the Enter A Name For The New Catalog dialog box, type **CIB Catalog** as the name for your new catalog. Disable Import Free Music Into This Catalog, and then click OK.

5 In the Organizer, choose File > Get Photos And Videos > From Files And Folders. In the Get Photos From Files And Folders dialog box, click My Documents to open the My Documents folder. Double-click the PSE8CIB folder to open it; then click once to select the Lessons folder that you copied from the CD. Don't double-click—you don't want to open the Lessons folder.

6 In the Get Photos From Files And Folders dialog box, confirm that the Get Photos From Subfolders option is activated in the list of options above the Get Media button. Disable the options Automatically Fix Red Eyes and Automatically Suggest Photo Stacks. You'll learn about these useful options as you work through the lessons, but you won't use them just yet.

7 Click the Get Media button. The Getting Media window opens showing the files being imported.

8 The Import Attached Keyword Tags dialog box opens. Click Select All below the left side of the Keyword Tags box, and then click OK.

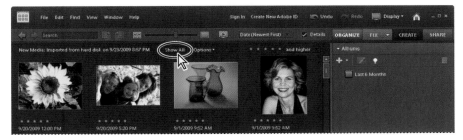

The images you are adding to your catalog contain information known as keyword tags, which have been applied to help you organize the images as you work through the lessons in this book. Once the image files have been imported, these keyword tags will be listed in the Keyword Tags panel. You'll learn about using keyword tags in Lessons 2 and 4.

9 A dialog box appears to inform you that the only items displayed in the Organizer are those you just imported. Click OK to dismiss this alert.

10 Click OK to close any other alert dialog box. The imported images are displayed in the Media Browser in the main display area. Use the scrollbar at the right side to browse through the images.

11 Click the Show All button above the thumbnail images in the Media Browser.

Reconnecting missing files to a catalog

● **Note:** To avoid the problem of missing files in your catalog, use the File > Move, File > Rename, and Edit > Delete From Catalog commands to move, rename, or delete files in Photoshop Elements, rather than doing so outside the application.

When you bring a photo or video clip into Photoshop Elements, the name and location of the file is recorded in the catalog. If you move, rename, or delete a file outside Photoshop Elements after it has been added the catalog, Photoshop Elements may no longer be able to find it. If a file cannot be located, the missing file icon (?) appears in the upper left corner of its thumbnail in the Photo Browser to alert you that the link between the file and your catalog has been broken.

If there are no files missing, you can now go on to the first lesson.

If Photoshop Elements alerts you that it cannot find an image file, you will need to carry out the following procedure to reconnect the file to your catalog.

1   Choose File > Reconnect > All Missing Files. If the message "There are no files to reconnect" appears, click OK, then skip the rest of this procedure.

2   If a message "Searching for missing files" appears, click the Browse button. The Reconnect Missing Files dialog box opens.

3   In the Browse tab on the right side of the Reconnect Missing Files dialog box, navigate to and open the moved folder.

4   Continuing to work in the Browse tab, locate and click once to select the folder that has the same name as the folder listed underneath the image thumbnail. The folder name is listed on the left side of the Reconnect Missing Files dialog box, directly under the image thumbnail.

5   After you select the appropriate folder and the correct thumbnail picture appears in the right side of the dialog box, click the Reconnect button.

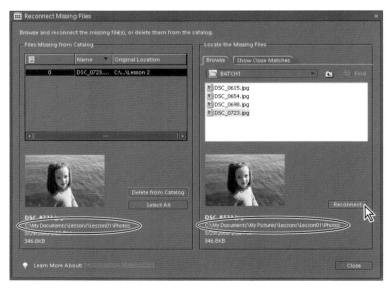

6 Repeat steps 4 and 5, continuing to select the appropriate folders and clicking the Reconnect button as you find matching files. When all the files are reconnected, click the Close button.

You can now use the Photoshop Elements Organizer to select and open files in the Photoshop Elements Editor.

● **Note:** This procedure also eliminates error messages regarding missing files when you're creating Photo Projects, or printing from the Organizer.

Additional resources

Adobe Photoshop Elements 8 Classroom in a Book is not intended to replace the documentation that comes with the program, nor is it designed to be a comprehensive reference for every feature in Photoshop Elements 8. For additional information about program features, refer to any of these resources:

- Photoshop Elements Help, which is built into the Adobe Photoshop Elements 8 application. You can view it by choosing Help > Photoshop Elements Help. If you're connected to the Internet you will be directed to the Photoshop Elements Help and Support Center, your hub for community-based instruction, inspiration, and support that combines the product Support pages, Design Center and Help Resource Center. If you're not connected to the Internet, you'll access a subset of Help that is installed with your software. For regular updates, it's best to connect to the Web for Help.

- Adobe TV, where you'll find programming on Adobe products, including a How To channel. New Movies are added regularly, so be sure to check back if you don't find what you're looking for on your first visit to http://tv.adobe.com/.

1 PHOTOSHOP ELEMENTS FOR WINDOWS - A QUICK TOUR

Lesson Overview

This chapter provides an overview of Photoshop Elements 8 for Windows. For a quick tour of the Photoshop Elements workspace on Mac OS, please go on to chapter 3, "Basic Organizing on Mac OS."

This lesson will familiarize you with the Adobe Photoshop Elements 8 workspace and provide you with an overview of the tools and procedures you'll use to capture and edit your digital images.

As you work through the exercises in this lesson you'll be introduced to the following basic skills and concepts:

- Working with the Organizer and the Editor
- Creating and loading Catalogs
- Attaching media
- Using the Photo Downloader
- Reviewing and comparing photos
- Sending photos in e-mail
- Using Photoshop Elements Help

 You'll probably need between one and two hours to complete this lesson.

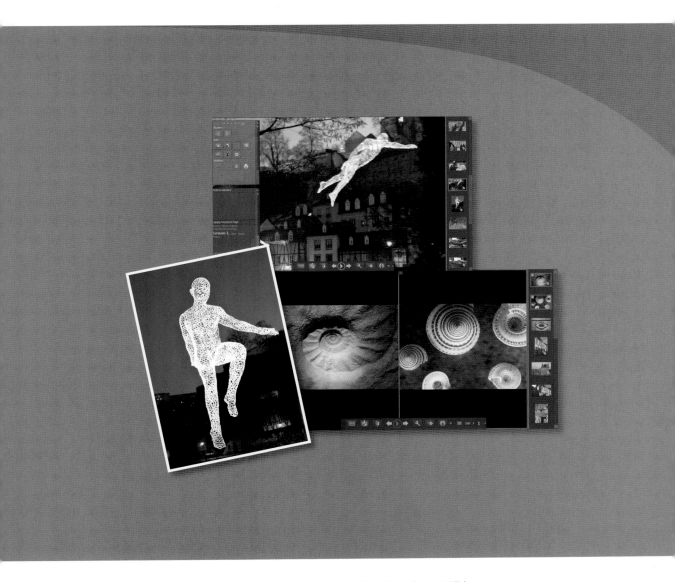

Welcome to Adobe Photoshop Elements! Take a quick tour and get to know the Photoshop Elements workspace. You'll find all the power and versatility you'd expect from a Photoshop application in an easy-to-use, modular interface that will help you take your digital photography to a new level.

How Photoshop Elements works

● **Note:** This chapter provides an overview of Photoshop Elements 8 for Windows.
For a quick tour of the Photoshop Elements workspace on Mac OS, see chapter 3, "Basic Organizing on Mac OS."

Photoshop Elements has two primary workspaces: the Elements Organizer and the Editor. You'll use the Organizer to locate, import, manage, and share your photos and media files, and the Editor for editing and adjusting your images and for creating presentations to showcase them.

About the Photoshop Elements workspaces

Once you've imported a photo and selected it in the Organizer, you can open it in the Editor by clicking the white triangle on the orange Fix tab above the Task Pane at the right, and then choosing one of the Editor's three editing modes.

While you're working in the Editor, you can open the Organizer by clicking the Organizer button (▦) located near the top right corner of the Editor workspace.

Once both the Organizer and the Editor windows are open, you can also move quickly between the two workspaces by clicking on the corresponding buttons in the Windows task bar at the bottom of your screen.

The Organizer workspace

In the Organizer workspace, the main work area is the Media Browser pane where you can find, sort, and organize your photos and media files and preview the presentations you've created to showcase and share them. At the right of the Organizer window is the Task Pane, with tabs for the Organize, Fix, Create, and Share modes.

● **Note:** The Elements Organizer is an integral part of both Adobe Photoshop Elements and Adobe Premiere Elements video editing software. You can import, manage, and view both your photos and video clips in Elements Organizer, which serves as a hub, allowing seamless integration of the two editing applications.

The Media Browser pane can display a single photo or media file or show thumbnails of all the files in your catalog arranged in a variety of ways. Display your files sorted by import batch, folder location, or keywords—or if you prefer viewing your photos and media files by date, the Organizer includes a Date View workspace that lets you work with your files arranged in a calendar format.

The Media Browser makes it easy to browse through all the photos and assets in your catalog in one comprehensive window. It can even show previews of files that you keep stored remotely—on a CD-ROM or other removable media.

On the Organize tab of the Task Pane are the control panels you'll use to sort, search and manage your photos by applying keyword tags and grouping them in albums. The Fix panel offers tools for the most common photo editing tasks, such as color correction and red eye removal. (For more complex editing tasks, you'll switch to one of the Editor's three editing modes.) On the Create tab you'll find options for creating projects and presentations—from greeting cards to slide shows—and on the Share tab, a variety of ways to share your files with friends and family, clients, or the world at large by burning a CD or DVD, sending your photos as e-mail attachments or photo mail layouts, or creating an online album.

The Editor workspace

In the Editor you'll focus on editing, adjusting, and correcting your images and creating projects and presentations to showcase them. You can choose between the Full Edit mode—with tools for color correction, special effects, and image enhancement—the Quick Edit mode with simple tools and commands for quickly fixing common image problems, and the Guided Edit mode, which provides step-by-step instructions for a range of editing tasks. If you're new to digital imaging, the Quick Edit and Guided Edit modes make a good starting point for fixing and modifying your photos, and provide a great way to learn as you work.

The Full Edit mode provides a more powerful and versatile image editing environment, with commands for correcting exposure and color and tools for making precise selections and fixing image imperfections. The Full Edit tool bar also includes painting and text editing tools. You can arrange the flexible Full Edit workspace to suit the way you prefer to work by floating, hiding, and showing panels or rearranging them in the Panel Bin. You can work with your photos in separate floating windows or as tabbed documents, and even set up multiple views of the same image.

Using panels and the Panel Bin

In the Full Edit workspace, the Panel Bin provides a convenient location to organize the panels you use most often. By default, only the Effects and Layers panels are docked in the Panel Bin; other panels can be opened from the Window menu. All panels can either be kept docked in the Panel Bin or dragged to float in a convenient position above your image as you work.

It's a good idea to familiarize yourself with organizing the Full Edit workspace so that you'll always have the controls you need at your fingertips. Try the following tips and techniques:

* To open a panel that you don't see in the workspace, choose its name from the Window menu in the menu bar at the top of the workspace.

* To hide an open panel so that you see only its header bar, choose its name from the Window menu or click its header bar.

* To float a panel above your image in the work area, drag it out of the Panel bin by its header bar. You can also float the Project Bin and the toolbox by dragging them away from their default positions.

* To return a floating panel to the Panel Bin, drag it into the Panel Bin and release the mouse button when you see a blue line indicating the new position for the panel. You can either place the panel between two others or drag it onto another panel to create a tabbed panel group. Switch between grouped panels by clicking their name tabs. Drag the name tag to move a panel out of a group.

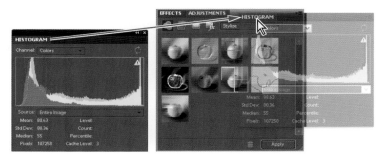

▶ **Tip:** Floating panels can also be grouped in this manner, or snapped together one above the other.

* To collapse a panel to an icon, click the two white triangles at the right of the header bar. You can collapse the entire Panel Bin, or a group of panels that are snapped together, in the same manner. Click the triangles again to expand the panel or group.

* To expand a single panel in a collapsed group, choose its name from the Window menu.

* To close a panel, drag it out of the Panel Bin and click the close button (x) at the right of its header bar or choose its name from the Window menu.

* To adjust the width of the Panel Bin, drag its left border.

* To adjust the height of panels in the Panel Bin, drag the separator bars between panels up or down.

* To adjust the size of a floating panel, drag the panel's lower right corner. (Some panels can not be resized.)

* To return the workspace to the default arrangement, choose Window > Reset Panels or click the Reset Panels button (🔄) at the top of the workspace.

Workflow

A typical Photoshop Elements workflow follows these basic steps:

- Bring images and media into the Organizer from a digital camera, scanner, or digital video camera.

- Sort and group images and media by a variety of methods, including applying keyword tags and creating albums, in the Organizer.

- Edit, adjust, and correct images and media or add text in the Editor.

- Share your images and media by creating projects and presentations, using e-mail or an on-line sharing service, or by burning them to CD/DVD-ROM.

- Back up and synchronize your catalog to Photoshop.com and across multiple computers.

Importing media

Before you can view, organize, and edit your photos in Photoshop Elements, you first need to import them into your catalog. Bringing your digital files into Photoshop Elements is easy.

Getting photos

You can bring photos into Photoshop Elements from a variety of sources and in several different ways.

If your image files are already on your computer hard disk, you can either drag them directly into the Organizer workspace from Windows Explorer or import them from within Photoshop Elements by using the Get Photos And Videos > From Files And Folders command.

You can use the same methods to import images that you've download to your hard disk using the software that came with your digital camera, or files that have been stored on CD-ROM or other removable media.

By far the most streamlined option is to download images directly into the Elements Organizer from your camera or card reader using the Adobe Photo Downloader. Getting photos directly in this way will save you time and get you started working with them sooner. The Adobe Photo Downloader is a feature of Photoshop Elements that automatically searches for and downloads photos from attached card readers, cameras, or mobile phones.

If for some reason you prefer to download images to your hard disk using the software that came with your digital camera, you can disable automatic detection by the Adobe Photo Downloader in the Camera Or Card Reader section of the Organizer Preferences.

Even with automatic detection disabled, you can still manually access the downloader from within the Organizer by choosing File > Get Photos And Videos > From Camera Or Card Reader.

Photoshop Elements will register data about each imported image, including the location of the file, in a catalog. You can either use the catalog that is created by default when you first start the application or create your own.

Creating a new catalog

Photoshop Elements stores information about your images in catalog files, which manage the photos on your computer but are independent of the image files themselves. As well as digital photographs, a catalog can include video and audio files, scans, PDF documents, and any presentations and layouts you might create in Photoshop Elements such as slide shows, photo collages, and CD jacket designs. When you sort and group your media in Photoshop Elements, all your work is recorded in the catalog. A single catalog can efficiently handle thousands of files, but you can also create separate catalogs for different purposes if that's the way you prefer to work.

1 Start Photoshop Elements, either by double-clicking the shortcut on your desktop or by choosing Start > All Programs > Adobe Photoshop Elements 8.

2 Click the Organize button in the Welcome Screen, and then wait until the Elements Organizer has finished opening.

3 In the Organizer, choose File > Catalog.

Note: Before you start working on this exercise, make sure that you've installed the software on your computer from the application CD (see the Photoshop Elements 8 documentation) and that you have correctly copied the Lessons folder from the CD in the back of this book onto your computer's hard disk (see "Copying the Classroom in a Book files" on page 2).

4 In the Catalog Manager dialog box, click New.

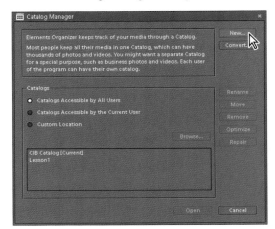

5 In the Enter A Name For The New Catalog dialog box, type **Lesson1** as the catalog name, disable the option Import Free Music Into This Catalog, and then click OK.

The new Lesson1 catalog is opened in the Organizer. The name of the currently active catalog is displayed in the lower left corner of the Organizer workspace. Now that you have a special catalog that you'll use just for this lesson, all you need is some pictures to put in it.

Using the Adobe Photo Downloader

The rest of this lesson is concerned with importing images into the Organizer.

If you have a digital camera or memory card at hand with your own photos on it, you can step through this exercise using those images. Alternatively, you can simply follow the process in the book without performing the exercise yourself, or skip to the section "Getting photos from files and folders" and return to this exercise when you are prepared.

Getting photos from a digital camera or card reader

The Adobe Photo Downloader makes it easy to import photos from your camera directly into your Photoshop Elements catalog.

1 Connect your camera or card reader to your computer. For instructions on connecting your device, refer to the manufacturer's documentation that came with it. Once your camera or card reader is connected to your computer, you're ready for the next step.

2 If the Windows Auto Play dialog box appears, you could choose the option Organize And Edit Using Adobe Elements Organizer 8, but for the purposes of this lesson click Cancel.

3 If the Photo Downloader dialog box now appears automatically, you can continue with step 4. If the Photo Downloader dialog box does not appear automatically, choose File > Get Photos And Videos > From Camera Or Card Reader.

4 Under Source at the top of the Photo Downloader dialog box, choose the name of the connected camera or card reader from the Get Photos From menu.

5 Under Import Settings, accept the folder location listed next to Location, or click Browse to choose a new location for the files.

6 Next to Create Subfolder(s), choose one of the date formats from the menu if you want the photos to be stored in subfolders named by capture or import date. You can also choose Custom Name to create a folder using a name you type in the text box, or choose None if you don't want to create any subfolders at all. Your selection is reflected in the Location pathname.

7 From the Rename Files menu, choose Do Not Rename Files and from the Delete Options menu choose After Copying, Do Not Delete Originals. If the Automatic Download option is activated, click the check box to disable it.

You'll learn more about customizing import settings and the advanced features of the Adobe Photo Downloader in Lessons 2 and 4.

8 Click the Get Photos button.

The photos are copied from the camera to the specified folder location.

9 If the Files Successfully Copied dialog box appears, click OK. The Getting Photos dialog box appears as the photos are imported into Photoshop Elements.

10 Click OK to close any other alert dialog box. Thumbnails of the newly imported photos appear in the Media Browser pane.

Getting photos from files and folders

Images stored on your hard disk can also be imported into Photoshop Elements.

1 Choose File > Get Photos And Videos > From Files And Folders.

2 In the Get Photos dialog box, navigate to and open the Lessons folder inside your PSE8CIB folder. Click once to select the Lesson01 folder.

3 Activate the Get Photos From Subfolders option. Ensure that the options Automatically Fix Red Eyes and Automatically Suggest Photo Stacks are disabled, and then click Get Media.

The Getting Photos dialog box appears as the photos are imported. Since the imported photos contain keyword metadata, the Import Attached Keyword Tags dialog box appears. You'll learn more about keyword tags in Lessons 2 and 4.

4 In the Import Attached Keyword Tags dialog box, click Select All, and then click OK. Click OK to close any other alert dialog box.

Thumbnails of the newly imported photos appear in the Media Browser pane.

About keyword tags

Keyword tags are personalized labels, such as "Vacation" or "Beach," that you attach to photos, video clips, audio clips and other creations in the Media Browser to make it easier to organize and find them.

When you use keyword tags, there's no need to manually organize your photos in subject-specific folders or rename files with content-specific names.

In fact, both of the latter solutions confine a given photo to a single group. By contrast, you can assign multiple keyword tags to a photo, allowing it to be included in several different groupings. You can then easily retrieve the selection of images you want by clicking the appropriate keyword tag or tags in the Keyword Tags panel.

For example, you could create a "Beach - Normandy" keyword tag and attach it to every photo you took at that location. You can then instantly find all the photos with the Beach - Normandy keyword tag by clicking the Find box next to that tag in the Keyword Tags panel, even if the photos are stored in different folders on your hard disk.

You can create keyword tags to group your images any way you want. For example, you could create keyword tags for individual people, places and events in your life.

You can attach multiple keyword tags to your photos and easily run a search based on a combination of keyword tags to find a particular person at a particular place or event.

For example, you can search for all "Pauline" keyword tags and all "Sophie" keyword tags to find all pictures of Pauline taken together with her sister Sophie.

Or search for all "Pauline" keyword tags and all "Beach - Normandy" keyword tags to find all the pictures of Pauline vacationing at the beach in Normandy.

Use keyword tags to organize and find photos by their content or any other association. See Lessons 2 and 4 for more information on keyword tags.

Reviewing and comparing

Photoshop Elements provides several options for quickly and easily reviewing and comparing your images in the Elements Organizer. Use the Full Screen view to assess your photos in detail, or to effortlessly present a selection of images as an instant slideshow. The Side By Side viewing mode lets you keep one image fixed on one side of a split screen while you cycle through a selection of photos on the other—great for comparing composition and detail or for choosing the best of a series of similar shots. In both Full Screen and Side By Side viewing mode you can add keyword tags, add photos to albums, and even perform a range of editing tasks.

Viewing photos at full screen or side-by-side

The Full Screen View and Side By Side View let you review your images without the distraction of other interface items such as windows, menus and panels.

1   Click the Display button (▣) near the upper right corner of the Organizer window, and then choose Compare Photos Side By Side from the menu.

As we made no selection of photos in the Media Browser, the Organizer treats all the images visible in the Media Browser as the selection. The Film Strip at the right of the screen displays thumbnails of the photos in the selection.

▶ **Tip:** If you don't see the Film Strip at the right of the screen, press Ctrl+F on your keyboard or click the button at the left end of the control bar at the bottom of the screen.

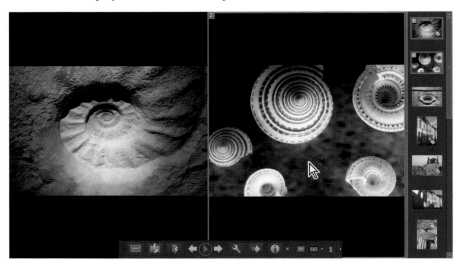

By default, the photo on the left—image #1—is active, as indicated by the blue line surrounding the preview. To activate image #2 instead, click it. Click the forward and back navigation buttons in the control bar at the bottom of the screen—or use the arrow keys on your keyboard—to cycle the active preview through all the images in the filmstrip, while the image on the other side of the screen remains fixed. If you don't move the pointer for a second or two, the control bar disappears; just move the pointer to make it reappear. As well as the forward and back navigation buttons, the control bar contains buttons that let you show and hide the Film Strip, the Quick Edit pane and the Quick Organize pane, where you can perform common editing tasks and tag images or group them by adding them to an album.

2 Click the triangle at the end of the control bar to extend it. Click the triangle beside the Side By Side View button ( ) to switch between the Side By Side and Above And Below split-screen arrangements.

3 Press the Esc key on your keyboard or click the Exit button (x) in the control bar to close the Side By Side view and return to the regular Organizer workspace.

4 Without selecting any of the thumbnail images in the Media Browser, click the View, Edit, Organize In Full Screen button in the bar above the thumbnails view.

5 The Full Screen view opens in slideshow mode, cycling through the images in the Film Strip. Experiment with the three buttons at the left of the control bar to show and hide the Film Strip and the Quick Edit and Quick Organize panes.

6 Try the two buttons to the right of the navigation controls to set Full Screen View and slideshow options and to choose a style for the transitions between slides. When you're done, press the Esc key to return to the Organizer.

Choosing files

To select more than one photo in the Media Browser, hold down the Ctrl key and click the photos you want to select. Ctrl-clicking enables you to select multiple non-consecutive files. To select a series of images that are in consecutive order, click the first photo, and then hold down the Shift key and click the last in the series. All the photos between the two images you Shift-click will be selected.

Sharing photos in e-mail

Have you ever had to wait a long time for an incoming e-mail to download, and then found that the e-mail contained photos at an unnecessarily high resolution? You can avoid imposing this inconvenience on others by using the Organizer's e-mail function, which exports images that are optimized specifically for sending via e-mail.

1 Select the photo (or photos) you'd like to send by e-mail in the Media Browser.

2 Click the Share tab above the Task Pane; then click the E-mail Attachments button.

Note: The first time you access this feature you may be presented with the E-mail dialog box. Choose your e-mail client (such as Outlook Express or Adobe E-mail Service) from the menu, and then click Continue. You can review or change your settings later by choosing Edit > Preferences > Sharing.

3 (Optional) Drag more photos from the Media Browser to the Items pane to add to your selection.

4 Choose Very Small (320 x 240 px) from the Maximum Photo Size menu and adjust the image quality using the Quality slider (the higher the quality the larger the file size and the longer the download time). The resulting file size and download time for a typical 56 Kbps dial-up modem are displayed for your reference. When you're done, click Next.

5 Select the example text in the Message box and type a message of your own.

6 Click the Edit Recipients In Contact Book button (■) above the Select Recipients box to create a new entry in the Contact Book dialog box. In the Contact Book dialog box, click the New Contact button (■). In the New Contact dialog box, type in the personal details and e-mail address of the

person to whom you wish to e-mail the picture. Click OK to close the New Contact dialog box and click OK again to close the Contact Book dialog box.

7   Click the check box next to the new contact in the Select Recipients box, and then click Next.

Your default e-mail application immediately creates an e-mail message. You can edit the message and Subject line as you wish. When you're finished and ready to send the e-mail, either click Send if you want to send this example e-mail, or close the message without saving or sending it.

8   Click the Organize tab above the Task Pane to switch back to the standard Elements Organizer workspace.

Creating an Adobe ID

Photoshop Elements users in the U.S. can create an Adobe ID to register their software and sign up for a free Photoshop.com account. Creating an Adobe ID enables Elements Membership services that are integrated with your software, giving you access to the Inspiration Browser as well as Organizer-based backup and sharing and other exciting Adobe-hosted services that extend the capabilities of your Photoshop Elements software.

● **Note:** At this stage, Elements Membership services are available only to users in the United States.

Basic Elements Membership is free and gives you your own storage space and a personal Photoshop.com URL where you can not only share and showcase your images but access your photos and videos anytime and from anywhere that you can connect to the Internet. You can also use your Photoshop.com account to back up your Photoshop Elements albums and even to synchronize albums on multiple computers. Basic membership includes access to the Inspiration Browser, with integrated tips, tricks and tutorials related to whatever you're currently working on, providing a powerful way to advance your skill set and helping you make the most out of your photos and creations.

You can upgrade to a Plus Membership to get more storage space as well as access to advanced tutorials. With Plus membership you also get regularly updated content such as project templates, themes, backgrounds, frames, and graphics delivered directly to your software to help you keep your projects fresh and appealing.

Signing up from the Welcome screen

1   Start Photoshop Elements or—if Photoshop Elements is already running—click the Welcome Screen button (🏠) at the top right of the workspace.

2   In the Welcome screen, click Create Adobe ID. Enter your name, e-mail address and a password, type a name for your personal Photoshop.com URL, and then click Create Account.

3 An e-mail message will be sent to you to confirm the creation of your account. Follow the instructions in the e-mail to activate your account.

Signing up from the Organizer or Editor

Tip: You don't have to start from the Welcome screen to create an Adobe ID. Links for registering and signing in are conveniently located throughout the Photoshop Elements workspace.

1 In the Organizer or Editor, click the Create New Adobe ID link in the menu bar.

2 Enter your personal details in the Create Your Adobe ID dialog box, and then click Create Account.

Signing in to your Photoshop.com account

1 Make sure your computer is connected to the Internet, and then start Adobe Photoshop Elements.

2 In the Welcome screen, enter your Adobe ID and password, and click Sign In.

If you didn't sign in at the Welcome screen, you can always click the Sign In link at the top of either the Organizer or Editor workspace.

Using Help

Help is available in several ways, each one useful in different circumstances:

Note: You do not need to be connected to the Internet to view Help in the application. However, with an active Internet connection you can see a more complete version of the user documentation and also access the latest updates as well as community-contributed content.

Help in the application A subset of the user documentation for Adobe Photoshop Elements is available as Help in the application, in the form of HTML content that you can access with your default browser. Help in the application provides easy access to summarized information on common tasks and concepts. Help in the application can be especially useful if you are new to Photoshop Elements or if you aren't connected to the Internet.

LiveDocs Help on the Web This is the most comprehensive and up-to-date version of Photoshop Elements Help. It is the recommended choice if you have an active Internet connection.

Help PDF Help is also available as a PDF that is optimized for printing; simply click View Help PDF at the top left of the online Help page. The Help PDF file is several megabytes in size and may take a considerable time to download when using a slow Internet connection.

Links in the application Within the Photoshop Elements application there are links to additional help topics, such as the "Tell me more" link at the bottom of the panel in each guided task.

Navigating Help

Depending on which module you're working with, choose Help > Elements Organizer Help or Help > Photoshop Elements Help, or simply press the F1 key. Your default Web browser will open and display the starting page of the Adobe Photoshop Help in the application or Help on the Web if you have a live Internet connection. Do any of the following: Click a topic heading in the table of contents. Click the plus sign (+) to the left of a topic heading to see its sub-topics. Click a topic or sub-topic to display its content. Type a search term in the Search text box at the top right of the page and press Enter on your keyboard.

Search tips

Adobe Help Search works by searching the entire Help text for topics that contain all the words typed in the Search box. These tips can help you improve your search results in Help:

- If you search using a phrase, such as "shape tool," put quotation marks around the phrase. The search returns only those topics containing that specific phrase.

- Make sure that the search terms are spelled correctly.

- If a search term doesn't yield results, try using a synonym, such as "photo" instead of "picture."

Links to help in the application

There are links to additional help connected to specific workflow tasks throughout the Photoshop Elements application. Clicking these links will take you to the corresponding topic in either Help in the application or on the Web.

Hot-linked tips

Hot-linked tips are available throughout Adobe Photoshop Elements. These tips either display information in the form of a typical tip balloon or link you to the appropriate topic in the help file.

You've reached the end of the first lesson. Now that you know how to import photos, understand the concept of the catalog, and are familiar with the essentials of the Photoshop Elements interface, you are ready to start organizing and editing your photos in the next lessons.

Before you move on, take a few moments to read through the review questions and answers on the next page.

Review questions

1 What are the primary workspaces in Adobe Photoshop Elements 8?

2 Define the typical Photoshop Elements workflow.

3 What is a catalog?

4 What are keyword tags?

5 How can you select multiple thumbnail images in the Media Browser?

Review answers

1 Photoshop Elements for Windows has two primary workspaces: the Organizer and the Editor. You'll use the Organizer to locate, import, manage, and share your photos and media files, and the Editor for editing and adjusting your images and for creating presentations to showcase them.

2 A typical Photoshop Elements workflow follows these basic steps:

- Bring images and media into the Organizer from a digital camera, scanner, or digital video camera.

- Sort and group images and media by a variety of methods, including applying keyword tags and creating albums, in the Organizer.

- Edit, adjust, and correct images and media or add text in the Editor.

- Share your images and media by creating projects and presentations, using e-mail or an on-line sharing service, or by burning them to CD/DVD-ROM.

3 Photoshop Elements stores information about your images in catalog files, which manage the photos on your computer but are independent of the image files themselves. As well as digital photographs, a catalog can include video and audio files, scans, PDF documents, and any presentations and layouts you might create in Photoshop Elements such as slide shows, photo collages, and CD jacket designs. When you sort and group your media in Photoshop Elements, all your work is recorded in the catalog. A single catalog can efficiently handle thousands of files, but you can also create separate catalogs for different types of work.

4   Keyword tags are labels with personalized associations that you attach to photos, creations, and video or audio clips in the Media Browser so that you can easily organize and find them.

5   To select more than one photo in the Media Browser, hold down the Ctrl key and click the photos you want to select. Ctrl-clicking enables you to select multiple non-consecutive files. To select a series of images that are in consecutive order, click the first photo, and then hold down the Shift key and click the last in the series. All the photos between the two images you Shift-clicked will be selected.

2 BASIC ORGANIZING ON WINDOWS

Lesson Overview

As you capture more and more images with your digital camera, it becomes increasingly important that you have effective ways to organize and manage your pictures on your computer so that those valuable memories are always accessible.

Adobe Photoshop Elements makes it easy to import your photos and other media files from a variety of sources and provides an array of powerful tools for sorting and searching your collection.

This lesson will get you started with the essential skills you'll need to import images and keep track of your growing photo library:

- Opening Adobe Photoshop Elements 8 in Organizer mode
- Creating a catalog for your images
- Importing photos from a digital camera
- Importing images from folders on your computer
- Switching between view modes in the Media Browser
- Working in the Date and Folder Location views
- Creating, organizing, and applying keyword tags
- Searching for files by keyword
- Finding and tagging faces in your photos

 You'll probably need between one and two hours to complete this lesson.

Import files to your catalog, and then explore a variety of ways to view and sort them. Learn how tagging and rating your photos can help you find just the pictures you want, just when you want them—easily and quickly. Once they share a keyword tag, a group of related photos can be retrieved with a single click, no matter how big your catalog is or across how many folders those images are scattered.

Getting started

Note: Before you start working on this lesson, make sure that you've installed the software on your computer from the application CD (see the Photoshop Elements 8 documentation) and that you have correctly copied the Lessons folder from the CD in the back of this book onto your computer's hard disk (see "Copying the Classroom in a Book files" on page 2).

For the exercises in this lesson you'll be working in the Organizer component of Photoshop Elements.

1 Start Photoshop Elements, either by double-clicking the shortcut on your desktop, or by choosing Start > All Programs > Adobe Photoshop Elements 8.

2 Do one of the following:

- If the Welcome screen appears, click the Organize button at the left.

- If the Editor window opens without first displaying the Welcome screen, click the Welcome Screen button (⌂) at the right of the menu bar. When the Welcome screen appears, click the Organize button. Alternatively, simply click the Organizer button (▦) located at the right of the Editor window menu bar, and then wait until the Organizer has finished opening.

- If the Organizer window opens without first displaying the Welcome screen, you don't need to do anything more—you're all set to start with this lesson.

Getting photos

The Organizer component of Photoshop Elements provides a workspace where you can view, sort and organize your media files. Before you print your photos, burn them to CD or DVD-ROM, or share them by e-mail or on the Web, the first step is to assemble them in the Organizer, as you'll learn later in this lesson.

Creating a new catalog

Photoshop Elements for Windows stores information about your images in catalog files, which manage the photos on your computer but are independent of the image files themselves.

A catalog can include digital photographs, video and audio files, PDF documents, scans, and any presentations or layouts you might create in Photoshop Elements.

When you organize your files in Photoshop Elements, all your work is recorded in the catalog. A single catalog can efficiently handle thousands of files, but you're free to create as many catalogs as you wish to suit the way that you prefer to work.

To begin this lesson you can create a new catalog so that you won't confuse the practice files for this lesson with files for the other lessons in this book.

1 In the Organizer, choose File > Catalog.

2 In the Catalog Manager dialog box, click New.

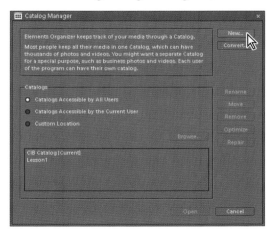

3 In the Enter A Name For The New Catalog dialog box, type **Lesson2** as the catalog name, disable the option Import Free Music Into This Catalog, and then click OK.

The new Lesson2 catalog is opened in the Organizer. The name of the currently active catalog is displayed in the lower left corner of the Organizer workspace.

In the following exercises you'll import the images for this lesson into your new catalog using a variety of different methods. You'll drag files directly into the Media Browser from Windows Explorer and use menu commands to import files from a known folder and to search for files on your hard disk.

Dragging photos from Windows Explorer

Perhaps the most direct and intuitive way to bring photographs and other media into the Organizer catalog is to use the familiar drag-and-drop method.

1 Minimize the Organizer by clicking the Minimize button (▬) at the right of the Organizer menu bar, or click the Organizer application button on the Windows taskbar.

2 Open the My Computer window in Windows Explorer; either double-click a shortcut icon on your desktop, or use the Start menu.

3 Navigate through the folder structure to locate and open the Lesson02-03 folder that you copied to your hard disk (see "Copying the Classroom in a Book files" on page 2). Open the sub-folder named Import.

4 Inside the Import folder you'll find the sub-folders: BATCH1, BATCH2, and BATCH3. Drag the BATCH1 folder icon and hold it over the Organizer application button on the Windows taskbar.

5 Wait until the Organizer becomes the foreground application; then drag the BATCH1 folder onto the Organizer workspace and release the mouse button.

Tip: If you can arrange the Windows Explorer window and the Organizer application window on your screen so that you can see both at once, you can simply drag the folder (or individual media files) directly from the Windows Explorer window into the Organizer, rather than going via the Windows taskbar.

The Organizer will briefly display a dialog box while searching inside the BATCH1 folder for files to import; then the Import Attached Keyword Tags dialog box opens, giving you the opportunity to choose whether or not to import any keywords that are attached to the images.

6 In the Import Attached Keyword Tags dialog box, click Select All; then click OK.

7 The Getting Photos dialog box appears briefly as the Organizer imports the images from the BATCH1 folder. If a message appears telling you that only the newly imported items will be visible in the Media Browser, click OK.

In the Media Browser, you can see thumbnails of the four images you've just added to the Lesson2 catalog. Don't drag the other two batches into the Organizer in this way; you'll use different methods to import them into your catalog.

8 Click the Maximize button (▣) towards the right end of the menu bar in the Organizer window. The workspace expands to fill the entire screen.

▶ **Tip:** If you'd prefer not to see this message each time you import, activate the option Don't Show Again. To reverse this action, click Reset All Warning Dialogs on the General tab of the Preferences dialog box.

▶ **Tip:** The timeline that you may expect to see above the Media Browser, if you've used Photoshop Elements 6 or an earlier version, is now hidden by default. To show and hide the timeline, choose Window > Timeline. To show and hide the information displayed under each thumbnail in the Media Browser, choose View > Details. If the View > Details option is activated, you can also show or hide file names, grid lines and thumbnail borders by activating View menu options.

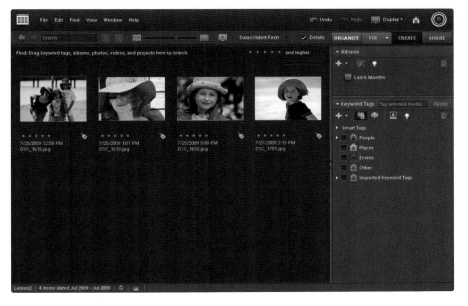

9 Click the Restore button (▣) in the menu bar to return to window mode.

Getting photos from a known location

In this exercise you'll use a menu command to import files to the Organizer.

1 Choose File > Get Photos And Videos > From Files And Folders. In the Get Photos From Files And Folders dialog box, navigate to your Lesson02-03 folder, open the Import folder, and then the BATCH2 folder.

2 Hold the pointer over a file in the BATCH2 folder to see detailed information about the photo; select the file to see a thumbnail image in the Preview pane.

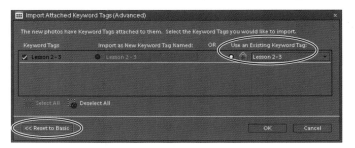

▶ **Tip:** Select a folder in the Get Photos From Files And Folders dialog box, and then click Get Media to import all items within that folder. Activate the Get Photos From Subfolders option to import files from any subfolders.

3 Select all four images, ensure that the options Automatically Fix Red Eyes and Automatically Suggest Photo Stacks are disabled, and then click Get Media.

4 Select the keyword "Lesson 2-3" in the Import Attached Keyword Tags dialog box. You'll notice that by default the new batch of images will pick up the Lesson 2-3 keyword tag that was added to the catalog in the previous import.

5 Click the Advanced button in the lower left of the dialog box. Now you have the option to either use the existing tag of the same name or to type a new one. For now, leave the settings unchanged. Click the Reset To Basic button; then click OK. Click OK to dismiss any other alert dialog box.

6 Click the Show All button above the Media Browser to see all eight images. In the Keyword Tags panel, click the triangle beside the Imported Keyword Tags category to see the Lesson 2-3 tag. Note that all the thumbnails in the Media Browser are marked with a tag icon to indicate they have attached keywords.

The name of the active catalog is displayed in the lower left corner of the Organizer. You can also see a count of the items currently visible in the Media Browser and an indication of the range of their capture dates. If you apply a search, these details will change to describe the search results.

Automatically fixing red eyes during import

The term "red eye" refers to the phenomenon common in photos taken with a flash, where the subject's pupils appear red instead of black. This is caused by the flash reflecting off the retina at the back of the eye.

While none of the images for this lesson require red eye correction, for photos taken with a flash you can have Photoshop Elements remove the red eye effect automatically while importing the images. To activate this option, click the check box beside Automatically Fix Red Eyes in the Get Photos From Files And Folders dialog box.

More methods for fixing the red eye effect will be discussed in Lesson 8.

Searching for photos to import

This method is useful when you're not sure exactly where on your hard disk you've stashed your photographs and other media files over the years. You might run a search of your entire hard disk or just your My Documents folder. For this exercise, you'll limit the search to just a portion of the folder hierarchy on your computer.

1   In the Organizer, choose File > Get Photos And Videos > By Searching.

2   In the Get Photos And Videos By Searching For Folders dialog box, choose Browse from the Look In menu under Search Options.

3   In the Browse For Folder dialog box, navigate to and select your Lessons folder, and then click OK.

4   Under Search Options in the Get Photos By Searching For Folders dialog box, disable the Automatically Fix Red Eyes option.

5   Click the Search button located at the upper right of the dialog box.

6   The Search Results box lists all folders inside the Lessons folder. A preview pane at the right shows thumbnails of the contents of a selected folder. Select the Lesson02-03\Import\BATCH3 folder and click Import Folders.

7   In the Import Attached Keyword Tags dialog box, click Select All, and then click OK. Click OK to close any other alert dialog box. Click the Show All button above the Media Browser to see all 12 imported images in your Lesson2 catalog.

Importing from a digital camera

If you have a digital camera or memory card at hand with your own photos on it, you can step through this exercise using those images. Alternatively, you can simply follow the process in the book without performing the exercise yourself, or skip to the next section of this lesson and return to this exercise when you are prepared.

1 Connect your digital camera or card reader to your computer, following the manufacturer's instructions.

2 Do the following:

- If the Windows Auto Play dialog box appears, click Cancel.

- If the Photo Downloader dialog box appears automatically, continue with step 3. If the Photo Downloader dialog box does not appear automatically, choose File > Get Photos And Videos > From Camera Or Card Reader.

3 In the Photo Downloader dialog box, choose the name of your connected camera or card reader from the Get Photos From menu.

4 Accept the default target folder listed beside Location, or click Browse to designate a different destination for the imported files.

5 From the Create Subfolder(s) menu, choose Today's Date (yyyy mm dd) as the folder name format; the Location path reflects your choice.

6 Choose Do Not Rename Files from the Rename Files menu. From the Delete Options menu, choose After Copying, Do Not Delete Originals.

7 Deactivate Automatic Download, and then click the Advanced Dialog button.

The Advanced Photo Downloader Dialog displays thumbnail images of the photos on your camera's memory card.

8 (Optional) Click the check box below a thumbnail—removing the green check mark—to remove that photo from the selection to be imported.

9 (Optional) Select one or more photos to rotate. Click the appropriate Rotate button in the lower left corner of the dialog box.

10 Under Advanced Options, if the options Automatically Fix Red Eyes, Automatically Suggest Photo Stacks, and Make 'Group Custom Name' A Tag are activated, disable them by clicking their checkboxes, and then click Get Photos.

The selected photos are copied from the camera to the specified folder on your hard disk. By default, imports from a camera are copied to your My Pictures folder.

11 If the Files Successfully Copied dialog box appears, click OK.

12 The Getting Photos dialog box appears briefly as the photos are being imported into Photoshop Elements. Click OK to close any other alert dialog box.

The imported photos appear in the Media Browser, already rotated where specified.

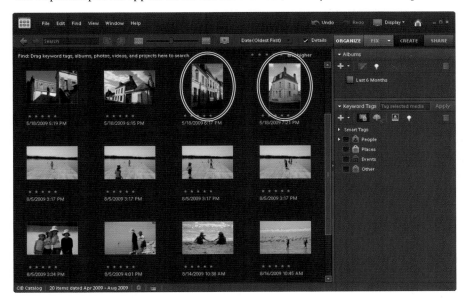

Using watched folders

You can simplify and automate the process of keeping your catalog up to date by using watched folders.

Designate any folder on your hard disk as a watched folder and Photoshop Elements will automatically be alerted when a new file is placed in (or saved to) that folder. By default, the My Pictures folder is watched, but you can add any number of additional folders to the Folders To Watch list.

You can choose to have any new files that are detected in a watched folder added to your catalog automatically or to have Photoshop Elements ask you what to do before importing the new media. If you choose the latter option, the message "New files have been found in Watched Folders" will appear whenever new items are detected. Click Yes to add the new files to your catalog or click No to skip them.

Now you'll add a folder to the watched folders list.

1   Choose File > Watch Folders.

2   Under Folders To Watch in the Watch Folders dialog box, click Add, and then browse to your Lesson02-03 folder (nested inside the Lessons folder in your PSE8CIB folder).

3 Select the Lesson02-03 folder and click OK.

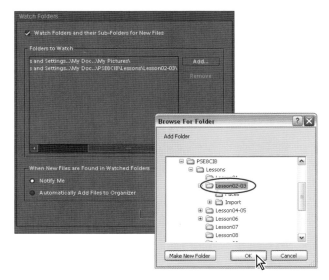

The Lesson02-03 folder now appears in the Folders To Watch list. To stop a folder from being watched, select it in the list and click Remove.

4 Ensure that the Notify Me option is activated, and then click OK to close the Watch Folders dialog box.

This concludes the portion of this lesson concerned with importing files into your catalog. You'll learn more ways to bring media into Photoshop Elements—along with time-saving techniques for sorting and managing your files even as you import them—in Lesson 4, "Advanced Organizing on Windows."

Viewing photo thumbnails in the Organizer

In the Organizer, there are several ways to view the images in your catalog. You can switch between the various viewing modes to suit different stages in your workflow or to make it easier and more efficient to perform specific organizing tasks.

Using the Media Browser views

Up to this point, you've been working in the default Media Browser view: the Thumbnail View, where your images are arranged by capture date and time. You can reverse the display order by choosing either Date (Oldest First) or Date (Newest First) from the menu to the right of the Thumbnail Size slider just above the Media Browser pane.

Let's look at some of the other display options in the Organizer.

1   Use the Thumbnail Size slider just above the Media Browser pane to reduce the size of the thumbnails so that you can see all the images in your Lesson2 catalog.

2   Click the Display button () near the upper right corner of the Organizer window, and then choose Import Batch from the menu to see the thumbnails organized by their separate import sessions.

3   Try the following:

   • Click the divider bar above any of the import batches ("Imported from hard disk on ...") to select all images imported in that session.

   • Increase the thumbnail size by dragging the slider above the thumbnail pane until only a few of the images in the catalog are visible in the Media Browser.

In the Import Batch view, a divider bar marked with a film canister icon (🎞) and an import session date separates each group of thumbnails.

   • Choose Window > Timeline. The timeline shows three bars representing the three import sessions that account for all the images in this catalog. Click each of the three bars in turn to jump to the first image imported in the corresponding session. A frame surrounds the currently selected bar.

As you click each bar in the timeline, the view changes to show the corresponding import batch; the first image in the batch is surrounded by a green border and its capture date flashes. The equal height of the bars indicates that each batch contains the same number of images.

   • Choose Window > Timeline once more to hide the timeline from view.

4 Click the Display button () near the upper right corner of the Organizer window and choose Folder Location to see the images organized in the folder hierarchy in which they are stored on your computer. Use the slider above the thumbnail pane to reduce the size of the thumbnails again so that you can see all the images in the catalog. Select an image to highlight its folder entry.

► **Tip:** To see file names displayed with the thumbnails in the Media Browser, first choose View > Details (or activate the Details check box above the thumbnails pane); then View > Show File Names.

The divider bars between the groups of thumbnails are now marked by folder icons—rather than the film canister icons that mark import batches—and display folder path-names, rather than the dates of import sessions. Note that although neither is the case for our exercise, a single folder may contain multiple import batches and a single import batch may include files from multiple folders.

5 Repeat the steps you performed in Step 3. This time, the three bars you see in the timeline represent the three folders containing the images in this catalog.

6 As you click each bar in the timeline, the corresponding source folder is highlighted in the folder hierarchy to the left of the Media Browser.

Using the Date View

The Date View can be a great way to organize and access your images, particularly once you are working with a large collection of photos that span a number of years.

1 Click the Display button () near the upper right corner of the Organizer window and choose Date View from the menu.

2 Click the Year view button below the calendar display, and then use the right and left arrows on either side of the year heading to see the page for 2009, if it's not already on view.

You can see at a glance that your Lesson2 catalog contains photographs taken on four separate dates during 2009.

3   Click May 17, 2009 on the calendar. A thumbnail preview of the first image captured on that date appears at the right of the Organizer window. An image count at the lower left of the preview indicates that there are four files in your catalog that share this creation date.

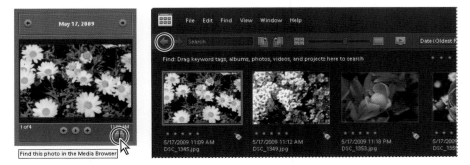

4   Click the Find This Photo In The Media Browser button (🔍) below the preview thumbnail to switch to the Media Browser with the currently previewed photo selected and ready for action.

5   In the Media Browser, click the Back To Previous View button (◀) near the upper left corner of the Organizer window to return to the Date View.

6 Click the Month view button at the bottom of the workspace; then click the month name at the head of the calendar page and choose July from the months menu. If you wished to move one month at a time, you could simply click twice on the Next Month button to the right of the month name.

7 The July page opens with the 25th already selected—that being the first date for which there are photos in your Lesson2 catalog. Click in the Daily Note box at the right of the calendar page and type **first day at the lake** to add a note to the selected date. An note icon appears on the thumbnail for March 25th.

8 Use the Next Item On Selected Day button (⬤) under the preview image to see the other photographs captured on the same date.

9 Click the Start Automatic Sequencing button (▶) under the preview image to view all the photos taken on the same day as a mini slide show.

Now that you know how to access photos via the calendar you'll be able to return and use the Date view whenever you wish, but for the remainder of this lesson you'll work with the Media Browser view.

10 Either click the Back To Previous View button (◀) near the upper left corner of the Organizer window or click the Media Browser button below the calendar page. You could also choose Media Browser from the Display menu.

Working with star ratings and keyword tags

Most of us find it challenging to organize our files and folders efficiently. It can be so easy to forget which pictures were stored in what folder—and so tedious when you're forced to examine the contents of numerous folders looking for the files you want. Photoshop Elements offers an array of powerful and versatile tools for organizing, sorting, and searching that can make all that frustration a thing of the past.

Earlier in this lesson you learned that even during the import process you can search your computer for the files you want to bring into your catalog. The next set of exercises will demonstrate how just a little time invested in applying ratings and tags to the files you import can streamline the process of locating and sorting your pictures, regardless of how many image files you have or where they are stored.

Applying keyword tags and rating photos

Applying keywords to your photos and grouping those tags in categories can make it quick and easy to find exactly the images you're looking for. With a single click you can rate each photo from one to five stars, adding a simple way to narrow a search. In this exercise, you'll apply a rating to one of the images you imported into your Lesson2 catalog, and then tag it with a keyword from the default set.

1 Click the Display button (▦) and choose Thumbnail View from the menu; then make sure the Details checkbox above the Media Browser pane is activated.

2 In the Media Browser, move the pointer slowly from left to right over the stars beneath the thumbnail image of the mother and two daughters. When you see four yellow stars, as in the illustration below, click to apply that rating.

3 To find images based on the ratings you've assigned, use the stars and the adjacent menu located at the right end of the Find bar above the thumbnail display. For this example set the search criteria at 2 stars and higher. Only the image with the 4-star rating is displayed in the Media Browser.

4 Click the Show All button.

5 In the Keyword Tags panel—on the Organize tab at the top of the Task Pane— click the arrow beside the People category so that you can see the nested sub- categories Family and Friends.

6 Drag the Family keyword tag to the thumbnail of the mother and her daughters.

7 Collapse the People keyword tag category, and then select the next three images in the Media Browser: the woman in a straw hat, the girl in pink and the girl with the orange sun-hat.

8 Click in the text box in the header of the Keywords Tags panel and type the letter "f". As you type a list of the existing keywords starting with "f" appears; choose Family, and then click Apply. The tag is applied to the three selected images.

9 Rest the pointer for a second or two over the tag icon beneath the thumbnail of any of your newly tagged photos; a Tooltip message appears identifying the keyword tags that are attached to that image file.

10 In the Keyword Tags panel, click the triangle to expand the People keyword tags category once more. Click the empty Find box beside the Family sub-category. The Media Browser is immediately updated to display only the four images to which you assigned the Family tag.

11 Click the Find box beside the Family tag again to clear the search. Once more the Media Browser displays all twelve images in the Lesson2 catalog.

● **Note:** In the Media Browser, the keyword tag icon or icons that you see below the thumbnails will vary in appearance depending on the size at which the thumbnails are displayed. If the thumbnail size is small, multiple color-coded tags may display as a single generic (beige) tag icon.

Using Star ratings and the Hidden tag

Star ratings—Use *Star ratings* to rank your photos. You can attach only one star rating value per photo. If you assign 5 stars to a photo that already has 4 stars assigned, the 5 star rating will replace the previous rating.

Hidden—The *Hidden tag* hides photos in the Media Browser, unless you select the Hidden tag as a search criteria. Use the Hidden tag, for example, to hide items that you want to keep, but prefer not to see every time you work in the Organizer.

—From Photoshop Elements Help

Creating new categories and sub-categories

It's easy to add or delete new keyword tag categories and sub-categories in the Keyword Tags panel to help you group and organize your keyword tags.

1   At the top of the Keyword Tags panel, click the Create New Keyword Tag, Sub-category, Or Category button (➕) and choose New Category from the menu.

2   In the Create Category dialog box, type **Garden** as the category name; then scroll the Category Icon menu and select the flower icon. Click OK.

3   In the Keyword Tags panel, expand the People category if necessary; then click to select the Family sub-category. Click the Create New button (➕) and choose New Sub-Category from the menu.

4   In the Create Sub-Category dialog box, type **Kids** as the new Sub-Category name. Ensure that Family is selected in the Parent Category or Sub-Category menu and click OK. Your new keyword tag category and sub-category have become part of this catalog.

Applying and editing category assignments

You can assign keyword categories to (or remove them from) several files at once.

1   In the Media Browser, click any of the six photos featuring children; then hold down the Ctrl key and click to add each of the other five images to the selection.

2   Click in the text box in the header of the Keywords Tags panel and type the letter "k"; choose Kids and click Apply. The tag is applied to the selected images.

3   Leaving the same six images selected, drag the Garden keyword tag to one of the un-selected images of flowers. The keyword tag is applied to just this picture. Selecting the thumbnail or deselecting the other thumbnails is not necessary.

4   Choose Edit > Deselect, and then Ctrl-click the remaining three flower photos. Drag your multiple selection onto the Garden tag in the Keyword Tags panel. The keyword tag Garden is applied to all three images at once.

5   Select the image of the mother and daughters to which you applied the 4-star rating earlier in the lesson. Choose Window > Properties to open the Properties panel, and then click the Keyword Tags tab (🏷) to see which keyword tags are attached to this image.

▶ **Tip:** You can also show and hide the Properties panel by holding down the Alt key on your keyboard, and then pressing Enter.

6   Remove the Family keyword tag from the image by doing one of the following:

   • In the Properties panel, right-click the listing Family, Kids, and then choose Remove Family Sub-Category Keyword Tag.

   • Right-click the thumbnail itself and choose Remove Keyword Tag > Family from the context menu.

   • Right-click the tag icon beneath the thumbnail in the Media Browser, and then choose Remove Family Sub-Category Keyword Tag from the menu.

7   Close the Properties panel by clicking the Close button (❎) in the upper right corner of the panel, or by choosing Window > Properties again.

Creating and applying new keyword tags

In the last exercise you created new keyword categories and sub-categories. This time you'll create, apply and edit a new keyword tag.

1   In the Keyword Tags panel on the Organize tab in the Task Pane, click the Create New button (➕) and choose New Keyword Tag from the menu. The Create Keyword Tag dialog box appears.

2 In the Create Keyword Tag dialog box, choose Kids (under People, Family) as the category and type **Lilly** for Name, and then click OK.

3 Drag the picture of the mother and daughters from the previous exercise to the new Lilly tag in the Keyword Tags panel.

The image becomes the icon for the new tag because it's the first image to have this keyword applied. You'll adjust the tag icon in the next steps, before applying the new keyword tag to additional photos.

4 In the Keyword Tags panel, select the Lilly keyword tag; then click the Create New button (➕) above the list of keyword tags and choose Edit from the menu. You could also right-click the Lilly keyword tag itself and choose Edit Lilly Keyword Tag from the context menu. The Edit Keyword Tag dialog box appears.

5 Click the Edit Icon button to open the Edit Keyword Tag Icon dialog box.

6 In the Edit Keyword Tag Icon dialog box, drag the corners of the bounding box in the preview image so that it surrounds just the little girl in a pink jacket at the center of the photo.

7 Click OK to close the dialog box; then click OK again to close the Edit Keyword Tag dialog box.

You'll update the keyword tag icon later to an image that works better as an icon for this tag.

8 Drag the Lilly keyword tag onto the close-up photo of Lilly. The Lilly tag is now attached to two images.

9 In the Keyword Tags panel, right-click the Lilly tag and choose Edit Lilly Keyword Tag from the context menu. The Edit Keyword Tag dialog box appears. Click the Edit Icon button to open the Edit Keyword Tag Icon dialog box.

10 In the Edit Keyword Tag Icon dialog box, click the arrow to the right of the Find button beneath the main preview image.

The Find arrows cycle through all photos with the same keyword tag. In our example, the second of two images is the close-up shot from step 8. A small tag preview at the top of the dialog box shows how the new image will look applied as the new tag icon.

11 Drag the bounding box on the main preview (and re-size it, if you wish) until you are satisfied with the way it looks in the small tag preview; then click OK to close the dialog box. Click OK again to close the Edit Keyword Tag dialog box.

Converting keyword tags and categories

Changing the hierarchy of categories and keyword tags in the Keyword Tags panel is easy. Doing so will not remove the tags or categories from the images to which you've attached them.

1 Click the Find box next to the Kids sub-category. A binoculars icon (🔍) appears in the box to remind you that it is now activated. Only the six photos tagged with the Kids keyword are displayed in the Media Browser. Click the Show All button above the Media Browser so that all the images in the catalog are visible.

2 Right-click the Kids sub-category and choose Edit Kids Sub-Category from the context menu. The Edit Sub-Category dialog box appears.

3 From the Parent Category or Sub-Category menu, choose None (Convert To Category) and click OK.

Now Kids is no longer a sub-category under People, Family but a category in its own right. Its new icon has been inherited from its former parent category.

4 (Optional) Right-click the tag and choose Edit Kids Category from the context menu to select a different icon for the new category.

5 Click the empty Find box beside the Kids category. Notice that the selection of six images tagged with the Kids tag did not change. Click the Show All button.

6 In the Keyword Tags panel, drag the Kids category onto the People category.

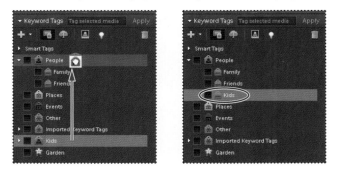

Now the Kids category appears as a sub-category under People. Because it's no longer a category, it has the generic sub-category icon.

7 Click the empty Find box next to the Kids sub-category. Note that the search still returns the same six images tagged with the Kids keyword. Click Show All.

8 Under the People category, right-click the Family sub-category and choose Change Family Sub-Category To A Keyword Tag from the menu.

9 (Optional) Right-click the new Family tag and choose Edit Family Keyword Tag from the context menu. In the Edit Keyword Tag dialog box, click the Edit Icon button and select a new image by clicking on the arrows under the main preview. Click OK to close the Edit Keyword Tag Icon dialog box; then click OK again to close the Edit Keyword Tag dialog box.

Applying more keyword tags to images

As well as the manual methods you have seen already, there are a few simple ways to tag multiple images automatically.

1   Click the Display button (![icon]) near the upper right corner of the Organizer window, and then choose Folder Location from the menu.

2   Click the BATCH2 folder in the folder hierarchy view. In the thumbnails pane, click the Instant Keyword Tag button at the right of the separator bar above the thumbnails in the BATCH2 group to quickly apply the same keyword tag to all of the photos in that group.

3   The Create And Apply New Keyword Tag dialog box appears. From the Category menu, choose Other. Accept BATCH2 as the name for the new tag or type another keyword if you wish; then click OK.

4   Repeat Steps 2 and 3 for the other folder groups in your Lesson2 catalog: BATCH1 and BATCH3.

5   Switch back to Thumbnail View using the Display button as you did in Step 1. Click Show All if it's visible above the thumbnails in the Media Browser.

Working with keyword tags in Full Screen mode

In Photoshop Elements 8 the Full Screen mode has been improved to give you even more ways to work with keyword tags while reviewing and organizing your photos.

1 Click the Full Screen button (▣) above the Media Browser, or click the Display button (▣) near the upper right corner of the Organizer window, and then choose View, Edit, Organize In Full Screen from the menu.

2 Move the pointer on the full screen image to see the control bar at the bottom of the screen. If necessary, click the Pause button, and then click the Toggle Film Strip button or press Ctrl+F on your keyboard so that you can see a strip of thumbnails at the right of the screen as shown below. Click to select the photo of the girl with the orange hat.

3 Move the pointer to the lower left edge of the screen to expand the Quick Organize panel. Click to deactivate the Auto Hide button at the top of the title bar of the Quick Organize panel so that the panel remains open while you work.

4 Click in the text box at the bottom of the Quick Organize panel and type **Pauline**; then click the Apply button (➕) at the right of the text box to attach the new keyword to this image. Move the pointer over the keywords in the Keyword Tags pane of the Quick Organize panel; as you move over each keyword a Tooltip message shows that you can click to either apply or remove any of these tags. The keywords already attached to this image are highlighted.

5 Click to activate the Auto Hide button once more; the Quick Organize panel closes after a second or so.

6 Right-click the image and choose Show Properties from the context menu.

7 In the Properties panel, click the Keyword Tags tab (🏷) to see the keyword tags attached to this image. Right-click the Pauline tag and choose Remove Pauline Keyword Tag. Click the Close button (✖) to close the Properties panel. You'll explore a different way to tag people later in this chapter.

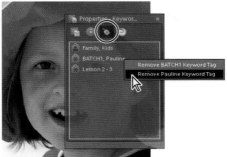

8 Press the Esc key on your keyboard or click the Close button at the right of the control bar to exit Full Screen mode to the thumbnail view. If Show All is visible above the Media Browser, click it.

Creating a keyword tag for your working files

You can create a keyword tag to apply to the files that you create and save as you work through the lessons in this book.

1 In the Keyword Tags panel, click the Create New button and choose New Category from the menu.

2 In the Create Category dialog box, type **Work Files** and select one of the Category icons. You can scroll to the right to see more icons. Click OK.

3 Apply this keyword tag to all the files you create and save to your My CIB Work folder as you complete the lessons in this book.

Editing In Full Screen mode

Full Screen mode in the Elements Organizer not only provides you with a fun way to view and deliver instant slideshows that include both photos and videos, but also lets you access tools to perform a range of common photo-editing adjustments without leaving the Organizer.

By using the Quick Edit panel in Full Screen mode you can make substantial improvements to an image with just a click or two, and assess the results at a conveniently high zoom level.

You can access the Quick Edit panel from the controls at the bottom of the screen (which appear when you move the pointer) or by moving the pointer to the left edge of the screen.

Using keyword tags to find pictures

The reason for creating, applying and sorting all these keyword tags is so that you can always find just the picture you want, just when you want it—easily and quickly. Once they share a keyword tag, a group of related photos can be retrieved with a single click; no matter how big your catalog is or across how many folders those images are scattered.

Before you go on to have fun with the People Recognition feature, let's become more familiar with using the Keyword Tags panel to sort and search your files. In Photoshop Elements 8 you now have even more ways to find files by keyword, with enhancements to both the text search feature and the tagging interface.

Perhaps the most intuitive method of searching by keyword is the Keyword Tag Cloud—new in Photoshop Elements 8—which displays all your tags in alphabetical order. Varying text sizes indicate the relative number of files tagged with each keyword, which means that those tags you use most often are the easiest to spot.

Ansonia Hotel, Asia, Bangkok, Beach, Belgium, Brooklyn Bridge, Elephant, Emma, Empire State Building, Europe, Family, Friends, Giraffe, Hippo, Holidays, Hong Kong, Imagine, Jefferson Market, Kate, Kids, Lilly, New York, Normandy, Ostrich, Patricia, Pauline, Road Trip, San Francisco, Sirani, Sofie, Summer, Tom, Vittorio, Winter, Zebra, Zoo

You can switch to the hierarchical view of your keyword categories, sub-categories and tags when you want extra organizational control.

1 If Show All is visible at the top of the Media browser, click it. Click the Keyword Tag Cloud button ( ) at the top of the Keyword Tags panel.

2 In the tag cloud, click BATCH1; then press Ctrl+A on your keyboard to select all four images. Type **Holidays** in the text box in the header of the Keyword Tags panel and click Apply to attach the new tag to the four images.

3 In the tag cloud, click BATCH2. Press Ctrl+A on your keyboard to select all four images, and then drag the keyword Holidays from the tag cloud to any one of the selected photos.

4 Click the Holidays keyword in the tag cloud to see all eight images displayed in the Media Browser.

5 Click the Keyword Tag Hierarchy button (▨) at the top of the Keyword Tags panel.

6 In the tag hierarchy, click the empty find box beside the new Holidays tag, in the keyword category Other; eight images show in the Media Browser. Leaving the Holidays find box active, click the empty find box beside the BATCH2 tag; the Media Browser display is reduced to the four images that have both of these tags attached. Finally, click the find box beside the Kids tag. Only three images are returned by the narrowed search. The Find bar above the thumbnails shows that these images have all three keywords: Holidays, BATCH2 and Kids.

7 From the Options menu in the Find bar above the Media Browser, select Show Close Match Results. The thumbnail display is updated to show five more photos: images that are tagged with some, but not all of the searched keywords. These close matches can be identified by a check mark icon in the upper left corner of the thumbnail.

8 Click Show All to display all images.

Automatically finding faces for tagging

Undoubtedly, your growing photo library will include many photos of your family and friends. Photoshop Elements 8 makes it quick and easy to tag the faces of friends and family members with the People Recognition feature, taking most of the work out of sorting and organizing a large portion of your catalog.

About People Recognition

The People Recognition feature automatically finds the people in your photos and makes it easy for you to tag them. Once you begin using the feature it learns to recognize the faces you've already tagged and will automatically tag new photos that picture the same faces—the more times a particular person is tagged, the better People Recognition will get at recognizing them.

Naming faces in the Media Browser

The first experience you'll have of People Recognition will probably be the "Who Is This?" prompt that pops up on thumbnails in the Media Browser when the Elements Organizer is idle for a few moments. People Recognition displays these hints to help you identify and tag all the people in your photos. You can ignore the hints if you wish, but remember that the more people you identify, the smarter People Recognition gets at tagging faces for you automatically.

● **Note:** Once People Recognition begins to recognize a particular face, the "Who is this?" hint changes to read "Is this Pauline?" and gives you the opportunity to confirm or cancel automatic tagging.

The automatic "Who Is This" hints and the People Recognition feature itself can be disabled in the Organizer Preferences. Before continuing with the exercises in this section, you need to make sure that both are activated. You can also import a few more images with faces for People Recognition to find.

1   In the Organizer, choose Edit > Preferences > Keyword Tags And Albums.

2   Under People Recognition Hints in the Preferences dialog box, click Show. In the list of preferences categories at the left of the dialog box, click Auto Analyzer Options. In the Auto Analyzer Options make sure that Recognize People Automatically is activated, and then click OK.

3   Choose File > Get Photos And Videos > From Files And Folders. In the Get Photos From Files And Folders dialog box, navigate to and open your Lesson02-03 folder, and then click to select the Faces folder. Click Get Media.

4   In the Import Attached Keyword Tags dialog box, click Select All, and then click OK. Click OK to close any other alert dialog box. The Media browser shows only the six newly imported images.

5   Above the Media Browser, choose Oldest First for the sorting order.

Finding people for tagging

Photoshop Elements helps you with every step of the face tagging process.

1   In the Media Browser, Ctrl-click to select the two images faces_1.jpg and faces_2.jpg, and then choose Find > Find People For Tagging or click the Start People Recognition button (🔲) at the top of the Keyword Tags panel.

The Organizer opens the first photo in the People Recognition - Full Size View dialog box. People Recognition has found three of the four girls in this photo and surrounded each of their faces with a white box. When you move the pointer over any of the boxes it displays a black text box with the "Who is this?" prompt.

2   Starting with the girl at the left, click the "Who is this?" text, type the name **Pauline**, and then press Return. Photoshop Elements creates a new keyword tag for Pauline, which appears by default in the People category in the Keyword Tags panel. Name the second girl **Sophie** and the girl on the right **Lilly**.

New keyword tags are created for Pauline and Sophie and added to the People category in the Keyword Tags panel, but Photoshop Elements does not create a new tag for Lilly; the existing tag that you created earlier is detected and added to the people recognition data for this catalog.

3   Click the Add Missing Person button at left below the tagging preview. Drag the new "Who is this?" box onto the face of the taller girl and use the handles around the box to surround her face neatly. Type the name **Emma** for this girl.

4   Click the arrow at the right of the image to move on to the next photo selected for tagging. This time, People Recognition has detected all four faces. Click the "Who is this?" box for the girl at the left. You have not yet tagged enough faces for People Recognition to name the girl, but you are offered a choice of the available tags. From left to right, name the girls Lilly, Emma Sophie and Pauline.

5 People Recognition thinks it has identified another face in the top right corner of the image. Click the Close button (x) to dismiss the "Who is this?" box or Photoshop Elements will register this as a person not yet named. You'll see a People Recognition alert asking you to confirm this person's exclusion from People Recognition; click Yes.

6 Double-click the face of Lilly, the girl at the left. The People Recognition dialog box changes, giving you the opportunity to confirm whether other faces detected in the photos in the Media Browser belong to Lilly. By default, all the faces are marked with a red Reject button (✖) and will be rejected unless you confirm them. As you move the pointer over an image the Reject button changes to a Confirm button (✔). Click to confirm the four thumbnails of Lilly.

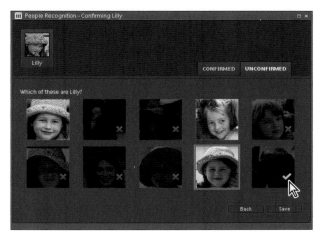

7 Click Save. A dialog opens asking if you'd like to name more people. Click No, and then click Done to close the People Recognition - Full Size View dialog box.

8 Ctrl-click to select the other ten images in the Media Browser that feature faces, and then choose Find > Find People For Tagging or click the Start People Recognition button (▣) at the top of the Keyword Tags panel.

9 Move the pointer over each of the faces in turn. Notice that Lilly is recognized as having already been tagged. Click the Name More People button at the lower right of the dialog box.

The People Recognition - Name People dialog box opens displaying thumb- nails of any faces from the selected images that have not yet been tagged or recognized by Photoshop Elements. As you move the pointer over the question mark below each thumbnail, the naming text box appears.

What you see in the People Recognition - Name People dialog box will vary depending on how many of the people in your photos you have already named, and how smart People recognition has become at recognizing and tagging them automatically. Once automatic tagging is occurring, the Name People dialog box will present you with groups of photos that have been tagged with a particular name, giving you the chance to confirm or reject the automatic naming, or show you pictures that may be people you don't know or sometimes objects that are not people.

10 Go ahead and name the rest of the people in your selection of images. The girls you have met already—their parents are Kate and Tom. When you're done, click Save. The People Recognition - Name People dialog box will continue to present groups of faces for tagging until all the people in the selected images have been named or recognized. A dialog box will appear to let you know when that is the case. Click OK to exit People Recognition and return to the Organizer.

In the keywords panel, the newly created tags are listed in the People Category, which is the default location for tags created by People Recognition. You can move the tags elsewhere if you chose and People Recognition will keep track of them.

11 In the keywords panel, click the Find box beside the Emma tag. All the photos featuring Emma are displayed in the Media Browser.

For more detailed information on People Recognition, as well as other aspects of the Auto-Analysis feature including Smart Tags, please refer to Adobe Photoshop Elements Help.

Congratulations, you've finished the lesson! You've imported files into the Elements Organizer using a variety of new techniques and learned several different ways to view and access the images in your catalog. You've also created, edited, and applied keyword tags to individual photographs so that they'll be easy to find in future.

You can skip chapter 3, which applies only to those using Photoshop Elements on Mac OS, and go directly to Lesson 4, "Advanced Organizing on Windows."

Before you move on, take a few moments to review the concepts and techniques presented in this lesson by working through the following questions and answers.

Review questions

1 How do you open the Elements Organizer component of Adobe Photoshop Elements?

2 Name three ways to import photos from your computer hard disk into your catalog.

3 What is a "watched folder"?

4 Summarize the characteristics of the Media Browser and Date views in the Organizer.

Review answers

1 Click the Organize button in the Welcome Screen when you start Photoshop Elements. Alternatively, if the Editor window is already open, click the Organizer button located to the right in the menu bar.

2 This lesson demonstrated three different ways to import photos into Photoshop Elements:

   • Drag-and-drop photographs from a Windows Explorer window into the Media Browser pane in the Organizer window.

   • In the Organizer, choose File > Get Photos And Videos > From Files And Folders, and then navigate to the folder containing your photos. You can import a whole folder, specify whether to include subfolders, or select just those images you want to add to your catalog.

   • In the Organizer, choose File > Get Photos And Videos > By Searching, and then select the folder on the hard disk that you wish Photoshop Elements to search. This method will locate all images in that folder and its subfolders and offer you the opportunity to select which images to import.

3 A watched folder is a folders on your computer that automatically alerts Photoshop Elements when a new photo is saved or added to the folder. By default, the My Pictures folder is watched, and you can add additional folders to the list. New images added to these folders can be automatically added to the Organizer.

4 In the default Media Browser view in the Organizer you can browse thumbnail images of your photos. You can choose to see them sorted by chronological order, by folder location, or by import batch. The Date view is organized in the form of a calendar where you can quickly find photos taken on a particular day, month, or year.

3 BASIC ORGANIZING ON MAC OS

Lesson Overview

On Mac OS, Photoshop Elements 8 works together with its companion product Adobe Bridge. You'll use Bridge to help you import, find and manage your photos, and then open them in Photoshop Elements to edit them, create presentations, and share your work.

In this lesson you'll begin to explore the Photoshop Elements and Adobe Bridge workspaces and learn a variety of ways to import your photos for editing. You'll find out how to review and compare images and get started with the essential skills you'll need to organize and keep track of your growing photo library:

- Using the Welcome screen
- Moving between Edit modes
- Using panels and the Panel Bin
- Switching between Photoshop Elements and Adobe Bridge
- Importing photos from a digital camera
- Importing images from folders on your computer
- Using pre-configured workspace modes in Bridge
- Reviewing and Comparing photos in Bridge
- Sharing Photos by e-mail

 You'll probably need between one and two hours to complete this lesson.

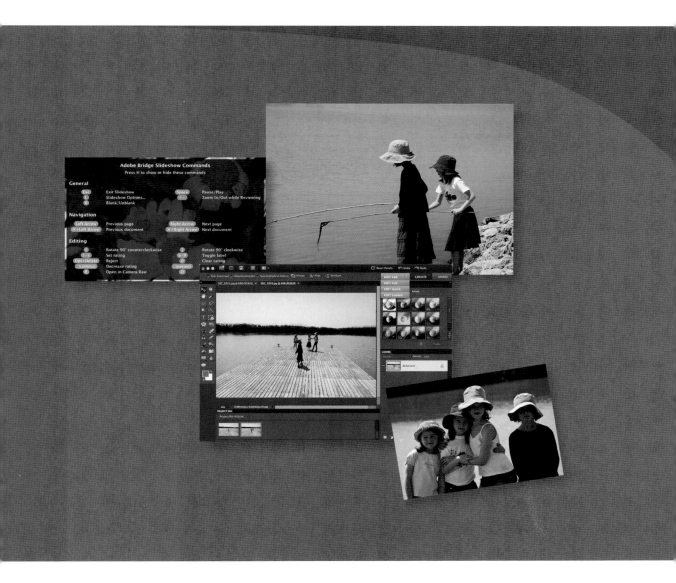

As you capture more and more images with your digital camera, it becomes increasingly important that you have ways to organize and manage your pictures on your computer so that your valuable memories are always accessible. Adobe Photoshop Elements makes it easy to import photos from a variety of sources and works closely together with Adobe Bridge—a powerful tool for sorting and searching your collection.

A Quick Tour of Photoshop Elements (Mac OS)

On Mac OS, Photoshop Elements works together with its companion product Adobe Bridge. You'll use Adobe Bridge to help you import, find and manage your photos, and then open them in Photoshop Elements to edit them, create presentations, and share your work. Although you don't have to use Bridge to open a photo in Photoshop Elements, the seamless integration of the two applications makes it by far the most convenient way to work.

Working in Photoshop Elements

When you start Photoshop Elements, the Welcome screen opens by default, serving as a convenient starting point or hub from which you can open a blank document, browse for files with Adobe Bridge, or import files from a camera or a scanner.

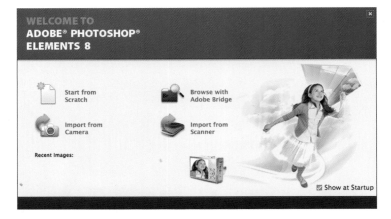

▶ **Tip:** If you prefer to skip the Welcome screen entirely when you start Photoshop Elements, disable the Show At Startup option by clicking the check box in the lower right corner.

To close the Welcome screen and start working directly in Photoshop Elements, click the Close button (x) in the upper right corner of the screen. You can reopen the Welcome screen at any time from within the Photoshop Elements workspace by choosing Window > Welcome.

The Bridge workspace

▶ **Tip:** If you wish to follow this description of the workspaces on your screen, start Photoshop Elements and click Browse With Adobe Bridge in the Welcome screen.

Adobe Bridge provides a flexible workspace where you can efficiently sort and organize your photos. In Adobe Bridge you can easily view, search, sort, filter, and manage, your files. You can use Bridge to rename, move, and delete files and also to work with keyword tags, labels, ratings and other metadata.

The Adobe Bridge workspace consists of three columns, or panes, that contain various panels. You can customize the workspace by moving or resizing panels.

You can save your customized workspace or select from several pre-configured arrangements listed across the top of the application window. For the purposes of the exercises in this book, you'll work mainly with the Essentials workspace preset.

▶ **Tip:** For more detailed information on the various Bridge panels and workspace configurations, please refer to Adobe Bridge Help.

The Essentials workspace gives you convenient access to your files and folders in the Favorites and Folders panels in the pane on the left. You can view thumbnails of the files in a selected folder in the Content panel in the center pane and a preview of a selected file in the Preview panel at the top of the right pane. The Filter and Collections panels on the left help you sort and search your files and the Keywords and Metadata panels on the right enable you to organize and manage them. You can customize the brightness of the user interface and the image backdrop (the background in the Content and Preview panels) separately in the General screen in Adobe Bridge Preferences, where you can also set the Accent Color that indicates a selected item.

Choosing files

To select more than one photo in the Bridge Content panel, hold down the Command key and click the photos you want to select. Command-clicking enables you to select multiple non-consecutive files. To select a series of images that are in consecutive order, click the first photo, and then hold down the Shift key and click the last in the series. All the photos between the two images you Shift-clicked will be selected.

The Photoshop Elements workspace

The Photoshop Elements workspace provides easy, intuitive access to all the tools and controls you'll need to fix and enhance your images, use them to create stylish photo projects, and share them with friends and family or the world at large.

The Photoshop Elements workspace consists of a central work and preview area surrounded by the toolbox on the left, the Project Bin below—displaying thumbnails of the images that are currently open—and the Panel Bin at the right.

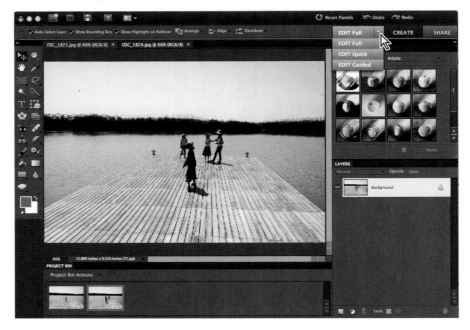

Above the Panel Bin are color-coded tabs for moving between Edit, Create and Share mode tasks and buttons for switching between the three Edit modes: Full Edit, Quick Edit, and Guided Edit.

The Full Edit workspace has tools to correct lighting and color problems, make complex selections, add text, create special effects, and enhance photos. In Quick Edit mode you'll find simplified tools for correcting color and lighting and other common image problems. The Guided Edit mode offers step by step instructions for a range of editing tasks, offering a great way to learn as you work.

You can rearrange the Full Edit workspace to suit the way you work by moving, grouping, hiding, and showing the Panel Bin or individual panels, as well as the toolbox and Project Bin. You can work with your photos in free-floating windows or consolidated on tabs in the work area, and open multiple views of a single image.

Using panels and the Panel Bin

In the Full Edit workspace, the Panel Bin provides a convenient location to organize the panels you use most often. By default, only the Effects and Layers panels are docked in the Panel Bin; other panels can be opened from the Window menu. All panels can either be kept docked in the Panel Bin or dragged to float in a convenient position above your image as you work.

It's a good idea to familiarize yourself with organizing the Full Edit workspace so that you'll always have the controls you need at your fingertips. Try the following tips and techniques:

- To open a panel that you don't see in the workspace, choose its name from the Window menu in the menu bar at the top of your screen.

- To hide a panel in the Panel Bin so that you see only its header bar, choose its name from the Window menu or click its header bar. To hide a free-floating panel so that you see only its header bar, click its header bar.

- To float a panel above your image in the work area, drag it out of the Panel bin by its header bar. You can also float the Project Bin and the toolbox by dragging them away from their default positions.

- To return a floating panel to the Panel Bin, drag it into the Panel Bin and release the mouse button when you see a blue line indicating the new position for the panel. You can either place the panel between two others or drag it onto another panel to create a tabbed panel group. Switch between grouped panels by clicking their name tabs. Drag the name tag to move a panel out of a group.

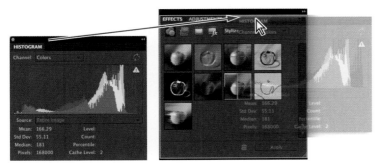

▶ **Tip:** Floating panels can also be grouped in this manner, or snapped together one above the other.

- To collapse a panel to an icon, click the two white triangles at the right of the header bar. You can collapse the entire Panel Bin or grouped floating panels in the same manner. Click the triangles again to expand the panel or group.

- To expand a single panel in a collapsed group, choose its name from the Window menu.

- To close a panel, drag it out of the Panel Bin and click the close button at the left end of its header bar or choose its name from the Window menu.

- To adjust the width of the Panel Bin, drag its left border.

- To adjust the height of panels in the Panel Bin, drag the separator bars between panels up or down.

- To adjust the size of a floating panel, drag the panel's lower right corner. (Some panels cannot be resized.)

- To return the workspace to the default arrangement, choose Window > Reset Panels or click the Reset Panels button ( ) at the top of the workspace.

Working with the Application Frame

The Application Frame groups all the Photoshop Elements workspace elements in an integrated window so you can treat the application as a single unit. When you move or resize elements such as panels, bins or the application window itself, all the elements within it are rearranged in response to each other, so that none overlap. Panels won't disappear from view when you switch applications or if you accidentally click out of the application. If you work with two or more applications, you can position them side by side on the screen or on multiple monitors.

If you prefer to work with the traditional, free-form user interface of the Mac, you can choose Window > Application Frame to toggle it on or off. When the Application Frame is turned off, you can also show or hide the Application Bar by choosing Window > Application Bar; the button controls in the Application Bar are also available as menu commands.

Opening Bridge from Photoshop Elements

From Photoshop Elements you can open Bridge in several ways:

- Click Browse With Adobe Bridge in the Welcome screen. While Photoshop Elements is running you can access the Welcome screen at any time by choosing Window > Welcome.

- Choose File > Browse With Bridge.

- Click the Bridge icon (Br) in the Application bar at the top of the workspace.

If you opened Bridge from Photoshop Elements, you can switch back without opening a file by choosing File > Return To Adobe Photoshop Elements. You'll learn how to open files in Photoshop Elements from Bridge in the next section.

Getting photos

In the next series of exercises you'll import and open images using a variety of methods.

Browsing for files with Adobe Bridge

First we'll look at browsing for files and opening them using Adobe Bridge.

1   Start Photoshop Elements. If the Welcome screen does not appear—or if Photoshop Elements is already running—choose Window > Welcome.

2   In the Welcome screen, click Browse With Adobe Bridge.

3   In Bridge, click Essentials in the row of workspace options at the top of the application window.

4   In the Favorites panel in the panel group at the left, click the shortcut to your Documents folder. If you don't see the Favorites panel, right-click / Control-click the header of any other panel and choose Favorites Panel from the context menu, or choose Window > Favorites Panel, and then click the shortcut to your Documents folder.

5   In the Bridge Content panel, locate the PSE8CIB folder that you created in Getting Started at the beginning of this book and do one of the following:

   •   Right-click / Control-click your PSE8CIB folder and choose Add To Favorites from the context menu.

   •   Drag the PSE8CIB folder into the Favorites panel.

   •   Select your PSE8CIB folder and choose File > Add To Favorites.

You'll use this link to your PSE8CIB folder to help you locate the lesson files for many of the lessons throughout this book.

6   Click the new entry for the PSE8CIB folder in the Favorites panel. In the Content panel, double-click to open the Lessons folder, and then double-click the Lesson02-03 folder. Open the Import folder, and then the BATCH1 folder.

7   Command-click to select all four images, and then do one of the following:

   •   Choose File > Open With > Adobe Photoshop Elements 8.

   •   Right-click / Control-click any of the selected files and choose Open With > Adobe Photoshop Elements 8 from the context menu.

The four images open in Photoshop Elements in floating image windows, one in front of the other. The Project bin displays thumbnails of all the open images.

● **Note:** Before you start working on the exercises, make sure that you've installed the software on your computer from the application CD (see the Photoshop Elements 8 documentation) and that you have correctly copied the Lessons folder from the CD in the back of this book onto your computer's hard disk (see "Copying the Classroom in a Book files" on page 2).

▶ **Tip:** If you don't see your Documents folder listed in the Favorites panel, open Bridge Preferences. On the General tab, activate the check box beside Documents in the Favorites pane at the bottom of the dialog box, and then click OK.

8 Choose Window > Images > Cascade.

9 Double-click each of the thumbnails in the Project bin in turn to bring each image window to the front, making it the active image to which any editing command would be applied.

10 Experiment with the other commands in the Window > Images menu.

11 Click the Arrange Documents button (⊞) at the top of the workspace and experiment with the layout options and commands available in the menu.

12 When you're done, choose File > Close All.

Opening files from Photoshop Elements

If you know the location of the files you wish to work with, you can open them from within Photoshop Elements without browsing in Bridge.

1 In Photoshop Elements, choose File > Open.

2 In the Open dialog box, navigate to and open the PSE8CIB > Lessons > Lesson02-03 folder; then open the Import folder, and then the BATCH2 folder. Select all four images in the BATCH2 folder and click Open.

3 The four images open in floating image windows, one in front of the other. The Project bin displays thumbnails of all the open images. Choose File > Close All.

You can also use this method to import images from a CD-ROM or other removable media.

Opening files from the Finder

You can open files in Photoshop Elements directly from the Finder.

1   In Photoshop Elements, switch to the Finder by clicking the Finder icon in the Dock.

2   In the Finder, press Command+N on your keyboard to open a new Finder window.

3   In the new Finder window, navigate to and open the PSE8CIB > Lessons > Lesson02-03 folder; then open the Import folder, and then the BATCH3 folder. Select all four images in the BATCH3 folder and drag them to the Photoshop Elements icon in the Dock.

The images open in floating image windows, one in front of the other. The Project bin displays thumbnails of all the open images.

4   Choose File > Close All.

5   Repeat steps 1 through 3, this time dragging the files directly into the Photoshop Elements workspace.

This time, the four images open as tabbed documents, consolidated in the Edit pane. The Project bin displays thumbnails of all the open images.

6   Click each of the four tabs in turn to bring the corresponding image to the front, making it the active image to which any editing command would be applied.

The file name text on tab of the active image is highlighted, while the tabs of the inactive images are dimmed. In the Project Bin, the currently active image is surrounded by a blue border.

Getting photos from a camera or card reader

You can download (copy) photos from cameras and card readers in several ways:

•   The recommended method is to copy photos from your camera and import them into Photoshop Elements using the Adobe Photo Downloader. Using this method is not only quick and easy, but also allows you to improve and organize your photos during the import process.

•   Open the Welcome screen and click the Import From Camera option.

•   If your camera or card reader displays as a drive in the Finder, you can drag them directly into Photoshop Elements, or open them from within Photoshop Elements with the File > Open command.

In some cases, you need to install the software driver that came with your camera before you can download pictures to your computer.

Using the Adobe Photo Downloader

The Adobe Photo Downloader makes it easy to import photos from your camera directly into your Photoshop Elements catalog.

If you have a digital camera or memory card at hand with your own photos on it, you can step through this exercise using those images. Alternatively, you can simply follow the process in the book without performing the exercise yourself, or skip to the next section and return to this exercise when you are prepared.

1 Connect your camera or card reader to your computer. For instructions on connecting your device, refer to the manufacturer's documentation that came with it. Once your camera or card reader is connected to your computer, you're ready for the next step.

2 If the Photo Downloader dialog box does not appear automatically, choose File > Adobe Photo Downloader in Photoshop Elements or File > Get Photos From Camera in Bridge.

3 Under Source at the top of the Photo Downloader dialog box, choose the name of your camera or card reader from the Get Photos From menu. If the menu doesn't display the specific device name, choose Untitled.

4 Under Import Settings, accept the default folder location (your *username* > Pictures folder) listed next to Location, or click Choose to choose a new location for the files.

5 Next to Create Subfolder(s), choose one of the date formats from the menu if you want the photos to be stored in subfolders named by capture or import date. You can also choose Custom Name to create a folder using a name you type in the text box, or choose None if you don't want to create any subfolders at all. Your selection is reflected in the Location pathname.

6 From the Rename Files menu, choose Do Not Rename Files and ensure that all the other options are disabled except for Open Adobe Bridge.

You'll learn more about customizing import settings and the advanced features of the Adobe Photo Downloader in Lesson 5.

7 Click the Get Photos button. The photos are copied from the camera to the specified folder location, and then Bridge opens a new window in which the newly downloaded images are displayed in the Content panel.

▶ **Tip:** Your camera or card reader must be switched on to appear in the Get Photos From menu. If your camera is connected and switched on but the menu doesn't display the specific device name, choose Untitled. If no option for the device is available, choose Refresh List.

Reviewing and comparing photos

Adobe Bridge offers a range of ways to preview and compare your images. You can quickly review a selection of images in the Preview panel, view your photos as large as possible in Full Screen Preview or as a Slideshow, or review and refine a selection of images without distraction in Review mode.

Full Screen Preview displays images one at a time at full-screen size. Review mode displays images in a full-screen view that lets you navigate the images; refine your selection; label, rate, and rotate images; and open images in Camera Raw.

Viewing a selection of photos in the Preview panel

The Preview panel displays up to nine thumbnail images for quick comparisons.

1   In Bridge, make sure you are in the Essentials workspace, and then click the entry for your PSE8CIB folder in the Favorites panel. In the Content panel, double click to open the Lessons folder, and then open the Lesson02-03 folder.

2   Choose View > Show Items From Subfolders, and then choose View > Show Folders to hide the folder icons so that you see only the photo thumbnails.

3   Choose Edit > Deselect All or press Shift+Command+A to ensure you have no images selected.

4   Click Filmstrip in the row of workspace options at the top of the application window.

The Preview panel now occupies most of the workspace; the Content panel shrinks to a narrow strip below the Preview panel.

5   Click any of the thumbnails in the Content panel film strip to see a large preview in the Preview panel. Command-click more images to add to the selection. Command-click any of the selected images again to remove it from the selection and from the Preview panel.

6   Click in any of the images in the Preview panel to see a magnified Loupe view of the area you clicked. Drag in the image to magnify the area beneath the pointer. Zoom in or out in the Loupe view by pressing the plus sign (+) or minus sign (-) key. Click inside the magnified view to close it, or click the Close button (x) in the lower right corner.

7   Right-click / Control-click any of the images and take note of the options available in the context menu. You can apply a star rating, label a photo, or rotate it—all without moving the pointer outside the Preview panel.

Viewing photos at full-screen size

The Preview panel displays up to nine thumbnail images for quick comparisons.

1   Keeping the same group of images selected, choose View > Full Screen Preview or press the Space bar on your keyboard.

2   Use the arrow keys on your keyboard to cycle through the selected images. Press the plus sign (+) or minus sign (-) key to zoom in or out of an image. You can also use a mouse scroll wheel to increase and decrease magnification. To pan the image, zoom in and then drag.

▶ **Tip:** If you open Full Screen Preview with a single image selected, the arrow keys will cycle the preview through any other images in the same folder.

3   Press the Esc key to exit from Full Screen Preview.

Viewing a full-screen slideshow

1   Choose View > Slideshow to see a full-screen slideshow of the selected images. Press the Space bar to pause or restart the slideshow. By default the slideshow ends automatically after playing through the selection once. If the slideshow continues playing, press the Esc key to stop it.

2   Choose View > Slideshow Options and experiment with the settings, and then play the slideshow again to see the results.

3   Press H while the slideshow is playing to see the slideshow controls. Notice that as well as commands for zooming and navigating in the slideshow there are commands to rotate an image and to apply or remove ratings and labels without leaving the slideshow.

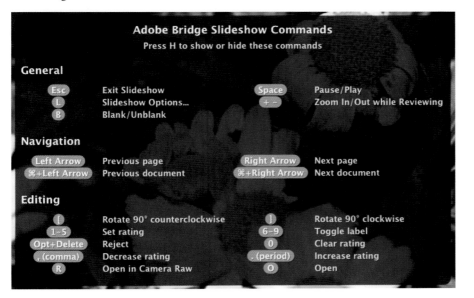

● **Note:** You'll learn about using ratings, labels and keywords to organize your images in Lesson 5 "Advanced Organizing on Mac OS."

4   Press the Esc key to stop the slideshow.

Compare and select photos using Review mode

Review mode is a dedicated full-screen view for reviewing a selection of images, refining—or narrowing—the selection, and performing basic editing tasks. Review mode displays the selected photos in a rotating "carousel" that you can navigate interactively.

1   Choose Edit > Select All or press Command+A, and then choose View > Review Mode or press Command+B on your keyboard.

2   Try each of these actions:

*   Click the Left or Right Arrow buttons in the lower left corner of the screen, or use the arrow keys on your keyboard, to go to the previous or next image.

*   Drag the foreground image right or left to bring the previous or next image forward. Click any image in the background to bring it to the front.

*   To remove an image from the selection, drag it off the bottom of the screen or click the Down Arrow button in the lower left corner of the screen.

*   Click the foreground image to activate the Loupe tool.

*   Right-click / Control-click any image to rate it, apply a label, rotate it. These commands and more be accessed by pressing H on your keyboard.

*   Press] to rotate the foreground image 90° clockwise. Press [to rotate the image 90° counterclockwise.

You can access the Loupe tool by clicking its button in the lower right of the screen where you'll also find the New Collection button. Clicking the New Collection button creates a collection from the selected images and exits Review mode. You'll learn about Collections in Lesson 5, "Advanced Organizing on Mac OS."

3   Press Esc or click the Close button (x) in the lower right corner of the screen to exit Review mode.

4   Click Essentials in the row of workspace options at the top of the Bridge application window.

5   Choose View > Show Folders to make your folders visible once more in the Content panel, and then choose View > Show Items From Subfolders to disable that option.

Sharing photos by e-mail

Photoshop Elements streamlines the process of sharing photos by e-mail.

1   Open one or more photos in Photoshop Elements, and then select the photo or photos you want to share in the Project Bin. Click the Share tab, and then click the E-mail Attachments button.

Your default e-mail application opens a new message with the attachments already in place—it's that easy! If you're e-mailing a photo for the first time and you're asked to choose the e-mail service you wish to use, make your choice and click OK.

2   Compose your message.

3   Select recipients for the e-mail and click Send.

▶ **Tip:** If your image files are large, you may wish to use the File > Save For Web command to reduce the file size before e-mailing them. See "Saving copies of your images for use on the Web" in Lesson 7.

Using Help

Help is available in several ways, each one useful in different circumstances:

Help in the application   A subset of the user documentation for Adobe Photoshop Elements is available as Help in the application in a form that you will display in your default browser. Help in the application provides easy access to summarized information on common tasks and concepts and can be especially useful if you are new to Photoshop Elements or if you aren't connected to the Internet.

Help on the Web   This is the most comprehensive and up-to-date version of Photoshop Elements Help. It is the recommended choice if you have an active Internet connection.

Help PDF   Help is also available as a PDF that is optimized for printing; simply click View Help PDF at the top left of the online Help page. The Help PDF file is

● **Note:** You do not need to be connected to the Internet to view Help in the application. However, with an active Internet connection you can see a more complete version of the user documentation and also access the latest updates as well as community-contributed content.

several megabytes in size and may take a considerable time to download with a slow Internet connection.

Navigating Help

Choose Help > Photoshop Elements Help (or Help > Adobe Bridge Help) or simply press the F1 key. Your default Web browser will open and display the starting page of the Adobe Photoshop Help in the application or Help on the Web if you have a live Internet connection. Click the plus sign (+) to the left of a topic heading in the table of contents to see its sub-topics. Click a topic or sub-topic to display its content. Type a search term in the Search text box at the top right of the page and press Enter on your keyboard.

Search tips

Adobe Help Search works by searching the entire Help text for topics that contain all the words typed in the Search box. These tips can help you improve your search results in Help:

* If you search using a phrase, such as "shape tool," put quotation marks around the phrase. The search returns only those topics containing that specific phrase.

* Make sure that the search terms are spelled correctly. If a search term doesn't yield results, try using a synonym, such as "photo" instead of "picture."

Links to help in the application

There are links to additional help connected to specific workflow tasks throughout the Photoshop Elements application. Clicking these links will take you to the corresponding topic in either Help in the application or on the Web. In some cases, such as the Print dialog box, you'll see a Help button; elsewhere you'll find "Tell Me More" text links and hot-linked tips, recognizable by the light bulb icon.

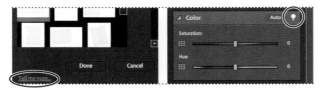

You've reached the end of the first lesson. Now that you know how to import and open photos and are familiar with the essentials of the Photoshop Elements and Adobe Bridge workspaces, you're ready to move on to Lesson 5 "Advanced Organizing on Mac OS" where you'll learn about some advanced importing options and how to sort, organize, group and search your photos.

Before you move on, take a few moments to read through the review questions and answers on the facing page.

Review questions

1   How do you open Adobe Bridge from Photoshop Elements?

2   Name three methods to import photos located on your computer hard disk into your catalog.

3   What are the advantages of using the Adobe Photo Downloader to download images from your camera or card reader?

4   What are your options for reviewing and comparing images before you open them for editing or inclusion in a project or presentation?

Review answers

1   There are several ways to open Adobe Bridge from Photoshop Elements. You can click Browse With Adobe Bridge in the Welcome screen, which can be accessed even while Photoshop Elements is running by choosing Window > Welcome. You can also choose File > Browse With Bridge or click the Bridge icon (Br) in the Application bar at the top of the workspace.

2   This lesson demonstrated three different methods for importing photos into Photoshop Elements from your hard disk:

   • Drag photographs directly from a Finder window into the Photoshop Elements workspace or onto the Photoshop Elements icon in the Dock.

   • Browse for files using Adobe Bridge.

   • Open files from within Photoshop Elements by choosing File > Open.

3   The Adobe Photo Downloader enables you to rename, organize, and improve photos while importing them to your computer. Properly organizing photos during import makes finding them later much easier and faster.

4   In Adobe Bridge, you can quickly review a selection of images in the Preview panel, view your photos as large as possible in Full Screen Preview or as a Slideshow, or review and refine a selection of images without distraction in Review mode. The Preview panel displays up to nine thumbnail images for quick comparisons. Full Screen Preview displays images one at a time at full-screen size. Review mode displays images in a full-screen view that lets you navigate the images; refine your selection; label, rate, and rotate images; and open images in Camera Raw.

4 ADVANCED ORGANIZING ON WINDOWS

Lesson Overview

As your collection grows to hundreds or even thousands of images, keeping track of your photos can be a daunting task. Photoshop Elements 8 delivers advanced organizing tools that not only get the job done, but in fact make the work quite enjoyable.

In this lesson you'll learn a few new methods of importing images and some of the more advanced techniques for organizing, sorting, and searching your growing photo collection:

- Using advanced Photo Downloader options

- Acquiring still frames from video

- Importing pictures from a PDF document

- Importing pictures from a scanner

- Using Version Sets and Stacks to organize photos

- Sorting photos by location using the Map view

- Viewing and managing files in the Folder Location view

- Finding photos by similarity, metadata, and text search

- Hiding unwanted files from view

- Grouping photos in Albums and Smart Albums

 You'll probably need between one and two hours to complete this lesson.

Discover some advanced import options that will make organizing your photos even easier. Have Photoshop Elements apply tags and group images automatically during import so your files will already be organized by the time they arrive in your catalog! Simplify navigating your catalog with Stacks, Version Sets and Albums and learn about a range of powerful search features to help you find exactly the right files.

Getting started

Note: Before you start working on this lesson, make sure that you've installed the software on your computer from the application CD (see the Photoshop Elements 8 documentation) and that you have correctly copied the Lessons folder from the CD in the back of this book onto your computer's hard disk (see "Copying the Classroom in a Book files" on page 2).

In this lesson you'll be working mainly in the Organizer workspace, though you will switch to the Editor to capture frames from a video and import images from a PDF document. You'll start by creating a new catalog so that you won't confuse the practice files for this lesson with files for the other lessons in this book.

1   Start Photoshop Elements, either by double-clicking the shortcut on your desktop or by choosing Start > All Programs > Adobe Photoshop Elements 8.

2   Do one of the following:

- If the Welcome Screen appears, click the Organize button at the left.

- If the Editor window opens without first displaying the Welcome Screen, click the Welcome Screen button (🏠) at the right of the menu bar. When the Welcome Screen appears, click the Organize button. Alternatively, simply click the Organizer button (▦) located at the right of the Editor window menu bar, and then wait until the Organizer has finished opening.

- If the Organizer window opens without first displaying the Welcome Screen, you don't need to do anything more—you're all set to continue with step 3.

3   In the Organizer, choose File > Catalog.

4   In the Catalog Manager dialog box, click New.

5   In the Enter A Name For The New Catalog dialog box, type **Lesson4** as the catalog name, disable the Import Free Music Into This Catalog option, and then click OK.

Now you have a special catalog that you'll use just for this lesson; all you need is some pictures to put in it.

Advanced import options

In Lesson 2 you learned various methods for importing images into the Organizer and how to apply keyword tags manually as a way of organizing photos once they are in your catalog.

In the following exercise you'll discover some advanced import options that will make organizing your photos even easier. By having Photoshop Elements apply tags and create groups automatically during the import process, your images will already be organized by the time they arrive in your catalog! You'll also learn how to import photos from some different sources—capturing a frame from a movie, extracting images embedded in a PDF document, and acquiring an image from a scanner.

Photo Downloader options

If you have a digital camera or memory card at hand with your own photos on it, you can step through this first exercise using those images. To get the best results from this exercise, you should have several batches of pictures taken at different times on the same day.

Alternatively, you can simply follow the process and refer to the illustrations in the book, without actually performing the exercise yourself.

1   Connect your digital camera or card reader to your computer, following the manufacturer's instructions.

2   Do the following:

- If the Windows Auto Play dialog box appears, click Cancel.

- If the Photo Downloader dialog box appears automatically, continue with step 3.

- If the Photo Downloader dialog box does not appear automatically, choose File > Get Photos And Videos > From Camera Or Card Reader.

3 If the Photo Downloader dialog box opens in the Advanced mode, click the Standard Dialog button located near the lower left corner of the dialog box. From the Get Photos From menu at the top of the Photo Downloader dialog box, choose the name of the connected camera or card reader.

4 Under Import Settings, accept the default destination folder listed next to Location, or click Browse to choose a different destination. By default, the image files are saved to your My Pictures folder.

5 Without making any other changes to the settings, click the Advanced Dialog button in the lower left corner of the dialog box.

The Advanced Photo Downloader dialog displays thumbnails of the photos on your camera's memory card. Here you'll find access to a range of options for organizing your photos during import that are not available in the Standard dialog box. In the following steps you'll set up the automatic creation of subfolders and keyword tags.

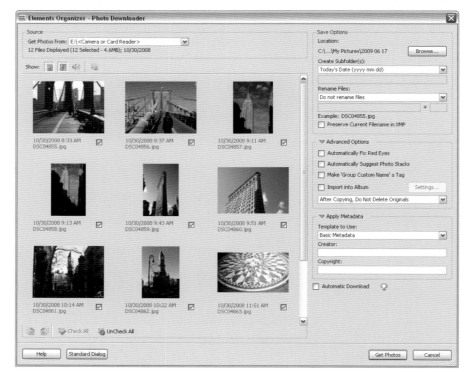

6 From the Create Subfolder(s) menu under Save Options, choose Custom Groups (Advanced). Your selection is reflected in the Location pathname.

You can see that the images have been automatically divided into groups, based on capture time and date. A slider below the Create Subfolder(s) menu enables you to adjust the granularity of the subdivision and the box to the right of the slider shows the resulting number of groups. In our example, the automatic grouping based on capture time has done a good of job separating our subjects, producing six groups.

7 Experiment by moving the slider to the left to generate fewer groups (sub-folders) or to the right to generate more. Scroll down the list of thumbnails to review the effect of the slider on the grouping of your photos. Note that the number of groups created is displayed in the box to the right of the slider.

Tip: To increase or decrease the number of groups by one at a time, press Ctrl-Shift-M or Ctrl-Shift-L respectively on your keyboard.

8   Next you'll apply custom names to the subfolders for your grouped photos. From the Group Name menu, choose Shot Date (yyyy mm dd) + Custom Name.

9   On the right end of the separator bar above the thumbnails of the first group, click the Custom Name field and type **Brooklyn Bridge** in the text box.

10 Repeat step 9 for the other groups in the list, giving each group a distinct name.

In our example, we used the group names: **Brooklyn Bridge, Empire State Building**, **Flatiron Building**, **Jefferson Market**, **Imagine** and **Ansonia Hotel**.

11 Under Advanced Options, activate the option Make 'Group Custom Name' A Tag, by clicking the check box. This will automatically create keyword tags corresponding to the group custom names and apply them to your photos as they are imported into the Organizer. If the options Automatically Fix Red Eyes and Automatically Suggest Photo Stacks are currently activated, disable them by clicking their checkboxes.

12 Click Get Photos. The photos are copied from the camera or memory card reader to the specified group subfolders on your hard disk.

13 If the Files Successfully Copied dialog box appears, click OK.

The Getting Media dialog box appears briefly while the photos are being imported into your Lesson4 catalog. The imported images appear in the Media Browser. You can see that Photoshop Elements has automatically created and applied tags for the groups during the import process. The new tags have been created inside the keyword tag category Other.

The Advanced Photo Downloader dialog box also offers other options: you can choose to import only a specified selection of the images on your memory card, rotate images as they are imported, fix red eye effects automatically, have your photos grouped into stacks, rename them, and add a range of metadata.

The more of these advanced options you take advantage of when importing your photos into the Organizer, the less time and effort you'll need to spend sorting and organizing your files later—and the easier it will be to find that specific photo months or even years after you added it to your catalog.

Later in this lesson you'll learn further techniques for organizing your catalog, but first let's look at some more methods of bringing images into Photoshop Elements.

Acquiring still frames from a video

You can capture frames from digital videos in any of the file formats supported by Photoshop Elements. These include: ASF, AVI, MLV, MOV, MPG, MPEG, and WMV. To capture and import frames from video, you'll need to open the Editor.

1   If you still have any images selected in the Organizer from the previous exercise, choose Edit > Deselect.

2   Click the small arrow on the orange Fix tab at the top of the Task Pane and choose Full Photo Edit from the menu. When the Editor opens choose File > Import > Frame From Video.

3   In the Frame From Video dialog box, click the Browse button. Navigate to your Lesson04-05 folder, select the file Tiger.mov, and click Open.

4   To start the video, click the Play button ( ). Click the Pause button ( ) after 3 or 4 seconds, and then use the arrow keys on your keyboard to move forward or backward one frame at a time until you find a frame you want to capture.

5   To capture any frame of the video as a still image, click the Grab Frame button or press your spacebar when the frame you want is visible on the screen.

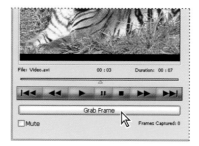

6   (Optional) You can continue to move forward and backward in the video to capture additional frames. When you have all the frames you want, click Done.

Depending on your video footage and which frames you captured, you might notice artifacts in the still image resulting from the fact that a video picture consists of two interlaced half-pictures. The odd-numbered scanlines of the image, also called odd fields, constitute one half of the picture, and the even-numbered scanlines, or even fields, the other. Since the two halves of the picture were recorded at slightly different times, the captured still image might look distorted.

For the purposes of this exercise, it's worthwhile to deliberately choose a frame with this kind of distortion, which is most easily identified as a 'zigzag' effect and is particularly noticeable on vertical detail, as can be seen in the image on the right.

In Photoshop Elements you can remedy this problem with the De-Interlace filter, which will remove either the odd or even fields in an image captured from video, and then replace the discarded lines either by duplication or by interpolation from the remaining lines, depending on the options you specify.

7 Choose the captured image you wish to use for this exercise. You can discard the others by clicking the Close button in the top right corner of each image window. Click No in the alert dialogs that ask if you wish to save the images.

8 With the image you've chosen still open in the Editor, switch from Full to Quick Edit mode. Click the triangle on the orange Edit tab at the top of the Panel Bin and choose Edit Quick.

9 From the View menu in the lower left corner of the Editor window, choose Before & After - Vertical.

10 Click the number in the Zoom value box in the lower right corner of the image display window, type **300**, and then press Enter. Use the Hand tool to move the image in either the Before or After pane so that you can see the tiger's eyes. (When you're working with tigers, it's *always* a good idea to watch the eyes!)

11 Choose Filter > Video > De-Interlace. Position the De-Interlace dialog box so that you can see both the Before and After views, and then choose either Odd Fields or Even Fields under Eliminate and either Duplication or Interpolation under Create New Fields By, and then click OK. The combination of options that will produce the best results depends on the image at hand. You can Undo after each trial and repeat this step until you are satisfied with the result.

12 Return to the Full Edit mode, save the image (File > Save) in your My CIB Work folder, and then close the image window in the Editor.

Importing from a PDF document

Photoshop Elements enables you to import either whole pages from a PDF document or to select and extract just the images you want.

1 In the Editor, choose File > Open.

2   In the Open dialog box, navigate to your Lesson04-05 folder, select the file ZOO.pdf, and then click Open. If you can't see the file ZOO.pdf in the Open dialog box, click the Files Of Type menu at the bottom of the dialog box and choose either All Formats or Photoshop PDF (*.PDF,*.PDP).

In the Import PDF dialog box, you can choose to import entire pages or just the images from a PDF file. If you choose to import pages from a multiple-page PDF file, you can Ctrl-click the page thumbnails to select those pages you wish to import. Pages are rasterized (converted to bit-mapped graphics) according to your choice of image size, resolution, and color mode. The imported result will be an image of the page similar to that acquired by scanning a printed document.

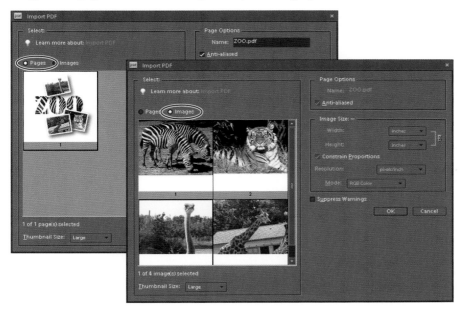

If you choose to import the images embedded in a PDF file rather than full pages, you can use the same method to multiple-select the images you want.

3   Under Select in the Import PDF dialog box, choose Images.

4   From the Thumbnail Size menu, select Fit Page to see the image previews at the largest possible size. Use the scrollbar at the right of the preview pane to scroll down to the last image.

5   Select Large from the Thumbnail Size menu. This enables you to see all four of the images in this file. Click to select an image you wish to import. Ctrl-click any additional images you would like to add to the import, and then click OK.

6   If any alert dialogs appear to let you know that the image files use an unsupported color mode, click Convert Mode.

Each image imported from the PDF file opens in its own document window in the Editor, ready for further processing.

7   For each imported image choose File > Save As, navigate to your My CIB Work folder, and save the file with a descriptive name in Photoshop (*.PSD,*.PDD) file format. If you wish to add the files to your catalog, activate the option Include In The Organizer before you click Save.

Scanning images

This exercise is optional; it requires that you have a scanner available.

1   To prepare for acquiring images from a scanner, switch to the Organizer, choose Edit > Preferences > Scanner, and then do the following:

*   If you have more than one scanner or an additional video input source installed, make sure that the correct device is selected in the Scanner menu.

*   Either accept the default settings for Save As (jpeg), and Quality (6 Medium) or, if you prefer different settings, change them now.

*   Disable the Automatically Fix Red Eyes option. You will learn about fixing red eye in the Organizer in Lesson 10, "Repairing, Retouching and Recomposing Images."

*   If you want to change the location to which the scanned files will be saved, click Browse, and then find and select the folder you want to use.

*   Click OK to close the Preferences dialog box.

2   Place the picture or document you want to scan on the scanner bed and make sure your scanner is turned on.

> **Tip:** Photoshop Elements 8 also allows you to scan images using a video input source—such as a web camera—attached to your computer.

3 If the scan dialog box does not appear automatically, go to the Organizer and choose File > Get Photos And Videos > From Scanner.

4 In the Scan dialog box, click the Preview button and examine the result.

Note: The general appearance of the dialog box and the options available for your scanner may differ from what you see in the illustrations.

5 (Optional) If you are not satisfied with the preview, change the scanner settings as preferred.

6 Click Scan. When the scan is complete, the thumbnail of the scanned image appears in the Media Browser pane in the Organizer.

7 Click Back To All Images to see your all the images in your catalog.

Tip: When you scan several photographs at once, Photoshop Elements can crop the scan into individual photos automatically and will also straighten them for you. For more information on the Divide Scanned Photos feature, see Photoshop Elements Help.

Organizing photos

Organizing your files and folders efficiently can be challenging. It's easy to forget what pictures are stored in which folder—and being forced to open and examine the content of numerous folders to find files can be both time consuming and extremely frustrating.

The Organizer can make the whole process much simpler and more enjoyable. The next set of exercises will show you how investing a little time in organizing your catalog can streamline the process of sorting through your image files, regardless of where they are stored.

Working with version sets

A version set automatically groups the original imported image file with any edited versions you've created. In the Media Browser, you'll see all versions of the image in a single stack rather than scattered amongst the rest of the items in your catalog—making it much easier for you to find the version you want.

For this exercise you'll use Auto Smart Fix to edit an image in the Organizer and Photoshop Elements will automatically create a version set grouping the original and the edited version. To prepare for the exercise, you'll clear any images that you've added to your Lesson4 catalog since the beginning of this lesson.

▶ **Tip:** The name of the currently active catalog is always displayed in the lower left corner of the Organizer window.

1   In the Organizer make sure the Lesson4 catalog is open. If the Show All button is visible above the Media Browser, click it. Choose Edit > Select All, and then choose Edit > Delete Selected Items From Catalog. The Confirm Deletion From Catalog dialog box appears; if you see the options Delete All Photos In Collapsed Stacks and Delete All Items In Collapsed Version Sets, activate both options by clicking their checkboxes, and then click OK.

2   Choose File > Get Photos And Videos > From Files And Folders.

3   In the Get Photos And Videos From Files And Folders dialog box, navigate to the Lesson04-05 folder and select the Photos Zoo folder. Activate the option Get Photos From Subfolders. If the options Automatically Fix Red Eyes and Automatically Suggest Photo Stacks are activated, disable them by clicking their check boxes.

4   Click Get Media. The Import Attached Keyword Tags dialog box appears; click Select All, and then click OK. Click OK to close any other alert dialog box. Click the Show All button above the Media Browser.

In the Media Browser, you can now see thumbnails of the images you've just added to your Lesson4 catalog.

5   In the Keyword Tags panel, click the triangle beside the Imported Keyword Tags category to see the newly added tags.

6 In the Media Browser, select the first photo of the Elephant and choose Edit > Auto Smart Fix. The Auto Smart Fix command corrects the overall color balance and improves shadow and highlight detail, if necessary. The edited copy of the photo is automatically grouped with the original photo in a version set, with the edited version topmost. A version set can be easily identified in the Media Browser by the version set icon in the upper right corner of the thumbnail.

Note: If you edit a photo in the Organizer, Photoshop Elements automatically creates a version set for you. If you edit an image in the Editor you need to choose File > Save As, and then activate the option "Save In Version Set With Original."

7 Click the expand button to the right of the thumbnail image to see the original and edited images in the version set displayed side by side.

Note: If you edit a photo that's already in a version set, the edited copy is placed at the top of the existing version set. To specify a different photo as the topmost, select it in the expanded view of the version set, and then choose Edit > Version Set > Set As Top Item.

8 To see only the topmost photo in a version set, click the collapse button to the right of the last thumbnail image in the expanded set, or right-click any image in the set, and then choose Version Set > Collapse Items In Version Set from the context menu. Notice the other commands available from the same context menu—as well as from the Edit menu—such as Version Set > Convert Version Set To Individual Items.

About stacks

You can create stacks to group a set of related photos in the Media Browser, making them easier to manage. Stack photos that make up a series or multiple images of the same subject to help reduce clutter in the Media Browser.

For instance, you might create a stack for several photos of your family taken in the same pose—keeping the candidates together until you have a chance to pick the best shot—or for photos taken at a sports event using your camera's burst mode or auto-bracket feature. Generally, when you take photos this way you end up with many variations of what is essentially the same photo, but you only want the best version to appear in the Media Browser. Stacking the photos lets you easily access them all in one place instead of having them scattered across rows of thumbnails.

1 In the Keyword Tags panel, click the empty Find box next to the Zebra tag in the Imported Keyword Tags category.

2 Click below the first thumbnail and drag upwards and to the right. When you release the pointer, all images intersected by the selection marquee are selected.

3 Choose Edit > Stack > Stack Selected Photos. The Zebra photos are now grouped in a stack.

A stack can be easily identified in the Media Browser by the stacked photos icon in the upper right corner of the image thumbnail.

You can expand and collapse a stack in the Media Browser the same way that you would with a version set—by clicking the expand or collapse button that you'll find on the right side of the stack frame.

4 Click the Show All button above the Media Browser, and then click the empty Find boxes next to the imported Hippo and Ostrich keyword tags.

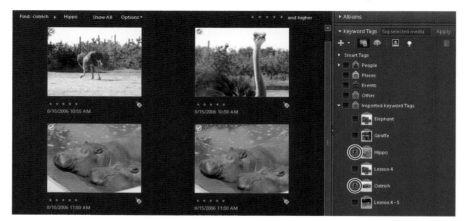

5 Marquee-select all four images, just as you did with the zebras, and then choose Edit > Stack > Automatically Suggest Photo Stacks.

The Automatically Suggest Photo Stacks dialog box appears. The two photos of the hippopotamus have been successfully placed in a group already, but the ostrich photos, which have less visual similarity, will need to be grouped manually.

6 In the Automatically Suggest Photo Stacks dialog box, scroll down to the bottom of the thumbnail list. Click the image of the ostrich in the last group and drag it upwards into the same group as the other ostrich.

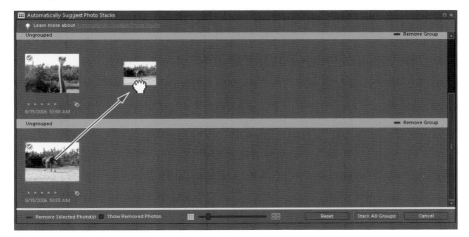

7 To split a suggested group, position the cursor between two images in the group. When the cursor changes to the scissors icon, click to divide the group.

8 To exclude all the photos in a group from being stacked, click the Remove Group button. Alternatively, you can select individual photos, and then click the Remove Selected Photo(s) button in the lower left corner of the dialog box.

9 If you change your mind about a photo that you've excluded from a group to be stacked, make sure the Show Removed Photos option at the bottom of the dialog box is activated, and then drag the thumbnail image from the removed photos bin and add it to the appropriate group in the main thumbnail area.

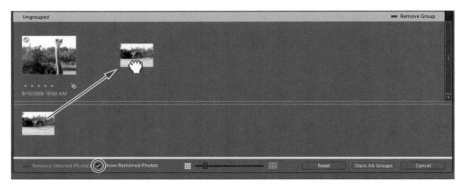

10 When you're done, click Stack All Groups to stack the photos in each group; then close the Automatically Suggest Photo Stacks dialog box. Click Show All in the Media Browser.

The two new stacks have simplified the view in the Media Browser considerably. Remember, a stack can be identified in the Media Browser by the stacked photos icon in the upper right corner of the thumbnail.

Tips for working with stacks

You should keep these points in mind when you're working with stacks:

- By default, the most recent photo is placed on top of the stack. To specify a new image as the topmost, expand the stack, right-click the desired photo, and then choose Stack > Set As Top Photo from the context menu.

- Combining two or more stacks merges them to form one new stack, with the most recent photo on top of the stack. The original groupings are not preserved.

- Many actions applied to a collapsed stack, such as editing, printing, and e-mailing, are applied to the topmost item only. To apply an action to multiple images in a stack, either expand the stack and select the individual images or un-stack them first.

- If you edit a photo that you've already included in a stack, the photo and its edited copy will be grouped as a version set nested inside the stack.

- If you apply a keyword tag to a collapsed stack, the keyword tag is applied to all items in the stack. When you run a search on the keyword tag, the top photo in the stack appears in the search results marked with the stack icon. If you want to apply a keyword tag to only one photo in a stack, expand the stack first and apply the keyword tag to just that photo.

Tip: You can access stack commands by right-clicking a stack, or by selecting the stack and choosing from the Edit menu.

Creating albums

Another way of grouping your photos is to organize them into albums. You might create a new album to group shots from a special occasion such as a wedding or a vacation, or to assemble the images that you intend to use in a project such as a presentation to a client or a slideshow.

The principal difference between grouping photos in an album and grouping them with a shared keyword tag is that in an album you can rearrange the order of the photos into any order you wish. In the Media Browser, each photo in an album displays a number in the upper-left corner, representing its order. You can drag the photos to rearrange their order within the album, which will effect the order in which they appear in a slideshow or their placement in a project layout.

A photo can be added to more than one album—the same image might be the first in a New York album and the last in a National Monuments album. You can also group albums—for example, you might group your New York and San Francisco albums inside your Vacations album. Your San Francisco album may also be included in a Road Trips album while the New York album is not.

Smart albums search your catalog and automatically collect the images that match any search criteria that you have specified. You'll learn about using smart albums later in this lesson in the section "Viewing and finding photos."

1 Choose File > Get Photos And Videos > From Files And Folders.

2 In the Get Photos And Videos From Files And Folders dialog box, navigate to the Lesson04-05 folder and select the Photos New York folder. Activate the Get Photos From Subfolders option and disable the other options.

3 Click Get Media. The Import Attached Keyword Tags dialog box appears; click Select All, and then click OK. Click OK to close any other alert dialog box.

In the Media Browser, you can now see thumbnails of the images you've just added to your Lesson4 catalog. In the Keyword Tags panel, you can see the newly added tags listed in the Imported Keyword Tags category.

4 If the Albums panel—on the Organize tab in the Task Pane—is collapsed, click the triangle in the header of the panel to expand it. (You may also find it convenient to collapse the Keyword Tags panel.)

5 To create a new album, click the Create New Album Or Album Category button (➕) below the panel header and choose New Album from the menu.

6 In the Create Album dialog box, type **New York** as the name of the new album.

7 Ctrl-click to select any six of the New York photos in the Media Browser, and then drag the group into the album Content pane. Click Done.

● **Note:** If you add a collapsed version set or stack to an album, only the topmost image in the version set or stack will be visible in the album. To add a picture other than the topmost photo to the album, expand the version set or stack, and select the desired image.

8 To see the contents of the new album, click the album name, or drag and drop the album icon onto the Find bar above the Media Browser. Notice the number in the top left corner of each photo, representing its order in the album.

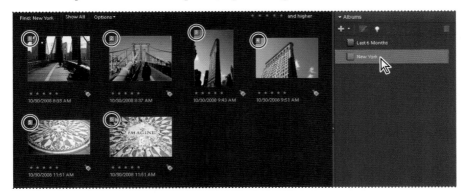

Note: It is not possible to view the contents of more than one album at a time, as images may appear in more than one album and occupy a different position in each.

9 Click the entry for the new album again to see all of the imported images in the Media Browser once more. If the thumbnails are set to display at a large enough size, photos that are included in an album are marked with a green album icon below their thumbnails. If you don't see the album icons, experiment with the thumbnail size slider above the Media Browser.

Tip: To see which album or albums a photo belongs to, hold the pointer over the album icon associated with the image in the Media Browser.

10 In the Media Browser, Ctrl-click to select the six New York photos that are not yet part of the new album, and then drag the selection directly onto the New York album icon. (Alternatively, you can drag the album icon onto any one of the selected photos, in the Media Browser.) All twelve images are now included in your New York album.

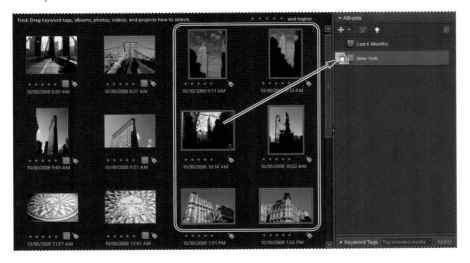

Tip: You can group related albums in an album category, as you group keyword tags in a category. To change an album's properties or icon, click the Edit Album button (▧) at the top of the Albums panel.

11 To change the order of the images in an album, first isolate the images in the album by clicking the album icon in the Albums panel. Select one or more photos in the Media Browser, and then simply drag the selection to the desired position. The photos are reordered when you release the mouse button.

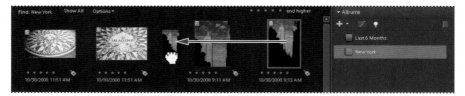

12 (Optional) To remove a picture from an album, right-click the picture in the album view, and then choose Remove from Album > [album name] from the context menu.

13 Click Show All above the Media Browser to see all the photos in your catalog.

14 To delete an album, right-click its icon in the Albums panel, and then choose Delete [album name] album from the context menu.

Note: Deleting an album does not delete the photos in the album from your catalog. Albums store only references to the actual photos.

15 Click OK in the Confirm Album Deletion dialog box.

The Map view

Note: You must have an active Internet connection to use this feature.

In the Map view of the Organizer, you can arrange and search for your photos by geographic location. You can link an image to a location either by typing an address or by simply dragging its thumbnail from the Media Browser directly onto the map.

1 In the Organizer, right-click the first thumbnail of the Empire State Building, and then choose Place On Map from the context menu.

2 In the Photo Location On Map dialog box, type **Empire State Building** in the text box, and then click Find.

3 In the Look Up Address dialog box, click OK to confirm the address: Empire State Building, New York, NY. 10001 US.

The Map view opens. The red pin indicates the location for your photo.

Below the map are the Zoom, Hand, and Move tools. You can zoom the view in or out, use the Hand tool to drag the map in any direction, or the Move tool to reposition the red pin if necessary.

4 Drag the second image of the Empire State Building to the pin you've already placed on the map. The pin is highlighted to show you when the new photo is in position; release the mouse button to locate the photo with its partner.

5 Choose Hybrid from the pop-up menu in the lower right corner of the Map panel, beside the Zoom, Hand, and Move tools.

6 Select the Zoom In tool (🔍) and click on the map twice, south of the pin you just placed.

7 Use the Hand tool to drag the map upwards and to the right so that you can see the Brooklyn Bridge, keeping the pin for the Empire State Building in view.

8 If you still have an image selected in the Media Browser, choose Edit > Deselect. Drag the Brooklyn Bridge tag from the Keyword Tags panel onto the map and release the mouse button when the tag is positioned over the Brooklyn Bridge.

9 Click on the new pin you just placed on the Brooklyn Bridge to display a preview of the photos assigned to that location.

10 Click the Limit Search To Map Area check box in the lower left corner of the Map View. Only photos mapped to the currently visible map area are displayed in the Media Browser.

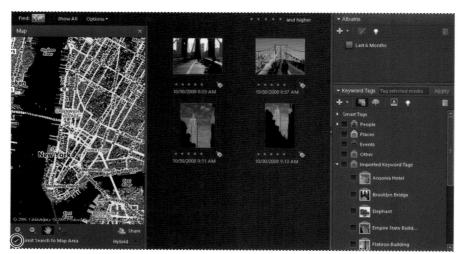

11 Right-click the Imagine tag and choose Place On Map from the context menu; then, type **Central Park New York, NY**. Click Find. Once you have a pin in Central Park, use the map's Move Tool to drag it a little inside the entrance at West 72nd St. (The Imagine mosaic is part of the John Lennon Memorial.)

12 (Optional) Place the other New York photos on the map, varying your method. The Ansonia Hotel is at 2109 Broadway New York, NY 10023. The Flatiron Building is at 175 Fifth Ave New York, NY 10011. The Jefferson Market branch of the New York Public Library is at 425 Sixth Avenue New York, NY 10011.

13 Click the Close button (⊠) in the upper right corner of the Map panel to close it. Click the Show All button above the Media Browser; then, right-click one of the Imagine photos and choose Show On Map from the context menu. The Map view opens, showing the location to which the photo was mapped.

14 Close the Map view.

This concludes the section on organizing your photos. You've learned about stacks and version sets, creating albums, and arranging photos by geographic location. In the next section, you'll learn how you can easily find your photos in the catalog, even when you haven't put a lot of effort into organizing them.

Viewing and finding photos

Photoshop Elements offers a variety of options for sorting and viewing the media in your catalog and a range of tools to help you quickly find just the files you need. In the Organizer you can search your catalog by media type, filename, date, folder location, star rating, album, keyword tag, text, or a range of other criteria, and then refine, sort and view the search results by album or in any chronological order.

- **The Find bar** You can drag a photo, keyword tag, creation, or album onto the Find bar across the top of the Media Browser to locate similar photos and media files. The Find bar also offers options for sorting the search results.

- **The Find menu** Use the Find menu commands to search your catalog by date, caption or note, file name, history, media type, metadata, or visual similarity. The Find menu also provides options for finding photos and media files that have unknown dates, are un-tagged, or are not included in any album.

- **Keyword Tags, Albums and Star Ratings** View only those files with a selected keyword tag, or combination of tags, by clicking in the Keyword Tags panel, or files in a particular album by clicking in the Albums panels. Use the Star Ratings filter in the Find bar to see just those photos and media files with a specified rating, or to refine a search based on any other criteria.

- **Text Search box** Type in the text box above the Find bar to locate media with matching text—whether it's in the filename, caption, metadata, or album name. The Text Search box also includes a dynamic list of existing keywords.

- **The Timeline** Choose Window > Timeline to display the timeline above the Media Browser. Use the Timeline as a search tool in its own right, or in combination with any of the other tools and views to help you refine a search or navigate the results. You might search for photos with the keyword tag "Kids", and then use the Timeline to limit the search to a particular date range.

  In the Timeline, click a month or set a date range to find photos and media files by capture date in Thumbnail view. See a breakdown by import date in the Import Batch view or a folder by folder distribution in Folder Location view. The height of the bars in the timeline indicate the number of files in each group. The Timeline becomes particularly helpful when your catalog contains a large number of files captured over a period of several years.

Finding photos by visual similarity

You can search for photos containing similar shapes, color, or general appearance.

1 If you are in another display mode, click the Click the Display button (🖥) above the Task Pane and switch to Thumbnail View. If you still have any images selected in the Media Browser, choose Edit > Deselect. If you see the Show All button in the Find bar, click it.

2 Drag either photo of the Ansonia Hotel (the last two photos in the New York set) to the Find bar.

The images you see in the Media Browser are now displayed in descending order of similarity in visual appearance to the photo you dragged to the Find bar. A marker displaying the calculated percentage of visual similarity for each image appears in the bottom left corner of its thumbnail. Photoshop Elements has done well to find the other shot of the same building as the most visually similar, despite the different aspect and detail. At lower percentages, the giraffes are more of a long shot!

3 Click the Show All button to clear this search.

Finding photos using details and metadata

Searching your catalog by metadata detail is useful when you want to narrow a search by applying multiple criteria. For example, you could configure a single search to find any photo in landscape orientation that was captured on a specific date, has been tagged with a nominated keyword *and* assigned a rating of five stars.

Some metadata is generated automatically by your camera when you capture an image; some is added when you spend time organizing your catalog. Searchable metadata includes filename, file type, keyword tags, albums, notes, author, map location, capture date, camera model, shutter speed, F-stop—to name just a few! For the following exercise you'll search for photos taken near a specific location.

1   Choose Find > By Details (Metadata) in the Organizer. The Find By Details (Metadata) dialog box appears. Under Search Criteria, click the first menu and scroll down the list, noting the many options available. Choose Map Location.

2   From the menu next to Map Location, choose Within, and then click the magnifying glass icon. The Photo Location On Map dialog box appears; type **350 5th Ave, New York, NY 10001** in the address box, and then click Find. Click OK to close the Photo Location On Map dialog box.

3   In the Find By Details (Metadata) dialog box, type **2** as the distance and choose Miles from the menu at the right.

● **Note:** To include more metadata values in your search, click the plus (+) button and specify new values using the menus that appear. To remove criteria from the search click the minus (-) sign to the right side of the item you wish to remove. If you specify multiple search criteria, activate the appropriate option to search for files matching any or all of the search criteria.

4   Disable the Save This Search Criteria As Smart Album option and click Search. Only images that match the specified criteria are displayed. (The results will depend on how far you progressed with the Map View exercise.)

5   (Optional) To modify the search, click Options in the Find bar, and then choose Modify Search Criteria from the menu. The Find By Details (Metadata) dialog box opens, showing the current search criteria set. Make the changes you want, and then click Search to display the new results in the Media Browser.

6   Click the Show All button in the Find bar.

Find photos using a text search

You can quickly find the photos you want using a text-based search. Type a word in the Text Search box at the left of the Find bar just above the Media Browser, and the Organizer will display images that match the text across a wide range of criteria. Matches can include items such as author, captions, dates, filenames, keyword tags, metadata, notes, album names, album groups, and camera information; Photoshop Elements will look for the search term in any text that is associated with the file.

You can use a text search as a convenient shortcut—for example, type the name of a tag, rather than navigating to the Keyword Tags panel. For Photoshop Elements 8, the feature has been enhanced to make it even easier and quicker to use. The search box has been augmented with a dynamic list of existing tags. As soon as you type a letter, the search box displays a list of tags starting with that letter; as you type more text the list changes to offer tags that match whatever you type. Click the item you want in the list and only the images tagged with that keyword are displayed.

Text search also supports the operators "and," "or," and "not" if they are preceded and followed by a space. For example, you could type "vacation and kids" to find only images with both words in their metadata, not just either one. Some words can be processed by Photoshop Elements as special instructions, not as specific search criteria. For example, you may want to search for a file tagged "Birthday," but only among your video files. You can use the Media "Type" and "Video" keywords. So, you would type "Type: Video Tag: Birthday."

For more information on using Text Search, and for a list of supported operators and special tags, please refer to Photoshop Elements Help.

Metadata support for audio and video files

Photoshop Elements 8 provides improved metadata support for audio and video files in the Organizer.

In the Properties - Metadata panel, metadata information is categorized into separate audio and video sections. In the Brief view, you'll find information such as pixel aspect ratio for video, while the audio section includes artist, album name, etc, if that information is present in the file. The File Properties section displays the filename, document type, creation and modification dates, and—if you activate the Complete view—the file size for your audio and video files.

1 Right-click on the audio file Temple of the Moon.wav and choose Show Properties to open the Properties - Metadata panel. To view all the available metadata, click the Info button (ⓘ) at the top of the panel, and then enable the Complete view options below the Info pane.

2 Repeat step 1 for the video file Tiger.mov.

⬤ **Note:** You cannot edit the metadata for audio and video files in Photoshop Elements.

3 Close the Properties panel by clicking the close button in the top right corner.

Viewing and managing files by folder location

In the Folder Location view you can manage your folders, add files to your catalog, automatically tag files with their folder name, and add or remove folders from Watched Folder status.

1 Click the Display button (🖥) above the Task Pane and choose Folder Location from the menu.

The Folder Location view divides the Media Browser into two parts: the folder hierarchy panel on the left, and the image thumbnail panel on the right. The folder hierarchy panel displays all the folders on your hard disk. The Media Browser displays the contents of a selected folder. Folders containing managed files (files that you've imported into a Photoshop Elements catalog) are marked with a Managed folder icon (📁). Watched folders have a Watched folder icon (📁).

2   To familiarize yourself with navigating your catalog via the Folder Location view and with the viewing options available, try each of these actions:

- To see thumbnails of all of your managed files in the Media Browser grouped by folder location, right-click in the folder hierarchy panel and activate the option Show All Files in the context menu. (When the option is activated a check mark appears beside it.) This option is useful when you want to search all your managed files while in Folder Location view.

- To see only those managed files in the folder that is currently selected in the hierarchy, right-click the folder entry in the folder hierarchy panel and disable the menu option Show All Files.

- To find the folder location of a file, click the file's thumbnail in the Media Browser. The folder containing the file is highlighted in the hierarchy.

- To find files in a specific folder—whether the Show All Files option is activated or not—click the folder in the left panel. Thumbnails for the files in that folder appear in the Media Browser, grouped under the folder name.

3   To familiarize yourself with managing your files and folders from the Folder Location view, try each of the following operations:

- To instantly tag a group of files by their folder locations, click the Instant Keyword Tag icon above that group of thumbnails in the Media Browser panel. In the Create And Apply New Keyword Tag dialog box you can accept the folder location as the keyword tag, or type a different keyword and apply it simultaneously to all managed files in that folder.

- To move a managed file to a different folder, simply drag the file's thumbnail from the Media Browser panel to a folder in the folder hierarchy panel.

- To view a folder in Windows Explorer, right-click the folder entry in the folder hierarchy and choose Reveal in Explorer from the context menu.

- To add or remove a folder from watched-folder status, right-click the folder entry in the folder hierarchy panel and choose Add to Watched Folders or Remove from Watched Folders.

- To add the unmanaged files in a folder to your catalog, right-click the folder in the hierarchy and choose Add Unmanaged Files To Catalog.

- To rename or delete a folder, right-click its entry in the hierarchy and choose the appropriate menu option.

- To create a new folder, right-click the entry for what will become the parent folder and choose New Folder from the context menu.

4   To return to the standard thumbnail view in the Media Browser, click the Display button (🖥) and choose Thumbnail View from the menu. In the Media Browser, click the Show All button above the thumbnails.

Note: You can change the default viewing option for the Folder Location view in the Organizer preferences. Choose Edit > Preferences > Folder Location View and activate either All Files Grouped By Folder or Only Files In The Selected Folder.

Hiding files

You've already learned how you can simplify the process of working with your growing catalog by creating stacks and version sets to help reduce clutter in the Media Browser. Stacking related shots and grouping edited versions with their originals effectively reduces the number of images on view; you can choose the most interesting image in a stack or version set as the topmost and keep the other images tucked out of view until you choose to work with them.

In many cases it may be more effective to hide those images from view entirely. Once you've settled on the best of a stack of similar photos, or of several edits in a version set, you can hide the other images from view so that they will no longer appear in search results, distract you when making selections, or need to be taken into consideration when applying commands. Hiding a photo does not delete it from its folder on your hard disk, remove it from your catalog, or even from an album—you can un-hide it at any time if you start a new project where it might be useful or if you find that you could make use of a differently edited version.

1 Ctrl-click to select both photos of the Empire State Building, and then choose Edit > Auto Smart Fix Selected Photos. Auto Smart Fix is applied to both images and both are automatically grouped in separate version sets with the edited versions topmost.

2 Ctrl-click to select both version sets and choose Edit > Version Set > Convert Version Set To Individual Items. There are now four images of the Empire State Building in the Media Browser: two originals and two edited copies.

3 Ctrl-click to select the second Brooklyn Bridge photo, both of the original photos of the Empire State Building, and the first image of the Jefferson Market. Choose Edit > Visibility > Mark As Hidden. The Hidden File icon now appears in the lower left corner of all four Thumbnails.

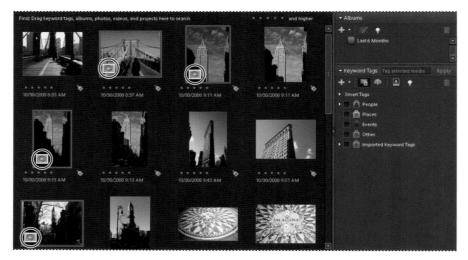

4   Choose Edit > Visibility > Hide Hidden Files. The four images marked as Hidden
    are removed from the Media Browser view.

5   Expand the Imported Keyword Tags category and click the empty Find boxes
    beside the Brooklyn Bridge, Empire State Building and Jefferson Market tags.
    The four hidden files do not appear in the search results.

6   In the Media Browser, click Show All. Choose Edit > Visibility > Show Only
    Hidden Files, and then choose Edit > Visibility > Show All Files. Finally,
    Ctrl-click to select all four thumbnails with the Hidden File icon and choose
    Edit > Visibility > Mark As Visible. The Hidden File icons are removed.

7   Ctrl-click to select both of the edited images of the Empire State Building and
    choose Edit > Delete Selected Items From Catalog. In the Confirm Deletion
    From Catalog dialog box, activate the option Also Delete Selected Items From
    The Hard Disk, and then click OK.

Working with smart albums

Rather than manually selecting individual photos as you do for an ordinary album,
you only need to specify search criteria to create a smart album. Once you set the
criteria for a smart album, any photo in a catalog that matches the specified conditions will automatically appear in that smart album. As you add new photos to your
catalog, those photos matching a smart album's criteria will appear automatically in
that smart album. In other words, Smart Albums keep themselves up-to-date.

1   To set up search criteria for a new smart album, choose Find > By Details
    (Metadata). In the Find By Details (Metadata) dialog box, select multiple search
    criteria for the smart album. Click the plus sign (+) to add a criterion, or click
    the minus sign (-) to remove one. Beside Search For Files Which Match, activate
    the option All Of The Following Search Criteria.

2   Activate the option Save This Search Criteria As Smart Album. Type **My first
    smart album** as the album name, and then click Search.

3 To change the name of your smart album, make sure the smart album is selected in the Albums panel and click the Edit button () at the top of the panel. In the Edit Smart Album dialog box, type a new album name (we entered Lesson 4, no ratings), and then click OK.

You cannot change the order of photos in a smart album, as you can for other albums. Nor can you add photos to a smart album by dragging them onto the album's icon; you need to modify the album's search criteria to change the content. The content of a smart album may change over time even without modifying the search criteria if photos matching the search criteria are added or removed from the catalog; for example, a smart album may be set up to contain photos captured within the last six months from the current date. Photos included in the album today may not fall within that date range tomorrow.

4 To change the search criteria for your smart album, first make sure the smart album is selected in the Albums panel; then click Options in the Find bar and choose Modify Search Criteria from the menu.

Note: If you wish to save the modified search criteria as a new smart album, you should enter a new name. It's possible to create more than one smart album with the same name, but this is not recommended. A second smart album with the same name will be created, rather than the first smart album being over-written. A dialog box will alert you about the duplicate file name.

5 Modify the search criteria in the Find By Details (Metadata) dialog box, and then click Search.

6 To delete the smart album, right-click its entry in the Albums panel and choose Delete *[smart album name]* Album from the menu. Click OK to confirm.

Congratulations—you've reached the end of Lesson 4! In this lesson, you've learned about the advanced import options in the Photo Downloader, how to acquire still frames from a video, and how to import images from a PDF file or acquire them from a scanner. You've organized images into version sets, stacks and albums, placed photos on a map, and learned some advanced techniques for finding and managing the files in your catalog.

You can skip chapter 5, which applies only to those using Photoshop Elements on Mac OS, and go directly to Lesson 6, "Creating Projects".

Before you move on, take a moment to review what you've learned and test your command of the concepts and techniques presented in this lesson by working through the following questions and answers.

Review questions

1 How can you automatically create and apply keyword tags to images while importing them from a digital camera or card reader?

2 What does the Photoshop Elements De-Interlace filter do?

3 What does the Auto Smart Fix command do?

4 What are Version Sets and Stacks?

5 What is the main difference between grouping files using shared keyword tags and grouping them in an album?

Review answers

1 In the Advanced Photo Downloader dialog box, choose Custom Groups (Advanced) from the Create Subfolder(s) menu. Next, choose an option including Custom Name from the Group Name menu, and then enter a Group Name in the Custom Name field in the separator bar above each group of thumbnails. Finally, activate the option Make 'Group Custom Name' A Tag before clicking Get Photos.

2 The Photoshop Elements De-Interlace filter can improve the appearance of a still frame acquired from a video by removing the artifacts caused by the fact that a video picture consists of two interlaced half-pictures taken at slightly different times. The De-Interlace filter removes either the odd or even fields in a still image from video and replaces the discarded lines by duplication or interpolation from the remaining lines.

3 The Auto Smart Fix command corrects the overall color balance and improves shadow and highlight detail, if necessary. The Auto Smart Fix command automatically groups the edited copy of the photo with the original in a version set.

4 A version set groups an original photo and its edited versions. Stacks are used to group a set of similar photos, such as multiple shots of the same subject or photos taken using your camera's burst mode or auto-bracket feature. A version set can be nested inside a stack: if you edit a photo that's already in a stack, the photo and its edited copy are put in a version set that is nested inside the original stack.

5 The main difference between grouping files in an album, rather than with a shared keyword tag, is that in an album you can rearrange the order of the files.

5 ADVANCED ORGANIZING ON MAC OS

Lesson Overview

As your collection grows to hundreds or even thousands of images, keeping track of your photos can be a daunting task. Photoshop Elements 8 works together with Adobe Bridge, which delivers a range of advanced organizing tools that not only get the job done but in fact make the work quite enjoyable.

In this lesson, you'll learn a few new methods of importing images as well as some of the more advanced techniques for organizing, sorting, and searching your growing photo collection:

- Using advanced Photo Downloader options

- Acquiring still frames from video

- Importing pictures from a PDF document

- Importing pictures from a scanner

- Using keywords, labels and ratings to organize photos

- Searching for photos with the Find command

- Finding photos using the Filter panel

- Using the Quick Search feature

- Grouping photos in Collections and Smart Collections

 You'll probably need between one and two hours to complete this lesson.

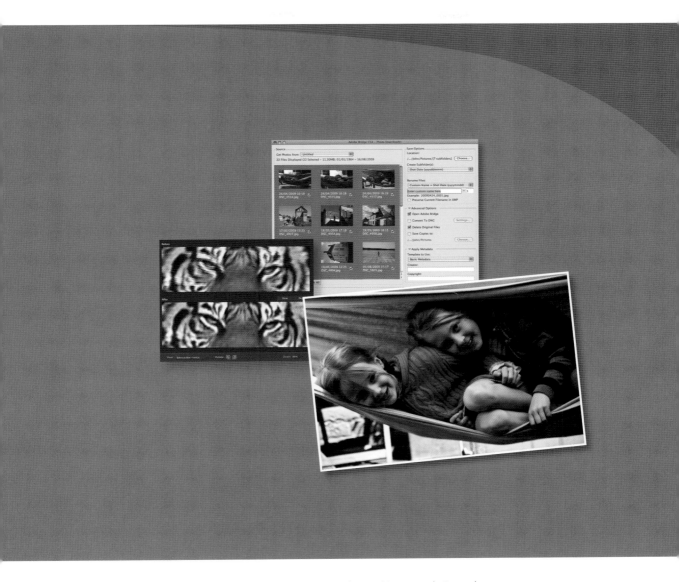

Discover some advanced import techniques that will extend your options for bringing images into Photoshop Elements. Get your photo library organized with keyword tags, labels, and ratings. Group your photos conveniently in virtual Collections and learn about a range of powerful search features that make it easy to find just the files you want, just when you need them.

119

Getting started

Before you start working on this lesson, make sure that you've installed the software on your computer from the application CD (see the Photoshop Elements 8 documentation) and that you have correctly copied the Lessons folder from the CD in the back of this book onto your computer's hard disk (see "Copying the Classroom in a Book files" on page 2).

In Lesson 3 you learned the fundamentals of working between Photoshop Elements and Adobe Bridge to import and open your images and some basic skills for navigating your folders and viewing files in Bridge. In this lesson you'll be introduced to some more advanced import options and find out how to use Bridge to keep your growing photo library organized.

Advanced import options

In Lesson 2 you used several methods for importing images. In this section you'll look at the Adobe Photo Downloader's advanced options and learn how to import photos from some different sources—capturing a frame from a movie, extracting images embedded in a PDF document, and acquiring an image from a scanner.

Photo Downloader options

If you have a digital camera or memory card at hand with your own photos on it, you can step through this exercise using those images. Alternatively, you can simply follow the process in the book without performing the exercise yourself, or skip to the next section and return to this exercise when you are prepared.

1   Start Photoshop Elements and close the Welcome screen by clicking the Close button (x) in the upper right corner.

2   Connect your digital camera or card reader to your computer, following the manufacturer's instructions.

3   If the downloader does not appear automatically, choose File > Adobe Photo Downloader.

4   Under Source at the top of the Photo Downloader dialog box, choose the name of your camera or card reader from the Get Photos From menu.

Your camera or card reader must be switched on to appear in the Get Photos From menu. If your camera is connected and switched on but the menu doesn't display the specific device name, choose Untitled. If no option for the device is available, choose Refresh List.

5   Without making any other changes to the settings, click the Advanced Dialog button in the lower left corner of the Photo Downloader dialog box.

The Advanced dialog box of the Adobe Photo Downloader offers several options not available in the Standard dialog box. It displays thumbnail images of the photos on your camera's memory card so that you can select which images you wish to download, lets you preview videos before importing them, and gives you the opportunity to add copyright details and other metadata.

6 Make your choices for the settings under Save Options:

- Accept the default folder listed under Location, (*username* > Pictures) or click Choose to browse for a new destination for the downloaded files.

- Choose whether you want the Photo Downloader to create subfolders for the downloaded files and select a naming option for the folders from the Create Subfolder(s) menu. Your selection is reflected in the Location pathname.

- In the Rename Files menu, choose whether you want the image files to be renamed as they are downloaded, and a select a naming option. If you choose a file renaming option that includes a custom name, type the name in the text box. Sequence numbers will be appended automatically.

> **Tip:** Creating subfolders with names based on Shot Date is a great way to organize your photos by subject or occasion during the downloading process.

7 Under Advanced Options you can choose whether to open Bridge to display the downloaded files, whether to delete the original files from your memory stick after they've been copied to your hard disk, and whether to convert files to DNG format (see Lesson 13). You can also choose whether to save backup copies and specify a destination folder for those copies.

8 Under Apply Metadata, you can enter a Creator name and copyright date. You won't be able to select a Metadata Template menu unless you've already created a custom template in Bridge. For information on using metadata templates, please refer to Adobe Bridge Help.

9 Select the photos you wish to download by doing any of the following:

- To deselect a photo, click the box below the thumbnail to remove the check mark. To deselect all images, click Uncheck All at the lower left of the Photo Downloader dialog box.

- To select individual photos, click the box below each thumbnail. To select all photos, click Check All at the bottom left of the dialog box.

- To select multiple photos, drag a selection marquee around their thumbnails, and then right-click and select Check Selected, or click a box below any of the selected images to check them all.

10 Click Get Photos.

A dialog box opens briefly showing the progress of the download. If you activated the Open Adobe Bridge option, a new Bridge window opens. If the photos were downloaded to a single folder, the downloaded images are displayed in the Content panel; otherwise Bridge displays the newly created subfolders.

Acquiring still frames from a video

▶ **Tip:** To be able to capture images from the broadest range of video formats, install the latest version of the QuickTime Player on your computer. You can download it free at www.apple.com/ quicktime/download/.

You can capture frames from digital videos saved in any of the file formats supported by Photoshop Elements. These include: AVI, MPG, MPEG, and MOV.

1 If Photoshop Elements is already running, go on to step 2; otherwise, start Photoshop Elements now. Close the Welcome screen by clicking the Close button (x) in the upper right corner.

2 In Photoshop Elements, choose File > Import > Frame From Video. In the Frame From Video dialog box, click the Browse button and navigate to your PSE8CIB > Lessons > Lesson04-05 folder. Select the file Tiger.mov, and then click Open.

● **Note:** Some video formats do not support rewind or fast-forward. When these functions are not available, the Rewind (◄◄) and Fast Forward (►►) buttons are dimmed.

3 Click the Play button (►) to start the video. After 3 or 4 seconds, click the Pause button (❚❚), and then use the arrow keys on your keyboard to move forward or backward one frame at a time until you find an image you want.

4 To capture any frame of the video as a still image, click the Grab Frame button or press your Space bar when the frame you want is visible on the screen.

5 Move forward and backward in the video to capture additional frames. When you have all the frames you want, click Done. The frames you captured open in separate image windows and a thumbnail of each appears in the Project Bin.

Depending on your video footage and which frames you captured, you might notice artifacts in the still image resulting from the fact that a video picture consists of two interlaced half-pictures. The odd-numbered scanlines of the image, also called odd fields, constitute one half of the picture, and the even-numbered scanlines, or even fields, the other. Since the two halves of the picture were recorded at slightly different times, the captured still image might look distorted.

For the purposes of this exercise, it's worthwhile to deliberately choose a frame with this kind of distortion, which is most easily identified as a 'zigzag' effect and is particularly noticeable on vertical detail, as can be seen in the image on the right.

In Photoshop Elements you can remedy this problem with the De-Interlace filter, which will remove either the odd or even fields in an image captured from video, and then replace the discarded lines either by duplication or by interpolation from the remaining lines, depending on the options you specify.

6 Choose the image you wish to use for this exercise and discard the others by clicking the red Close button at the top left of each image window. Click Don't Save in the alert dialogs that ask if you wish to save the images.

7 With the image you've chosen still open in the Editor, switch from Full to Quick Edit mode. Click the triangle on the orange Edit tab at the top of the Panel Bin and choose Edit Quick.

8 Hide the Project Bin by clicking its header bar. From the View menu in the lower left corner of the workspace, choose Before & After - Vertical.

9 Double-click the number in the Zoom value box in the lower right corner of the image display pane, type **300**, and then press Enter. Use the Hand tool to move the image in either the Before or After view so that you can see the tiger's eyes. (When you're working with tigers, it's *always* a good idea to watch the eyes!)

10 Choose Filter > Video > De-Interlace and position the De-Interlace dialog box so that you can see both the Before and After views. Under Eliminate, choose either Odd Fields or Even Fields. Under Create New Fields By, choose either Duplication or Interpolation, and then click OK. The combination of options that will produce the best results depends on the image at hand. You can Undo after each trial and repeat this step until you are satisfied with the result. Compare your results to the illustration on the next page.

11 Use the menu on the Edit tab to return to Full Edit mode, save the image (File > Save) in your My CIB Work folder, and then close the image window.

Importing from a PDF document

Photoshop Elements enables you to import either whole pages from a PDF document or to select and extract just the images you want.

1 In Photoshop Elements, choose File > Open. In the Open dialog box, navigate to your Lesson04-05 folder, select the file ZOO.pdf, and then click Open. If you can't see the file ZOO.pdf in the Open dialog box, click the Enable menu at the bottom of the dialog box and choose All Readable Documents.

In the Import PDF dialog box, you can choose to import entire pages or just the images from a PDF file (*see the illustration on the next page*).

If you choose to import pages from a multiple-page PDF file, you can Command-click the page thumbnails to select those pages you wish to import. Pages are rasterized (converted to bit-mapped graphics) according to your choice of image size, resolution, and color mode. The imported result will be an image of the page similar to that acquired by scanning a printed document.

If you choose to import the images embedded in a PDF file rather than full pages, you can use the same method to multiple-select the images you want.

2   Under Select in the Import PDF dialog box, choose Images.

3   Select Large from the Thumbnail Size menu in the lower left of the dialog box. This enables you to see all four of the images in this file. Click to select an image you wish to import. Command-click any additional images you would like to add to the import, and then click OK.

4   If any alert dialogs appear stating that the image files use an unsupported color mode, click Convert Mode.

Each image imported from the PDF file opens in its own document window and thumbnails of the imported images appear in the Project Bin.

5   For each image choose File > Save As, navigate to your My CIB Work folder, and save the file with a descriptive name in Photoshop or JPEG file format.

Scanning images

You can import scanned images directly into Photoshop Elements from any scanner that has a Photoshop Elements-compatible plug-in module or that supports the TWAIN interface. To use your scanner's plug-in module, see your scanner documentation for instructions on installing the scanner plug-in, and then choose the device name from the File > Import submenu.

If your scanner does not have a Photoshop Elements-compatible scanner driver, you can import the scan by choosing the TWAIN interface from the File > Import submenu.

Another option is to use the stand-alone software that came with your scanner to scan and save your images, and then bring them into Photoshop Elements using the File > Open command.

Note: Before you try to import an image to Photoshop Elements from your scanner, read carefully through the manufacturer's documentation and make sure that you've installed any software that came with the device. Make sure also that the scanner is connected properly to your computer.

This exercise is optional; it requires that you have a scanner available.

1   Make sure that your scanner is connected and switched on.

2   If Photoshop Elements is already running, go on to step 2; otherwise, start Photoshop Elements now. Close the Welcome screen by clicking the Close button (x) in the upper right corner.

Tip: If you begin the process by clicking Import From Scanner in the Welcome screen, you will be presented with the Select Import Source dialog box. The Import menu in the Select Import Source dialog box lists the same options that are available from the File > Import submenu.

3   Choose File > Import. If you see your scanner listed in the Import submenu, choose the scanner's name. If you don't see your scanner listed, choose the TWAIN option from the Import submenu.

4   Click Browse to select a destination folder for the scanned files. Choose a file format from the Save As menu. The default format, JPEG is usually the best choice.

5   Select a Matte color for the background. Set the image quality either by entering a value between 0 (lowest) to 12 (highest), by choosing Low, Medium, High, or Maximum, or by dragging the Quality slider. The higher the quality setting, the larger the resulting file size.

Tip: When you scan several items at the same time, Photoshop Elements can crop the scan into individual images automatically and will also straighten them for you. For more information on the Divide Scanned Photos feature, see Photoshop Elements Help.

6   In Formats Options, set the format for the image. The Baseline option causes images to display line-by-line on the screen. Baseline Optimized encodes the image to reduce the file size. Progressive causes the image to display in multiple passes on the screen. Set the number of passes in the Scans box.

7   Click OK. If your scanner uses a TWAIN driver, Photoshop Elements launches the driver that came with your scanner. Follow the instructions that came with the scanner software to scan your photo. Typically, you can set the area to be scanned and make some adjustments to color and tonal balance.

When the scan is complete, the image opens in Photoshop Elements in an untitled image window.

Organizing photos

Organizing your files and folders efficiently can be challenging. It's easy to forget what pictures are stored in which folder—and being forced to open and examine the contents of numerous folders to find files can be both time consuming and extremely frustrating.

Adobe Bridge can make the whole process much simpler and more enjoyable. Bridge offers a variety of ways to navigate your files and folders and powerful yet easy-to-use tools for grouping, sorting, filtering and searching your photos.

The remainder of this lesson will show you how investing a little time in organizing your photo library can streamline the process of managing your photos and other media files, regardless of where they are stored.

About keyword tags, labels, and star ratings

Keyword tags, color labels and star ratings are all powerful tools for organizing your ever-growing library of media files.

Keyword tags are text labels, such as "Vacation," "Beach," or "Sophie"—personalized labels that you can attach to photos and other media files in Adobe Bridge to make it easier to organize and find them. You can use keyword tags to sort and find photos intuitively by their content or any other association that you attach to them.

When you use keyword tags, there's no need to manually organize your photos in subject-related folders or rename files with content-specific names. In fact, both of the latter solutions confine a given photo to a single group. By contrast, you can assign multiple keyword tags to a single photo, allowing it to be included in several different groupings. You can then easily retrieve the selection of images you want by simply clicking the appropriate keyword tag or tags in the Filter panel or by configuring a search to find files with exactly the right combination of keywords.

Assigning color labels and star ratings to your photos is another way of grouping them by a different set of associations, at the same time adding even more criteria by which you can narrow a search to find just the files you want quickly and easily.

Assigning labels and ratings

Labeling files with different colors or assigning ratings of zero to five stars is an easy way to mark a large number of photos quickly. You can then sort your images according to their color label or rating. You can do this in several passes, refining your categorization as you go.

Tip: You can label and rate folders as well as the files inside them.

In Lesson 3 you learned that you can assign labels and ratings quickly and easily even when reviewing and comparing photos in a slideshow or in Review mode (see pages 77 and 78). This makes a great way to create a "first pass" grouping. In this exercise you'll apply labels and ratings as you browse in the Content panel.

1 Start Photoshop Elements and open Bridge either by clicking Browse With Adobe Bridge in the Welcome screen, by choosing File > Browse With Bridge, or by clicking the Bridge icon (**Br**) at the top of the workspace.

2 In Bridge, click Essentials in the row of workspace options at the top of the application window.

3 Click the link to your PSE8CIB folder that you added to the Favorites panel in Lesson 3 (if necessary, refer to steps 4 and 5 on page 71).

4 In the Content panel, double-click to open the Lessons folder, and then double-click to open the Lesson04-05 folder.

5 Choose View > Show Items From Subfolders. To hide the folders themselves from view in the Content panel, choose View > Show Folders.

6 Command-click to select three or four images in the Content panel to which you'd like to apply a 3-star rating. Be sure to select images both from the New York City and zoo series. Immediately below the thumbnail of each selected image you can see a row of five dots; click the third dot below any of the selected images to apply a 3-star rating to the entire selection.

7 Command click to select three or four different images to which you'd like to apply a 5-star rating, making sure to include images from both series. Click the Label menu and choose the five stars or press Command+5 on your keyboard to apply a 5-star rating to all the selected photos.

8 Command click to select five or six images across both series and including photos both with and without ratings. Right-click / Control-click any of the selected images and choose Label > Select to apply a red label to the selection.

Assigning labels and ratings is that simple! A little later in the lesson you'll see how these labels and ratings can help you sort and search your photos. For now, take a few moments to note all of the labeling and rating commands in the Label menu and in the context menu that appears when you right-click / Control-click a photo.

You can assign your own names to the different colored labels in the Labels section in Bridge preferences. Naming the red label "To Print" may be of more use in your workflow than keeping the default name "Select." When you change the name of a label, any files already marked with that label retain the old label name but appear with white labels in the Content panel.

Working with keyword tags

In Adobe Bridge you can use the Keywords panel to create, apply and manage keywords. You can use keywords to identify files based on their content or on any other association. For example, you may choose to tag a single photo with the keywords New York, Vacation, Winter, Pauline, and Blue. You could then use the Find command or the Filter panel to search each of those keywords in turn and locate the same image included in five very different groups of photos. You could also configure a search to include all five keywords to find just that image.

The sample photos for this lesson are all tagged with keywords. In this exercise you'll use the Keyword panel to find out which tags are attached to each file and create and apply some new keywords.

1 If you're starting a new session, please perform steps 1 to 5 in the preceding section "Assigning labels and ratings" before continuing with this exercise.

2 In the Keywords panel, click the triangle beside Other Keywords if necessary, to expand the category so that you can see the keywords nested inside it.

Drag the panel divider at the top of the Keywords panel upwards until you can see all the keywords listed.

3   Click the upper left image in the Content panel, and then use the arrow keys on your keyboard to select each photo in turn, keeping an eye on the Keywords panel. The Assigned Keywords area at the top of the Keywords panel, as well as the check-marked boxes beside the keyword names, show you that each selected image already has two keywords attached.

4   Choose Edit > Select All, or press Command+A. The check boxes show that all the selected images share the Lesson 4-5 keyword (indicated by a check mark) while the other keywords present are shared by only some of the images (indicated by check boxes marked with a hyphen).

5   Choose Edit > Deselect All, or press Shift+Command+A.

6   Right-click / Control-click the Other Keywords category and choose New Sub Keyword from the context menu. Type **Architecture** in the name box for the new tag and press Enter.

7   In the Content panel, Command-click to select the eight images that feature landmark buildings in New York City (omitting the shots of the Brooklyn Bridge and the Imagine mosaic). Click the check box beside the new Architecture keyword to apply the tag to all eight selected images.

8   In the Content panel, Command-click the other four New York City images to add them to the selection. Click the triangle beside the Places keyword category to see the sub-keywords inside it. Click the check box beside the New York keyword to apply the New York tag to all twelve selected images.

9   Right-click / Control-click the Other Keywords category again, but this time choose New Keyword from the context menu. Type **Animals** in the name box for the new tag and press Enter. The new keyword appears on the same level of the hierarchy as the Other Keywords tag.

10 In the Content panel, select all thirteen zoo photographs by clicking the first in the series, and then Shift-clicking the last. Command-click to add the video file Tiger.mov to the selection, and then click the check box beside the Animals keyword to apply the new tag to all fourteen selected files.

11 Drag the Elephant keyword out of the Other Keywords category and drop it onto the Animals keyword. Repeat the process for the Giraffe, Hippo, Ostrich, and Zebra keywords. Click the triangle beside the Animals tag to see the sub-keywords nested inside it.

12 Control-click to select the two images of elephants. Click the check box beside the Elephant keyword to remove the tag from both files, and then click the check box beside the Animals keyword to remove that tag also.

13 With the two Elephant photos still selected in the Content panel, Shift-click the check box beside the Elephant keyword. Shift-clicking has re-applied not only the Elephant tag, but also the parent tag Animals.

For more detail on using the Keywords panel and working with hierarchical keyword tags, please refer to Adobe Bridge Help.

Searching by keywords, labels, and ratings

The reason for creating, applying and sorting all these keyword tags, labels, and ratings is so that you can always find just the picture you want, just when you want it. Once they share a keyword tag and other metadata markers, a group of related photos can be retrieved easily and quickly; no matter how big your photo library is or across how many folders those images are scattered.

Searching for photos with the Find command

This demonstration builds on the previous exercise, "Working with keyword tags."

1 Click the shortcut to your PSE8CIB folder in the Favorites panel, and then choose View > Show Folders to make folders visible in the Content panel.

2 Choose Edit > Find. In the Find dialog box, the PSE8CIB folder is already listed as the Look In folder under Source, having been selected when the Find command was invoked. Under Criteria, choose Keywords from the first menu, choose Equals from the second menu, and then type **New York** in the text box.

3 To add a second criteria to the search, click the Add button (+) to the right of the first criteria. To define the new search criteria, choose Keywords from the first menu and Equals from the second; then type **Architecture** in the text box.

4 Under Results, choose If All Criteria Are Met from the Match menu. Activate the option Include All Subfolders and disable Include Non-indexed Files; then click Find. The Content panel displays the eight files in the PSE8CIB folder and all its subfolders that are tagged with both of the specified keywords.

5 Click New Search at the top of the Content panel. The Find dialog box opens, still configured as it was for the last search. To add a third criteria to the search, click the Add button (+) to the right of the second criteria. To define the new search criteria, choose Rating from the first menu, select Is Greater Than Or Equal To from the second menu, and then choose three stars from the menu on the right.

6   Click Find. The Content panel displays any files in the PSE8CIB folder and all its subfolders that are tagged with both the New York and Architecture keywords and also have a rating of three or more stars.

Tip: Hold the pointer over the Find Criteria text at the top of the Content panel to see the complete configuration for the current search.

7   Click New Search at the top of the Content panel. The Find dialog box opens, still configured as it was for the last search. Take a few moments to note all the options available in the menus for configuring a search, and then click Cancel.

8   Click the Cancel button (x) in the upper right corner of the Content panel to clear the search results.

Finding photos using the Filter panel

The Filters panel offers another way to configure a complex search as well as providing visual feedback on the metadata attributes of your files and folders.

1   Click the link to your PSE8CIB folder that you added to the Favorites panel in Lesson 3 (if necessary, refer to steps 4 and 5 on page 71).

2   In the Content panel, double-click to open the Lessons folder, and then double-click to open the Lesson04-05 folder.

3   In the Path bar across the top of the Content panel, click the chevron (arrow) to the right of the Lesson04-05 folder and choose Show Items From Subfolders from the menu.

Tip: Experiment with using the Path bar to navigate your files and folders. For detailed information on how to work with the Path bar, please refer to Adobe Bridge Help.

4   Open the Filter panel menu by clicking the menu icon (▼☰) at the right end of the Filter panel's header bar. Use this menu to customize the Filter panel to your workflow by showing or hiding Filter categories. For now, choose Collapse All.

5 If you can't see all the Filter categories, drag the panel divider at the top of the Filter panel upwards.

6 Click the triangles beside the Labels, Ratings, and Keywords categories to expand those categories.

Each of the three expanded Filter categories displays information that relates to the images currently on view in the Content panel—in this case, all the photos in the Lesson04-05 folder and its subfolders.

The Labels pane shows which labels are present amongst the files displayed, and shows how many files are marked with each. You can see at a glance that most of the files in this group have no label and a small number have the red Select label that you assigned earlier in this lesson.

The Ratings category gives a file count for files with no rating and shows how many images you rated at 3 and 5 stars.

The Keywords category shows all the keywords associated with the files in this group.

Clicking any of the entries in the expanded Filter categories filters (or searches) this group of images for files with that attribute.

7 Click the red Select label in the Labels filter category. The Content panel displays only those photos to which you applied this label earlier. Click the Select label filter again to disable it.

8 Click both the 3-star and 5-star filters in the Ratings category and the Architecture entry in the Keywords filter category to filter the files in the Lesson04-05 folder and its subfolders for any photo tagged with the Architecture keyword that has a rating of three or more stars.

9 Experiment with different combinations of filters. When you're done, clear all active filters by clicking the Clear Filter button (⊘) in the lower right corner of the Filter panel. If necessary, drag the panel divider at the top of the Filter panel downwards so that the Favorites panel is visible.

Performing a Quick Search

You can use the Quick Search field in the application bar to perform simple text searches to find files and folders in Adobe Bridge. Quick Search gives you the chice of searching using either the Adobe Bridge search engine or Spotlight (the Mac OS search engine).

The Adobe Bridge search engine searches filenames and keywords. Spotlight looks for filenames, folder names, and keywords. Adobe Bridge search looks within the currently selected folder and all subfolders. You can choose whether Spotlight searches the currently selected folder or your entire computer.

1   Click the magnifying glass icon ($\mathcal{O}\cdot$) in the Quick Search field and choose Bridge Search or one of the Spotlight Search options.

2   Enter a search term, and then press Enter on your keyboard.

Creating Collections

Another great way of organizing your photos is to group them into Collections. A Collection is like a "virtual folder" that you create to group a selection of files for easy access even if they're located in different folders or on different hard drives. A single image can be included in any number of collections. You might create a new collection to group shots from a special occasion or to assemble the images that you intend to use in a project, a presentation to a client, or a slideshow.

1   In the Filter panel, enable the 3-star and 5-star filters in the Ratings category and the Animals filter in the Keywords category.

2   Press Command+A to select all the images in the Content window.

3   Click the Collections tab in the left panel group to open the Collections panel.

4   Click the New Collection button (⊞) at the bottom of the Collections panel. An alert dialog box appears asking if you want to include the selected files in the new Collection. Click Yes. A listing for the new Collection appears in the Collections panel.

5   Type **Zoo Brochure** to name the new Collection, and then press Enter. You can now retrieve this group of photos at any time by simply clicking the listing in the Collections panel. You can add images to the collection by dragging them from the content panel or from a Finder window.

Working with Smart Collections

In effect, a Smart Collection is a virtual folder containing the results of an ongoing search. Once you set the criteria for a Smart Collection, any photo in the searched folder or folders that matches the specified conditions will automatically appear in that Smart Collection. As you add photos to your library and apply keywords, tags and ratings, any new image matching a Smart Collection's criteria will be included automatically. In other words, Smart Collections keep themselves up-to-date.

1 Click your PSE8CIB folder in the Favorites panel, and then click the New Smart Collection button () at the bottom of the Collections panel.

2 In the Smart Collection dialog box, the PSE8CIB folder is already listed as the Look In folder under Source. The Criteria settings may have been retained from the last search. Make new selections from the criteria menus to define two search criteria. Set the first criteria to Keywords / Equals / Animals, and the second to Rating / Is Greater Than Or Equal To / 3 Stars. To remove a criteria, click the Remove (minus sign) button to the right of that criteria.

3 Under Results choose If All Criteria Are Met from the Match menu. Activate Include All Subfolders and disable Include Non-indexed Files; then click Save.

4 A listing for the new Smart Collection appears in the Collections panel. Type Zoo Promotions as the name for the new Smart Collection. At the moment the new Smart Collection contains the same group of photos as the Zoo Brochure Collection. The difference is that the Zoo Promotions Smart Collection will be updated automatically to include any new photo that you tag with the Animals keyword and assign a rating of three or more stars, at any time in the future.

About stacks

One very easy way to simplify working with a large number of images is to create stacks to group sets of related photos in the Content panel, making them easier to manage. Stack photos that make up a series or multiple images of the same subject to help reduce clutter in the Content panel. For instance, you might create a stack for several photos of your family taken in the same pose or for photos taken at a sports event using your camera's burst mode or auto-bracket feature. Stacking such photos lets you easily access them all in one place instead of having them scattered across rows of thumbnails. Select a group of images in the Content panel and experiment with the commands in the Stacks menu. For detailed information on working with stacks, please refer to Adobe Bridge Help.

Congratulations—you've reached the end of another lesson! In this lesson, you've learned about the advanced import options in the Photo Downloader, how to acquire still frames from a video, and how to import images from a PDF file or acquire them from a scanner. You've organized images by adding tags, labels and ratings and by grouping them in virtual collections. You've also learned some advanced techniques for finding and managing the files in your image library.

Before you move on, take a moment to review what you've learned and test your command of the concepts and techniques presented in this lesson by working through the following questions and answers.

Review questions

1   What are the advantages of using the Adobe Photo Downloader's advanced options?

2   What does the Photoshop Elements De-Interlace filter do?

3   What are keyword tags?

4   How can you narrow a Find command search in the Find dialog box?

5   What is the difference between a Collection and a Smart Collection?

Review answers

1   The Advanced dialog box of the Adobe Photo Downloader offers several options not available in the Standard dialog box. It displays thumbnail images of the photos on your camera's memory card so that you can select which images you wish to download, lets you preview videos before importing them, and gives you the opportunity to add copyright details and other metadata.

2   The Photoshop Elements De-Interlace filter can improve the appearance of a still frame acquired from a video by removing the artifacts caused by the fact that a video picture consists of two interlaced half-pictures taken at slightly different times. The De-Interlace filter removes either the odd or even fields in a still image from video and replaces the discarded lines by duplication or interpolation from the remaining lines.

3   Keyword tags are personalized text labels that you can attach to photos and other media files in Adobe Bridge to make it easier to organize and find them. You can use keyword tags to sort, group, and find photos intuitively by their content or any other association that you attach to them.

4   In the Find dialog box you can set up multiple search criteria quickly by choosing from a large range of options in the criteria menus, and then configure the search to look for files with any of the specified conditions and attributes or find only those files that meet all the criteria.

5   A Collection is like a "virtual folder" that you create to group a selection of files for easy access even if they're located in different folders or on different hard drives. You select files for a Collection manually. For a Smart Collection, you set search criteria rather than selecting files. In effect, a Smart Collection is a virtual folder containing the results of an ongoing search. Smart Collections keep themselves up-to-date, automatically adding any new image that has the specified attributes.

6 CREATING PROJECTS

Lesson Overview

Photoshop Elements makes it simple to create stylish, professional-looking projects to showcase your photos. Choose from the preset themes and layouts—or create your own designs from scratch—as you put together a range of creations from greeting cards and Photo Books to animated slide shows and online albums.

Use your own images in personalized CD or DVD jackets and labels, calendars, collages, and digital flip-books. Combine images, text, animation and even music and narration, to produce unique multimedia creations.

Whether you're designing your own coffee table book, sharing your photos online, or creating personalized gifts for family and friends, Photoshop Elements will help unleash your creativity.

This lesson will familiarize you with the Create mode by stepping you through some basic techniques and simple projects:

- Creating a personalized greeting card
- Producing a stylish Photo Book
- Telling a story with a Photo Collage
- Using the Content library
- Working with layers

 You'll probably need around two hours to complete this lesson.

Photoshop elements offers a huge library of design themes, layout templates, and clip graphics that make it easy to produce eye-catching projects using your own photos. Show loved ones how much you care with stylish personalized greeting cards; preserve and share your precious memories in a sophisticated Photo Book or combine pictures and mementos to tell an evocative story in an artistic Photo Collage.

Getting started

Before you start working on the exercises in this lesson, make sure that you have installed the software on your computer from the application CD (see the Photoshop Elements 8 documentation) and that you have correctly copied the Lessons folder from the CD in the back of this book onto your computer's hard disk. (See "Copying the Classroom in a Book files" on page 2.)

Finding the lesson files on Windows

While you're working on the projects in this lesson, you'll use images from the CIB Catalog that you created in the "Getting Started" section at the beginning of this book. To open your CIB Catalog, follow these steps:

1 Start Photoshop Elements and click the Organize button in the Welcome Screen. Wait until the Organizer has finished opening.

2 Choose File > Catalog.

3 In the Catalog Manager dialog box, select the CIB Catalog, and then click Open.

If you don't see the CIB Catalog file, review "Copying the Lessons files from the CD" on page 2 and "Creating a catalog file" on page 3 in the "Getting Started" section at the beginning of this book.

4 Click Show All if it's visible above the Media Browser. In the Keyword Tags panel, expand the category Imported Keyword Tags, and then click the find box beside the Lesson 6 tag to isolate the images for the projects in this lesson.

For the first project—which begins on the facing page—you'll use a vacation photo as the basis for a personalized greeting card.

Finding the lesson files on Mac OS

For the projects in this lesson, you'll be working with the sample image files in the PSE8CIB > Lessons > Lesson06 folder that you copied to your hard disk in the section "Copying the Classroom in a Book files" at the beginning of this book.

1   Start Photoshop Elements and click Browse With Adobe Bridge in the Welcome Screen. If Photoshop Elements opens without displaying the Welcome Screen, choose File > Browse With Bridge. Wait until Bridge has finished launching.

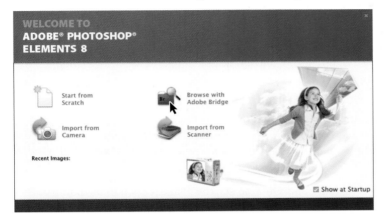

2   In Bridge, click Essentials in the row of workspace options across the top of the application window. Click the link to your PSE8CIB folder in the Favorites panel. If you don't see the Favorites panel, right-click / Control-click the header of any other panel and choose Favorites Panel from the context menu.

3   In the Content panel, double-click to open the Lessons folder, and then the Lesson06 folder, which contains the sixteen images for this lesson.

Now you're ready for the first project: making a personalized greeting card.

Creating a greeting card

Personalized greeting cards based on your own photos make a great way to show friends and family how much you care—a really attractive card can spend months on a loved one's mantelpiece and may even be framed and displayed with pride.

You can include one or more images on each page of a greeting card and either print it on your home printer, order prints online, or send it via e-mail.

The Projects panel, on the Create tab in the Panel Bin, offers easy access to an extensive library of themes, layout templates, backgrounds, frames and other artwork to help you to create sophisticated designs quickly and easily.

Choosing a theme and a layout

This project will show you how easy it is to use design themes, layout templates and clip graphics from the content library to present an image in a creative and stylish way. By the time you're done, you'll have learned to make use of the content library and created a delightful, professional-looking greeting card in the process.

▶ **Tip:** If you don't see file names displayed below the thumbnail images in the Media Browser, ensure that the Details check box in the bar above the browser pane is activated and choose View > Show File Names.

1   In the Organizer (Windows) / Bridge (Mac OS), select the image card.jpg, a photo of four girls at the seaside on a windy day.

2   Do one of the following:

   •   On Windows, click the purple Create tab above the Task Pane.

   •   On Mac OS, right-click / Control-click the image in the Bridge Content panel and choose Open With > Adobe Photoshop Elements 8; then click the purple Create tab above the Panel Bin to the right of the Media Browser.

3   In the Create panel, click the Greeting Card button.
    On Windows you need to choose a creation and printing method; click Print With Local Printer and wait while the Editor opens in Create mode.

The Projects panel opens and a thumbnail of the photo card.jpg appears in the Project Bin below the Edit pane. On Mac OS, the image is open in the Edit pane.

4   In the Projects panel, choose 5 inch × 7 inch from the Page Size menu.

5 In the Choose A Theme menu, scroll down to see the variety of designs available. Move the pointer over the theme swatches; a Tooltip appears with the name of each theme. Select the theme "Wedding, Beach With Seashells" at the bottom of the list.

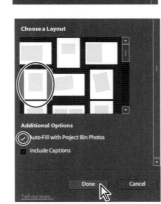

6 From the Choose A Layout menu, select the template "1 Portrait Vertical"—the design at the left of the second row—a vertical layout with a single photo frame in portrait format. Click the check box to activate the option Auto-Fill With Project Bin Photos, disable the option Include Captions, and then click Done. You may see a progress bar briefly while Photoshop Elements generates the page.

▶ **Tip:** Move the pointer over the layout swatches; a Tooltip appears with the name of each layout.

A new file is created and opens in the Edit pane. Your image has been placed in the theme and layout template you chose. The photo and its frame are surrounded by an active bounding box, indicating that they are selected.

▶ **Tip:** To move the framed photo, click inside the bounding box and drag the image to a new position. To re-size the image, move the pointer over any one of the corner handles of the bounding box and drag the handle when the diagonal double-arrow cursor appears. By default, the photo is scaled proportionally. To rotate a photo around its center point, move the pointer close to any handle, staying outside the bounding box; when the pointer becomes a curved double-arrow cursor, drag in either direction to rotate the image.

7 Ensure that you have the Move tool ( ) selected in the tool bar, and then right-click / Control-click inside the bounding box of the photo and frame. Choose Fit Frame To Photo from the context menu. The frame is re-sized so that its outside border conforms to the edge of the image.

Due to the fact that this frame is a bit-mapped graphic, it has been stretched to accommodate the non-standard proportions of our image. In attempting to find the best fit, Photoshop Elements has rotated the frame, which for this particular design, makes the distortion appear worse and spoils the graphic balance of the details. In the next exercise you'll replace the bit-mapped graphic with a vector frame.

A project theme from the content library consists of a preset combination of background artwork and image frame style. In some cases you may be happy with the un-edited result once your image has been placed in the layout but in other instances you may wish to treat the theme as a starting point or template and go on to customize the design. Both the background and frame can be replaced or even deleted. The frame can also be duplicated, which is one way to add more images to the layout if you wish.

Working with frames

In our example, it would be a good idea to change the frame even had it not been distorted; the theme is quite "busy" and in combination with an image that includes four faces the result is far too cluttered. A simpler frame will improve our design.

1   Leaving the framed photo selected, expand the Content panel by clicking its header bar in the Panel Bin. From the content sorting menu at the top left of the panel, choose By Type. From the content types menu, choose Frames.

2   Scroll down in the library of frames, noting the wide variety of designs available. Stop about half-way down the list and double-click the frame "Basic White 40px." The new frame is placed around the image in the Edit pane; the change is a marked improvement.

▶ **Tip:** Move the pointer over the frame swatches; a Tooltip appears with the name of each frame.

3   Move the pointer over one of the corner handles on the bounding box around the framed image. When the double-arrow cursor appears, hold down the Alt / Option key on your keyboard to scale the image from the center as you drag the handle outwards, enlarging the image together with its frame. Release the mouse button when the amount of background still visible at the sides of the image is roughly equivalent to the width of the white frame.

4   Move the pointer close to one of the corner handles, keeping it just outside the bounding box. When the curved double-arrow cursor appears, drag to rotate the image to the right. Hold down the Shift key as you drag to constrain the rotation to 15° increments; release the mouse button when you have rotated the image by 15°.

5   Click the Commit button (✓) beneath the image to commit the changes.

Adjusting a photo inside a frame

Note: The frame occupies the same layer as the image it contains, even though it appears to be overlaid.

The image frame and the photo it surrounds are on the same layer—when you scale, rotate or move the photo, the frame is transformed or moved with it.

To move or transform the image inside its frame, first right-click / Control-click the image and choose Position Photo In Frame from the context menu or alternatively, simply double-click the photo with the Move tool (🕂).

A control bar appears above the photo, with a scaling slider and buttons to re-orient the image or replace it with another.

- To re-size the image, either drag the slider or the handles on the bounding box.

- To rotate the photo inside the frame, move the pointer close to any handle; when the pointer becomes a curved double-arrow cursor, drag the handle in either direction.

- To reposition the image within the frame, simply drag it in any direction.

Working with backgrounds

You can also move, rotate, scale, delete or replace the preset background graphic in a Theme template.

1 The background for this theme is much larger than your 5 inch x 7 inch page. In order to see the bounding box around the entire background image, choose View > Zoom Out. Alternatively, press the Ctrl key (Windows) / Command key (Mac OS) together with the minus (-) key.

2 Right-click / Control-click the background and choose Move Background from the context menu. A bounding box appears around the background image.

3 Move the pointer close to one of the corner handles, keeping it just outside the bounding box. When the curved double-arrow cursor appears, drag to rotate the background image in a clockwise direction, holding down the Shift key as you drag to constrain the rotation to 15° increments. Release the mouse button when you've rotated the horizontal image by 90° into a vertical position, but don't click the Commit button just yet.

4 Click anywhere inside the bounding box, and then drag to move the background picture upwards and to the left until the lower right corner of the image snaps to the lower right corner of the card design. Click the Commit button (✓) to commit the changes.

Tip: When the Move tool is active, you can use the arrow keys on your keyboard to move the project elements in small increments instead of dragging them using the pointer.

Adding graphics from the Content library

1 From the content sorting menu at the top left of the Content panel, choose By Word; then type **beach** in the text box and click Find. The Content panel displays any themes, backgrounds, frames and graphics that are tagged with your search term.

2 Drag the yellow starfish from the content library onto the top right corner of your greeting card design.

3 Use the bounding box handles to scale and rotate the new object; then drag to position it as shown below. When you are satisfied with its placement, click the Commit button (✔) to commit the changes.

Refining a project in Full Edit mode

Now that all the elements of the design are in place, you can add a little polish to your project with a few quick touches in Full Edit mode.

1 Click the small arrow at the right of the orange Edit tab above the Panel Bin and choose Edit Full from the menu.

2 Click the Reset Panels button in the menu bar (Windows) / the application window header bar (Mac OS) or choose Window > Reset Panels. If you don't see the Effects and Layers panels in the Panel Bin, select their names from the Window menu.

3 In the Layers panel, right-click / Control-click the top layer "Star Fish" and choose Simplify Layer from the context menu.

4 Choose Enhance > Adjust Lighting > Brightness/Contrast. Use the sliders or type in the text boxes in the Brightness/Contrast dialog box to increase both values to 15, and then click OK.

5 In the Layers panel, click to select the middle layer "Basic White 40px 1" (the framed image), and then double-click the *fx* icon to the right of the layer name.

6 In the Style Settings dialog box, note that the Drop Shadow effect is already activated for this layer. Use the Lighting Angle wheel or type in the text box to set the lighting angle to 25°. In the Drop Shadow settings, set the values for both Size and Distance to 50 px and the Opacity to 80%.

7 Click the Drop Shadow Color box (currently black) to the right of the Size value. As you move the pointer over the image it becomes an eyedropper cursor; click with the eyedropper to sample the darkest shadow between the two seashells in the lower left corner. Click OK to close the Select Shadow Color dialog box, and then click OK to close the Style Settings dialog box.

8 Choose Layer > Layer Style > Copy Layer Style. Right-click / Control-click the layer "Star Fish" and choose Paste Layer Style from the context menu. Double-click the *fx* icon for the "Star Fish" layer to open the Style Settings dialog box. In the Style Settings dialog box, first deactivate the Stroke option (our white vector frame), and then set the Drop Shadow Size to 20 px, Distance to 10 px and Opacity to 60%. Click OK to close the Style Settings dialog box.

9 Choose File > Save. In the Save As dialog box, navigate to your My CIB Work folder and name the file GreetingCard_1.psd. On Windows, be sure to activate the option Include In The Elements Organizer. Click Save.

10 Congratulations; you've created your first photo project! Choose File > Close. On Mac OS you'll also need to close the original image file.

Working with multiple pages

You can create multiple-page layouts with Photoshop Elements, which are perfect for projects such as a photo album where you want a consistent theme from page to page, or for a set of invitations. In the Edit menu you'll find options for adding either new blank pages or new pages using the current layout.

Producing a Photo Book

A Photo Book is a multi-page digital project that offers an attractive way to present and share your memories and makes the perfect personalized gift for a loved one.

You can either have your completed Photo Book commercially printed and bound by ordering through an online service—great for a sophisticated gift—or print it yourself on your home printer. However, unless you have high-quality, double-sided paper in a large enough size you may have to make some design compromises and possibly scale your layout in the printer dialog box to fit standard paper sizes.

Rearranging the order of images in a project

You'll start by locating the images for this project and rearranging their order.

1   Check that you still have the images for this lesson visible in the Organizer (Windows) / the Bridge Content panel (Mac OS). If you do, you can skip this step; if not, do one of the following:

  •   On Windows, click Show All if it's visible above the Media Browser. In the Keyword Tags panel, click the find box beside the Lesson 6 tag to isolate the images for the projects in this lesson.

- On Mac OS, choose File > Browse With Bridge. In Bridge, click the link to your PSE8CIB folder in the Favorites panel. In the Content panel, double-click to open the Lessons folder; then the Lesson06 folder.

2 In the Organizer (Windows) / Bridge (Mac OS), click to select the image photobook_1.jpg; then Shift-click the image photobook_9.jpg to select all nine images for this exercise.

3 Do one of the following:

- On Windows, click the orange Fix tab above the Task Pane and choose Full Photo Edit from the menu. When the photos have opened in the Editor, click the purple Create tab above the Panel Bin.

- On Mac OS, right-click / Control-click any of the selected images in the Bridge Content panel, and then choose Open With > Adobe Photoshop Elements 8. If Photoshop Elements is not already in Create mode from the last exercise, click the purple Create tab above the Panel Bin.

4 In the Projects panel, click the Photo Book button. On Windows you'll then need to choose an option for the creation and printing method; click Print With Local Printer.

The Projects panel changes to Photo Book mode. The nine photos are open on tabs in the Edit pane and their thumbnails are displayed in the Project Bin at the bottom of the workspace.

The order of the images in the Project Bin will determine the order in which they are placed in your Photo Book. For our project, we need to rearrange them.

5 Right-click / Control-click any of the thumbnails in the Project Bin and choose Show Filenames from the context menu.

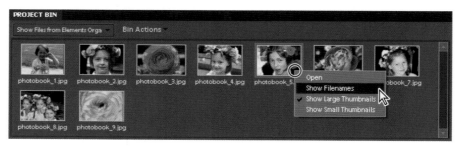

6 If you can't see all nine thumbnails, scroll downwards in the Project Bin so that you can see the last two images, photobook_8.jpg and photobook_9.jpg.

7 Reverse the order of the last two photos in the series by dragging the image photobook_9.jpg to a new position to the left of the image photobook_8.jpg. Release the mouse button when the insertion bar appears.

8 Hide the Project Bin by clicking its header bar or double-clicking its name tab; this will give you more space to work on your Photo Book design.

Choosing a theme and a photo layout

You can either use a Photo Book theme or layout "as is" or treat it as a basis and go on to customize your own design by deleting or replacing backgrounds and frames and either adding photos to the layout or removing them. For a Photo Book you can also have Photoshop Elements place your photos in the layout automatically by enabling the Random Photo Layout option.

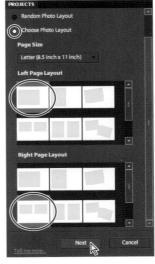

1 At the top of the project panel under Layout Options, click the radio button to activate the Choose Photo Layout option.

2 Choose Letter (8.5 inch x 11 inch) from the Page Size menu.

3 From the Left Page Layout menu, choose the first layout: "1 Landscape."

4 From the Right Page Layout menu, choose the template "2 Landscape" at the left of the second row, and then click Next.

▶ **Tip:** Move the pointer over the layout swatches; a Tooltip appears with the name of each layout.

5 Scroll down almost to the bottom of the Choose A Theme menu and click the theme "Texture Paper." Ensure that Auto-Fill With Project Bin Photos is activated, and that the number of pages is set to 6. (Photoshop Elements calculates the number of pages that will be needed to fit all the images from the Project Bin into the specified page layout.)

6 Click Create. Photoshop Elements generates the project pages, and then the Photo Book file opens in the right side of a split Edit pane.

▶ **Tip:** Move the pointer over the theme swatches; a Tooltip appears with the name of each theme.

7 Click once on the name tab of the foremost image in the left side of the Edit pane, and then click the tab of the Photo Book project file. The project file image window expands to fill the Edit pane. Don't change the magnification level yet—you'll want to be able to see a full two-page spread in the Edit pane.

A floating control bar presents controls that enable you to navigate backwards and forwards through the book and to quickly add or remove pages. Drag the floating control bar clear of the image and place it close to the bottom of the workspace.

Note: By default, the image on the title page is the first photo in the Project Bin. You could have chosen a different photo for the title page by changing the order of the thumbnails in the Project Bin before performing step 1 in this exercise.

The first page displayed is the title page, as indicated by a T in the control bar and in the page indicator at the bottom of the image window.

8 Use the forward and back arrows in the floating control bar to preview all the pages in the Photo Book, and then return to the title page for the next exercise.

Refining your Photo Book layout

In this exercise you'll polish your Photo Book design using some of the skills you picked up in the greeting card project.

Tip: When the Move tool is active, you can use the arrow keys on your keyboard to move the project elements in small increments instead of dragging them using the pointer.

1 Use the Move tool (⬩) to drag the image towards the upper right of the title page; then drag the handle at the lower left corner of the photo's bounding box to re-size the image as shown here. Click the Commit button (✓) to commit the changes.

2   Click the forward arrow in the floating control bar—or the one at the bottom of the image window—to advance to the next page. If you can't see the entire spread, double-click the Hand tool or choose View > Fit On Screen.

3   Using the Move tool (↖⊕), drag the photo on the left to center it on the page, and then move, re-size and rotate the images on the right page as shown in the illustration below. Remember that you need to click the green Commit button after every scaling or rotating operation.

▶ **Tip:** If your photos do not automatically fill their frames, right-click / Control-click each photo and choose Fit Frame To Photo, and then resize the frame and photo together using the handles on the bounding box. Alternatively, double-click the photo and resize it within its frame by using the slider, as discussed in "Adjusting a photo inside a frame" on page 144.

4   To reverse the layer order of the images on page 2 so that the photo of the orange flower lies on top of the portrait of the girl, right-click / Control-click the flower image and choose Bring Forward from the context menu.

5   Advance to the page 3 and 4 spread and reorganize the photos as shown in the illustration below, referring to steps 3 and 4 if necessary.

6   Advance to the final spread, pages 5 and 6. The photo of three girls on page 6 needs to be better positioned within its frame. Right-click / Control-click the photo and choose Position Photo In Frame from the context menu. Use the scaling slider to reduce the image slightly and the Move tool to drag it upwards inside the frame, and then commit the changes.

7 Select the empty frame on page 6 and press the Delete / Backspace key on your keyboard; then click Yes to confirm the action. Move, scale and rotate the other two images as shown in the illustration below.

8 Click the Go To First Page button in the floating Photo Book control bar.

Replacing design elements

Now that you've set up the overall layout of your Photo Book you can vary the design a little by replacing some of the preset theme elements with alternatives from the content library.

In this exercise, you'll give the Title page—the front cover of your Photo Book—a different look than the inside pages.

1 From the content sorting menu at the top left of the Content panel, choose By Word, and then type the word **handmade** in the text box. Click to deactivate the Frames, Graphics, Shapes, Text and Themes filter buttons below the sorting menu, leaving only the Backgrounds filter active; then click Find. The Content panel displays six background choices; click to select the last in the group: "Scrapbook 08," and then click Apply at the bottom of the Content panel.

2 Right-click / Control-click the new background and choose Move Background from the context menu. Drag the background to align its lower left corner with the corresponding corner of the page, and then click the Commit button.

3 Click to select the Title page photo.

4 Deactivate the Backgrounds filter button and activate the Frames filter. From the content sorting menu, choose By Style, and then choose Scrapbook from the styles menu. Scroll down in the search results and double-click the frame "Scrapbook 03" in the third row from the bottom.

▶ **Tip:** Move the pointer over the frame swatches; a Tooltip appears with the name of each frame.

Adding graphics

The Photo Book is almost complete. Before adding text, you can liven up the design with a judicious use of graphics from the content library.

1 Click the forward arrow in the floating control bar—or the one at the bottom of the image window—to advance to the page 1 and 2 spread.

2 Deactivate the Frames filter button and activate the Graphics filter. From the content sorting menu, choose By Object, and then choose Flower from the objects menu. Drag just one or two petals or flowers onto the spread, scaling and rotating them as desired. Right-click / Control-click a graphic on the page and choose from the context menu to bring it forward or send it backward in the layer order. Repeat the process for the remaining pages, but remember—be sparing; when it comes to design, less is more!

3 With the page 5 and 6 spread open, choose Speech Bubble from the objects menu in the Content panel and drag Speech Bubble 10 onto page 6. Use the bounding box handles to scale the graphic, positioning it as shown below.

Adding text to your project

In this exercise you'll personalize the Photo Book as a gift by adding some text.

1 Select the Horizontal Type tool; then choose a font from the font menu in the Tool Options bar across the top of the Edit pane. On Windows, we chose LTZapfino One (Zapfino on Mac OS) but any other calligraphic or script font such as Monotype Corsiva will suit the design. From the font size menu, we chose 72 pt—the largest size available—as a starting point.

2 Ensure that the Anti-aliased button is activated so that the edges of the letters are smoothed, and then choose Center Text from the text alignment menu.

3 Click the Text Color swatch. Move the Select Color dialog box away from the image on page 6 by dragging its title bar; then move the pointer onto the image and sample a deep grape color from one of the flowers in the photo. Click OK to close the dialog box.

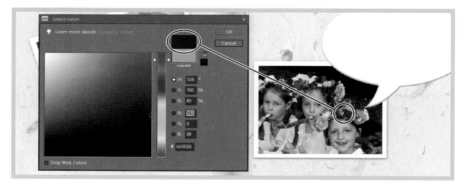

4 With the Type tool, click on the background below the image on page 5 and type **Happy Birthday Mom**. The text is placed on a layer above the background but below the framed photo. (If the text appears on top of the photograph, you can change the layer order when you scale and position the text a little later.) Click the Move tool to deactivate the text.

5 With the Move tool, click the speech bubble graphic on page 6. Select the Type tool again and choose Right Align Text from the text alignment menu. From the Leading menu on the left of the text color swatch, choose 60 pt. Click the text entry cursor in the upper right of the speech bubble and type **from your**; then press Enter / Return and type **darling blossoms**.

6 Select the Move tool to scale and position the text on both pages as you see in the illustration below.

7 Click the Go To First Page button in the floating control bar. Select the Type tool and choose Center Text from the alignment menu; then click on the background in the center of the title page and type **for you**. Use the Move tool to reposition and scale the text as shown here. Tweak the size and position of the photo if necessary.

8 As a final touch, you can soften the title page text by reducing its opacity. Use the Move tool to select the text. In the Panel Bin, expand the Effects panel, if necessary, by clicking its header bar. Click the Layer Styles button at the top of the Effects panel and choose Visibility from the adjacent Layer Styles menu. Double-click the left-most of the three swatches—the "Ghosted" effect—to make the text semi-transparent. If you wish, you can repeat this step for the text on pages 5 and 6.

Tip: On Windows, the Visibility effect swatches may be very difficult to see if your preferences are set for a dark user interface. Hold the pointer over the position indicated in the illustration to see a tooltip displaying the name of the effect.

9 The Photo Book is complete; choose File > Save. In the Save As dialog box, locate and open the My CIB Work folder you created earlier inside your Lessons folder. Type PhotoBook_1 as the file name. By default your project will be saved in Photo Project Format (.PSE), a multi-page document format that preserves text, layers and objects so that they can be edited later. You could also choose to save the project as a PDF file that can be shared as an email attachment. On Windows, make sure the option Include In The Elements Organizer is activated.

10 Click Save, and then choose File > Close.
Congratulations—you've completed another project!

Assembling a photo collage

In the next few exercises you'll create another project—this time, a Photo Collage. You can print your collage on your home printer, order prints on-line, or save it to your hard drive to send by e-mail or use as part of another digital document.

Start by locating the images for this project.

1   Check that you still have the images for this lesson visible in the Organizer (Windows) / the Bridge Content panel (Mac OS). If you do, you can skip this step; if not, do one of the following:

    •   On Windows, click Show All if it's visible above the Media Browser. In the Keyword Tags panel, click the find box beside the Lesson 6 tag to isolate the images for the projects in this lesson.

    •   On Mac OS, choose File > Browse With Bridge. In Bridge, click the link to your PSE8CIB folder in the Favorites panel. In the Content panel, double-click to open the Lessons folder; then the Lesson06 folder.

2   In the Organizer (Windows) / Bridge (Mac OS), click to select the file ChinaCalendar.jpg; then Shift-click the image ChinaScan4.jpg to select all six images for this project.

3   Do one of the following:

    •   On Windows, click the orange Fix tab above the Task Pane and choose Full Photo Edit from the menu. When the photos have opened in the Editor, click the purple Create tab above the Panel Bin.

    •   On Mac OS, right-click / Control-click any of the selected images in the Bridge Content panel, and then choose Open With > Adobe Photoshop Elements 8 from the context menu. If Photoshop Elements is not already in Create mode, click the purple Create tab above the Panel Bin.

4   In the Projects panel, click the Photo Collage button. The Projects panel changes to Photo Collage mode and thumbnails of the six photos are displayed in the Project Bin below the Edit pane. If the Project Bin is not visible click its header bar at the bottom of the Edit pane to expand it or choose Window > Project Bin.

As you can see, none of the images for this project are actually digital photographs as such. They are all scans of mementos from a trip to China: a cheaply printed calendar page, a much-used map and four paper photographs printed in sepia tone.

Most of us like to keep little reminders like these—an old concert ticket, a pressed flower, or the stamps on a torn envelope can hold as many memories as any photograph. A Photo Collage is a perfect way to preserve and present such evocative mementos. You can even scan or photograph three-dimensional keepsakes; a handful of seashells or colored pebbles could make a great background image.

Setting up your project page

In any Photoshop Elements project each image or object occupies its own layer. For a Photo Collage, which consists of multiple images on the same page, the order of the images in the Project Bin dictates their placement in the "stacking order" of the layers. The first image in the Project bin will be placed on the lowest layer—immediately above any preset background from the content library, which is assigned to the bottom layer by default. Each image, graphic or text object added subsequently will be placed above the last. Unoccupied space on a layer is transparent, enabling you to see through it to the layers below.

Although you can change the layering order later, it will simplify the process of assembling your collage if you do some basic planning and arrange your images to suit. For this project we wish to use the map as part of the background design, appearing below—or behind—the other elements.

1   Reverse the positions of the first two images in the Project Bin by dragging the scan of the calendar page to the right of the map. Release the mouse button when the insertion bar appears.

Set up your design by choosing a page size, design theme and layout template. As you've learned already, a theme consists of a preset combination of background artwork and a photo frame style, both of which can be edited or replaced. For this exercise however, you'll start without any theme preset—just a blank page.

2   From the Page Size menu near the top of the Projects panel, choose Letter (8.5 inch x 11 inch). Move the pointer over the theme swatches; a Tooltip appears with the name of each theme. Select the No Theme swatch in the top row.

3   Scroll down to the fourth row of Layout options and select the 2 Portrait Vertical layout. Make sure that the Auto-Fill With Project Bin Photos option is activated. Note that Photoshop Elements has calculated that for a two-image layout with six images in the Project Bin, three pages will be needed. To overrule this, double-click in the Number Of Pages text box and type **1**.

4   Click Done.

> ▶ **Tip:** Even if you chose a layout with more or fewer images, you could change it later, adding or removing images, repositioning them in the layout, changing their orientation, or rotating them to appear at an angle on the page.

5   The first two images are placed according to the specified template and the photo project opens in its own window in the Edit pane. The as yet untitled file appears as a new thumbnail in the Project Bin. Double-click the Hand tool or choose View > Fit On Screen to see the layout displayed as large as possible.

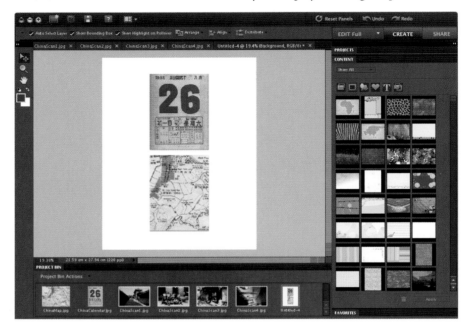

6   Select the Move tool. Right-click / Control-click each of the two placed images in turn and choose Fit Frame To Photo from the context menu.

7   Drag the calendar page down until it overlaps the map slightly; you can see that the calendar has been placed on a layer above—or in front of—the map.

Exploring the artwork library

Photoshop Elements makes it quick and easy to create distinctive photo projects by providing an extensive collection of themes, backgrounds, frames, text styles, clip-art shapes and graphics in the content library. In the following exercises, you'll choose a background for your collage and add graphics as you explore the options.

1   If necessary, expand the Content panel and collapse any other panels that are currently expanded, so that you can see as many of the sample swatches as possible, as shown in the illustration above.

What you see displayed in the Content panel depends on the options set with the sorting menus and filter buttons above the sample swatches.

2   In the Content panel, choose By Type from the menu on the left to see the contents of the library sorted by functional category. In the sorting menu on the

right, the options are Backgrounds, Frames, Graphics, Shapes, Text, Themes, and Show All. Choose each option in turn and scroll the sample swatch menu to see the options available.

  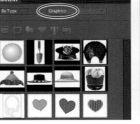 

3 Choose Show All from the sorting menu and make sure that all of the filter buttons below the menu are activated. Move the pointer over the left edge of the Content panel; when the double-arrow cursor appears, drag to the left to extend the panel out across the workspace.

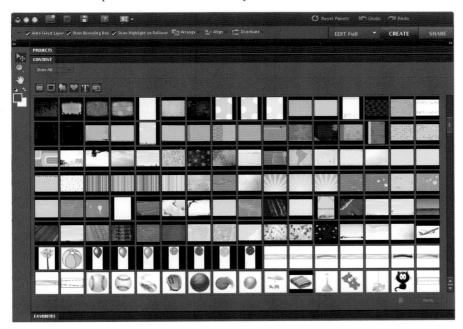

Scroll down to see the many backgrounds, frames, graphics, shapes and themes available in the library. In Show All mode, the number of choices may seem overwhelming, but Photoshop Elements provides several options that make it easy to sort and filter the library to locate the items you need. Another way to simplify working with library content is to make use of the Favorites panel.

4 Expand the Favorites panel by clicking its header bar below the Content panel. Drag a small assortment of items that interest you from the Content panel into the Favorites panel.

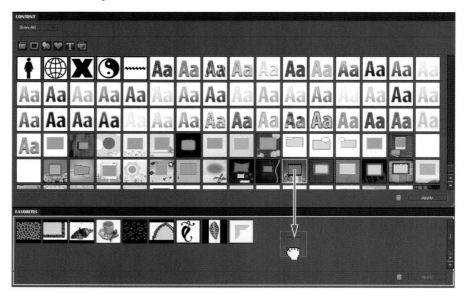

5 For now, collapse the Favorites panel once more and drag the left border of the Content panel to the right until the panel reaches its minimum width.

Adding a background

In this exercise you'll choose an appropriate background from the Content panel and add it to your collage.

1 In the Content panel, open the sorting menu on the left. Note the options in the menu; the content in the Artwork library has been tagged with keywords that allow you to search it intuitively—by activity, mood, season, and many other associations. For now, choose By Color. From the colors menu, choose Brown.

The Content panel now displays all the items in the artwork library that are tagged with the keyword "brown." Note the content filter buttons above the sample swatches. From left to right, these six buttons filter the items in the Content panel for Backgrounds, Frames, Graphics, Shapes, Text Effects, and Themes, providing a means for narrowing a search of the content library. To see all the items in the library irrespective of type, all six filter buttons should be activated.

2 Starting from the Filter For Themes button at the right, click to disable each of the content filters except Filter For Backgrounds. The Content panel now displays only the backgrounds that are tagged with the keyword "brown."

3 In the top row of swatches, click to select the Asia Map background and then click Apply. Alternatively, simply double-click the swatch to apply the background. The new background appears on the lowest layer—behind the images in your collage.

4 Choose View > Zoom Out. With the Move tool, right-click / Control-click the background image and choose Move Background from the context menu. If you don't see a bounding box surrounding the background image, choose View > Zoom Out once more.

▶ **Tip:** If you had started the process of creating your Photo Collage by choosing a theme that included a preset background, you could use the same technique to change it.

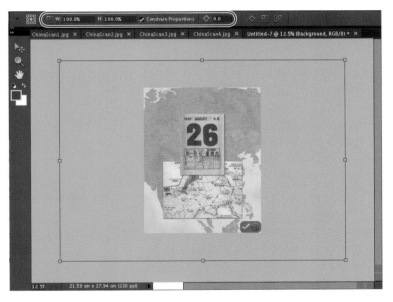

The bounding box shows clearly that the background graphic is considerably larger than your page.

5 In the options bar above the Edit pane, make sure that the option Constrain Proportions is activated (*see the illustration above*). Double-click either the width (W) or height (H) value and type **125**% to make the image even larger.

6 Drag the background to the left to position it as shown here. You can hold down the Shift key as you drag to constrain the movement horizontally. Click the Commit button (✔) at the bottom of the page preview to commit the changes, and then either double-click the Hand tool or choose View > Fit On Screen.

7 Drag the scanned map to the upper left corner of the page and the calendar to the lower right. Don't worry about precise placement at the moment; you'll work more with these elements later. Click the scanned map to select it.

Adding more images

In this exercise you'll add the rest of the images in the Project Bin to your collage. Selecting the map ensures that the next image added will be placed on the layer immediately above the map—and therefore, below the calendar page.

▶ **Tip:** On Windows, make sure that the menu below the Project Bin's name tab is set to Show Files From Elements Organizer, not Show Open Files.

1 Drag the image ChinaScan1.jpg from the Project Bin onto the page and place it a little below and overlapping the map. Don't drop it inside the bounding box surrounding the map or it will replace that image.

2 Leaving the new item selected, drag the image ChinaScan3.jpg from the Project Bin onto the page and place it a little below and overlapping the first image you added, being careful to place it outside the active bounding box. Repeat the process with ChinaScan4.jpg.

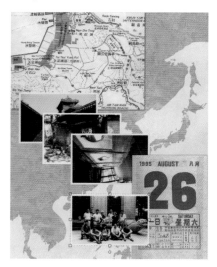

3 Click to select the calendar page. Drag the final image ChinaScan2.jpg from the Project Bin and place it a little outside the calendar's bounding box.

In the work area, you can now see the layering order of all the elements in your collage quite clearly.

Working with layers

● **Note:** Backgrounds chosen from the Artwork library will always appear on the bottom layer, even when they are added to the layout after the photographs—as was the case in this project.

Each element in your collage occupies its own layer. The background is at the bottom with the other images overlaid in successive layers in the order in which they were added to the project.

Layers are like transparent overlays on which you can paint or place photos, artwork, vector graphics or text. The checkerboard grid areas in layer thumbnails represent transparency through which you can see lower layers.

As well as photos and graphics from the content library layers can contain text, fills, gradients, or even saved photo projects. You can apply filters or special effects to any layer and specify the way those effects will affect other layers in the project. You can specify a layer's opacity and blending mode and also create adjustment layers, which do not contain images themselves but allow you to tune the appearance of the layer or layers below.

1 With the Move tool, Shift-click to select all four sepia photos, and then click the orange Edit Full tab above the Panel Bin and wait until Photoshop Elements has switched to Edit mode.

2 If you don't see the Layers panel in the Panels Bin, choose Window > Layers. Collapse any other panels that are currently expanded in the Panels Bin.

In the Layers panel, the layers containing the four sepia photographs are highlighted to indicate their selected state.

3 Click the eye icon beside the thumbnail for each selected layer in the Layers panel to hide the photographs for the time being.

Note: Layers that contain graphics from the content library are marked with a Smart Object icon in the lower right corner. A Smart Object is resolution independent; it can be scaled or rotated repeatedly without any degradation of the image, because the data is always drawn from the source file which remains in its original un-edited state.

▶ **Tip:** If you wish to further edit a Smart Object layer, you must first "simplify" the layer, making it a normal bit-mapped image and breaking its connection with the source file. Always scale and rotate the image first; then when you're ready for further editing, select the layer and choose Layer > Simplify Layer. You'll also find this command in the Layers panel Options menu.

4 Make sure you still have the Move tool selected. Click in the Layers panel to select the layer "No Theme 1"—the layer containing the scanned map. The selected layer is highlighted in the Layers panel and its contents are surrounded by a bounding box in the Edit pane. Use the handles on the bounding box to scale and rotate the image as shown below, and then click the Commit button. Use the Opacity slider at the top of the Layers panel to set the opacity of the map image to 50%.

5 Click in the Layers panel to select the layer "No Theme 2"—the second layer from the top containing the scanned calendar page. Drag the image in the collage to position it as shown here.

6 In the Layers panel, click the eye icon beside the thumbnail for each of the ChinaScan layers to make the photos visible again. Use the Move tool to select each of the four images in turn, moving and rotating them to arrange them in the collage.

7 Reverse the stacking order of the photographs ChinaScan1, 3, and 4 by dragging the respective layers in the Layers panel.

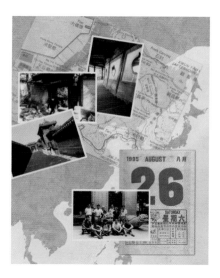

Adding graphics from the Content library

The design is almost complete, but it's all a little two-dimensional. Let's look for something in the content library to set it off.

1 If you don't see the Content panel, choose its name from the Window menu. From the sorting menu in the Content panel, choose the option By Word and type **travel** in the text box beside the menu. Click to activate the Filter For Graphics button, make sure that all the other content filters are disabled, and click Find.

2 Drag the graphics "Travel Compass" and "Plane Stamp" onto your Photo Collage page, and then scale and rotate them as shown in the illustration.

3 In the Layers panel, set the opacity of the Plane Stamp layer to 75%.

Applying effects

As a finishing touch you can apply a drop shadow effect to the compass and the four sepia photographs to give them greater presence and lift them from the flatness of the background elements; this will add contrast and increase visual impact.

1 Right-click / Control-click the image of the compass and choose Edit Layer Style from the context menu.

2 In the Style Settings dialog box, click the check box to activate the Drop Shadow option. Set the Lighting Angle to 135° and the Size, Distance, and Opacity values to 20, 25, and 50 respectively; then click OK.

3 With the compass still selected, choose Layer > Layer Style > Copy Layer Style, and then deselect the compass.

4 Shift-click to select all four sepia photographs and choose Layer > Layer Style > Paste Layer Style. Click the background to deselect the photos.

5 The collage design is complete. Save it to your My CIB Work folder as Collage_1.psd. Activate the Layers option so that the file is saved with its layers intact. On Windows, activate the option Include In The Elements Organizer.

A Photo Collage not only makes a great way to preserve and present fading mementos but, by combining a group of images and objects, can actually tell a story. The title of this particular picture-story is "Leaving Cheung Chau."

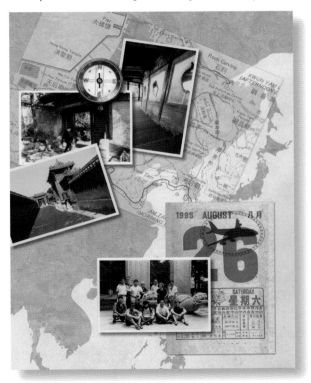

Congratulations! You've completed the last project in this lesson. You've learned about using the preset Theme and Layout templates, explored the content library, and become familiar with a variety of methods for locating the content you need. You've also learned the basics of working with layers and applying layer styles. Before you move on to the next lesson, "Printing, Sharing, and Exporting," take a moment to refresh your new skills by reading through the review on the next page.

Review questions

1 How do you begin a new project such as a greeting card, Photo Book or collage?

2 How do you scale and reposition a photo in a photo project?

3 How do you change the order of the pictures in a photo book?

4 How can you find the items you want amongst all the choices in the Content library?

5 What are layers, how do they work, and how do you work with them?

6 What is a Smart Object, and how does it affect your editing workflow?

Review answers

1 To create a project, select a project option on the Create tab in the Panel Bin by clicking one of the project buttons or choosing from the More Options menu. The Projects panel offers prompts to guide you through choosing theme and layout presets and the Content panel provides access to backgrounds, frames, graphics and more.

2 Once you've selected and applied a theme and a layout, an edit window opens with a bounding box around the photo. You can scale or rotate the photo by dragging the bounding box handles and move it on the page by dragging the image itself. To scale, rotate, or move a photo within its frame you need to double-click the image before using the same techniques, so that the changes affect the photo independently and are not applied to the photo and its frame together.

3 You can change the order of images in a photo book by dragging them to new positions in the Project Bin below the Edit pane.

4 You can sort and search the items in the Content library by using the menus and buttons at the top of the Content panel. From the first menu you can choose options to sort the content by type, activity, mood, season, color, keywords and other attributes. Once you have set up the first menu, you use the other menu to narrow the search—to specify which type, color, or mood you want. Use the content filter buttons to filter the search results to display only backgrounds, frames, graphics, shapes, text styles, or themes with the attributes you've specified. Use the favorites panel to assemble a collection of the items you're most likely to use, rather than looking through the entire library every time you want to add a library item to a project.

5   Layers are like transparent overlays on which you can paint or place photos, artwork, or text. Each element in a photo project occupies its own layer—the background is at the bottom and the other elements are overlaid in the order in which they are added to the project. Photos from the Project Bin are placed in the order of their capture date, so that the oldest is on the lowest layer. You can drag the thumbnails in the Project Bin to change that order. You work with layers in the Layers Panel, where you can toggle their visibility, change their order and add layer styles and effects. The checkerboard grid areas in the layer thumbnails represent the transparent parts of the layers through which you can see the layers below.

6   Layers that contain graphics from the content library are marked with a Smart Object icon in the lower right corner. A Smart Object is resolution independent; it can be scaled or rotated repeatedly without any degradation of the image, because the data is always drawn from the source file which remains in its original un-edited state. If you wish to further edit a Smart Object layer, you must first "simplify" the layer, making it a normal bit-mapped image and breaking its connection with the source file. Always scale and rotate the image first; then when you're ready for further editing, select the layer and choose Layer > Simplify Layer. You can also access this command in the Layers panel Options menu.

7 PRINTING, SHARING, AND EXPORTING

Lesson Overview

In previous lessons you imported photos, learned how to organize and find your files, and created projects to showcase your images. Now you'll learn how you can output your images and creations to share them with family, friends, or the world at large:

- Printing at home and ordering prints online
- Fine-tuning the composition of an image in the print preview
- Sharing photos by e-mail and Photo Mail
- Signing up for an Adobe ID and a Photoshop.com account
- Backing up and synchronizing your files
- Synchronizing multiple computers
- Creating your own Online Album or Web Gallery
- Using an online sharing service
- Burning your photos and projects to CD or DVD
- Exporting images for use on the Web

 You'll probably need between one and two hours to complete this lesson.

Now that you've learned how to find your way around the Photoshop Elements workspace, how to organize and find the photos and other media in your growing collection, and how to create photo projects and digital presentations, you're ready to share your images and creations with the world as printed output, by e-mail, or online.

Getting started

Before you start working on the exercises in this lesson, make sure that you have installed the software on your computer from the application CD (see the Photoshop Elements 8 documentation) and that you have correctly copied the Lessons folder from the CD in the back of this book onto your computer's hard disk. (See "Copying the Classroom in a Book files" on page 2.)

Setting up on Windows

For this lesson you'll use images from the CIB Catalog that you created in the "Getting Started" section at the beginning of this book. To open your CIB Catalog, follow these steps:

1   Start Photoshop Elements and click the Organize button in the Welcome Screen. Wait until the Organizer has finished opening.

2   The name of the active catalog is shown in the lower left corner of the Organizer window. If your CIB Catalog is already open you can skip to the next section, "About printing." If another catalog is currently loaded, continue with step 3.

3   Choose File > Catalog. In the Catalog Manager dialog box, click to select your CIB Catalog in the Catalogs list, and then click Open.

If you don't see the CIB Catalog file, review "Copying the Lessons files from the CD" on page 2 and "Creating a catalog" on page 3 in the "Getting Started" section at the beginning of this book.

4   Click Show All if it's visible above the Media Browser.

For the exercises in this section you'll be working from the Organizer, where you can explore a fuller range of printing options than are available in the Editor. Now you're ready to move on to "About printing" on the facing page.

Setting up on Mac OS

For the projects in this lesson, you'll be working with the sample image files in the PSE8CIB > Lessons folder that you copied to your hard disk in the section "Copying the Classroom in a Book files" on page 2.

1   Start Photoshop Elements and click Browse With Adobe Bridge in the Welcome Screen or choose File > Browse With Bridge.

2   In Bridge, click Essentials in the row of workspace options across the top of the application window. Click the link to your PSE8CIB folder in the Favorites panel. If you don't see the Favorites panel, right-click / Control-click the header of any other panel and choose Favorites Panel from the context menu.

3 To see all of the lesson images in your PSE8CIB folder at once, choose View > Show Items From Subfolders. If you see a check mark beside the Show Folders command in the View menu, choose View > Show folders to disable that option for now.

About printing

Whether you wish to use your home printer or order professional prints from an online service, Photoshop Elements offers a range of options for printing your photographs and Photo Projects such as photo books, greeting cards, and collages. You can print your photos individually or in picture packages with one or more photos repeated at a variety of sizes on the same page; preview a multiple selection of photos printed as thumbnail images arranged on a contact sheet, or produce your own photo labels using commercially available label paper.

Printing a contact sheet

A contact sheets is a great way to preview and assess a multiple selection of images by printing them at thumbnail size, arranged on a single page in a grid layout.

Printing a contact sheet on Windows

1 For the purposes of this demonstration, make a selection of twenty or more images in the Media Browser. To select a consecutive series of thumbnails, click the first image in the series, and then Shift-click the last; the images in-between will be selected. To select non-consecutive images, Ctrl-click their thumbnails.

2 Choose File > Print.

3 Set up the Prints dialog box as shown in the illustration on the next page:

- Choose a printer from the Select Printer menu and a paper size from the Select Paper Size menu.

- Choose Contact Sheet from the Select Type Of Print menu. The contact sheet layout includes all the photos in the thumbnail menu column at the left of the Prints dialog box. To remove a photo from the contact sheet, select it in the menu and click the Remove button (➖) below the menu pane.

- Experiment with the contact sheet layout by changing the number of columns under Select A Layout. Click the arrow buttons beside the Columns number or type a number between 1 and 9 in the text box.

● **Note:** If you choose the Print command without first making a selection of images, Photoshop Elements will ask if you want to print all the images currently visible in the Media browser.

The number of rows are adjusted according to your choice for the number of columns. If the number of photos selected for printing exceeds the capacity of a single page for the layout you've specified, more pages will be added to accommodate them. Use the Next Page and Previous page buttons below the page preview to navigate between the pages.

Tip: To display and print just a portion of an image in the contact sheet, select the image, and then use the slider beneath the print preview to zoom in. Drag the image to reposition it within its frame to display the area that interests you. Use the Rotate buttons to the left of the zoom slider below the print preview to change an image's orientation.

Note: Some words in the text label may be truncated, depending on the page setup and column layout.

4 To print image information labels below each image on the contact sheet, first click to activate Show Print Options (just below the Columns setting), and then activate any or all of the Text Label options. Activate Date to print the capture date recorded in the images' metadata, Caption to print any caption text, Filename to print the filename beneath each photo, or Page Numbers to print a page number on each contact sheet page.

5 Click Print or Cancel and skip to "Printing a Picture Package" on the next page.

Printing a contact sheet on Mac OS

1 For the purposes of this demonstration, make a selection of twenty or more images in the Bridge Content panel. To select a consecutive series of thumbnails, click the first image in the series, and then Shift-click the last; the images in-between will be selected. Command-click to select non-consecutive images.

2 Choose Tools > Photoshop Elements > Contact Sheet II.

3 Set up the Contact Sheet dialog box as shown in the illustration on the next page:

- Under Source Images, choose Selected Images From Bridge.

- Under Document, specify a size for your contact sheet.

- Under Thumbnails, specify the order in which the images will be arranged. Experiment with the number of rows and columns, referring to the layout preview at the right.

- Activate the Rotate For Best Fit, Use Auto-Spacing and Use Filename As Caption options

Tip: The other two Source Images options let you choose an entire folder of images or a selection of images that are already open in Photoshop Elements.

4   Click OK, and then wait while Photoshop Elements creates a new document for each page of the contact sheet and places the image thumbnails.

5   In Photoshop Elements, Command-click to select all the contact sheet pages in the Project Bin. Choose File > Print if you wish to see the contact sheet printed; otherwise choose File > Close All, and then click Don't Save.

Printing a Picture Package

A Picture Package layout you lets you print photos repeated at a choice of sizes on the same page, much as professional portrait studios do. You can choose from a variety of layout options with a range of image sizes to customize your picture package print.

Printing a Picture Package on Windows

1   Select one or more pictures in the Media Browser, and then choose File > Print.

2   In the Prints dialog box, choose a printer from the Select Printer menu and a paper size from the Select Paper Size menu. Choose Picture Package from the Select Type Of Print menu. If a Printing Warning dialog box cautioning against enlarging pictures appears, click OK. For this exercise you'll print multiple images at smaller sizes.

3   Choose a layout from the Select A Layout menu and activate the Fill Page With First Photo option. This will result in a page with a single photo repeated at a variety of sizes, according to the layout you have chosen. If you selected more than one photo in the Media browser, a separate Print Package page will be

Note: You can also access the Picture Package dialog from the Create panel. Select photos for printing in the Media Browser, click the purple Create tab above the Task Pane, and then click the Photo Prints button. In the Photo Prints panel, click the Print Picture Package button.

printed for each photo selected; you can see the previews for each page by clicking the page navigation buttons below the print preview.

The layout options available for a Picture Package will depend on the paper size specified in the Prints dialog box, the page setup, or the printer preferences. To change the paper size, choose from the Select Paper Size menu or click either the Page Setup button at the lower left of the Prints dialog box or the Change Settings button under Printer Settings. Depending on your printer, you may need to look for the paper size options in the Advanced preferences settings.

4   (Optional) Choose Antique Rectangle 2 (or another border of your preference) from the Select A Frame menu. You can select only one border style per picture package print; it will be applied to every picture in the layout.

5   If your photo is of non-standard proportions, the Crop To Fit option may fit the multiple images more closely to the layout and better fill the printable area.

● **Note:** The images in a Picture Package layout are automatically oriented to make the best use of the print-able paper area for the layout you have chosen. You cannot manually rotate the image cells (or print wells) in a picture package layout; however, you can still zoom or rotate each image within its print well using the zoom slider and orientation buttons below the preview. Drag an image to adjust its position in its print well.

6   (Optional) To add more photos from your catalog to the picture package, click the Add button (➕) under the thumbnails menu, select the photos you want in the Add Photos dialog box, and then click Done. The selected photos are added to the thumbnails column.

7   (Optional) To replace a photo in the layout with another, drag a thumbnail from the menu column onto an image in the print preview.

8   Click Print or Cancel and skip to "Printing individual photos" on page 178.

Printing a Picture Package on Mac OS

1 Do one of the following:

- Select one or more pictures in the Bridge Content panel. Right-click / Control-click a selected image and choose Open With > Adobe Photoshop Elements 8. In Photoshop Elements, choose File > Picture Package.

- Select one or more pictures in the Bridge Content panel, and then choose Tools > Photoshop Elements > Picture Package.

2 In the Picture Package dialog box, do one of the following, depending on your choice in step 1:

- If you invoked the Picture Package command in Photoshop Elements, choose Open Files from the Use menu under Source Images.

- If you invoked the Picture Package command from Bridge, choose Selected Images From Bridge from the Use menu under Source Images.

3 Make a selection from the Page Size and Layout menus, and then click the Edit Layout button below the Layout preview box.

4 In the Picture Package Edit Layout dialog box, adjust the Page Size if necessary.

5 Click to select an image in the layout preview and experiment by dragging the handles on its bounding box to scale the image or change its orientation. Option-click the image and try out some of the menu choices; then experiment with the settings and buttons in the Image Zones box. For now, click Cancel; clicking Save would overwrite the settings for the selected layout preset.

6 Click OK in the Picture Package dialog box, and then wait while Photoshop Elements creates a new document for each page of the Picture Package. If you wish to see the Picture Package printed choose File > Print; otherwise choose File > Close All, and then click Don't Save.

Printing individual photos

The Photoshop Elements Prints dialog box presents all your printing options in one convenient place and now also enables you to fine-tune the placement of each image within its own print well (its frame in the print preview). You can zoom or rotate an image with the controls beneath the preview and drag to reposition it, enabling you to get the image placed just right for printing without first editing it.

1 In the Organizer / Bridge Content panel, Ctrl-click / Command-click to make a multiple selection of eight or more images.

2 Do one of the following:

   • On Windows, choose File > Print.

   • On Mac OS, right-click / Control-click a selected image and choose Open With > Adobe Photoshop Elements 8. When the photos have opened in Photoshop Elements, choose File > Print.

3 In the Prints / Print dialog box, select a printer, paper size and print size from the menus at the right of the dialog box. On Windows, choose Individual Prints from the Select Type Of Print menu.

You may see a warning about print resolution, as some of the sample files are provided at low resolution. Click OK to dismiss this warning.

● **Note:** On Mac OS, some of the options in the Print dialog box differ from those illustrated here. For more information on printing from Photoshop Elements on Mac OS, please refer to Photoshop Elements Help and Adobe's online resources.

4 Experiment with the controls below the Print preview. Click to select an image in its print well and zoom in and out using the zoom slider. Use the Rotate Left and Rotate Right buttons beside the zoom slider to change the orientation of the

image within its print well frame. Drag the selected image to reposition it within the frame. Toggle the Crop To Fit option below the Select Print Size menu and observe the effect in the print preview.

5   To remove a photo from the selection of images to be printed, select its thumbnail in the menu column on the left side of the dialog box and then click the Remove button (➖).

6   To add a photo to the selection to be printed, click the Add button (➕) under the column of thumbnails and do one of the following:

- On Windows, activate one of the options in the Add Media From section of the Add Media dialog box, and then click the check box beside any image you'd like to add to the print job. Click Done.

- On Mac OS, browse for and select the image you want in the Open dialog box. From the Format menu, chose the file format in which you'd like to open the image, and then click Open.

Note: On Windows, you can print images from Photoshop Elements only if they are part of the currently active catalog. If you wish to add pictures to the printing batch that are not already in the currently active catalog, you must first import them using one of the methods described in Lessons 1, 2 and 4.

If you've selected more pictures than will fit on one page at the paper size and image dimensions you specified, Photoshop Elements automatically generates as many extra pages as necessary.

7   Check the page count below the Print Preview. If your print job has more than one page, preview the other pages by clicking the arrow buttons at each side of the page count.

8   Click the More Options button at the bottom of the dialog box and explore the settings available in the More Options dialog box. In the Printing Choices section, you can choose to print text details with your images, add image borders or a background color, and print crop marks to help you trim your images. The More Options dialog box also offers Custom Print Size and Color Management Settings. Click Cancel to close the More Options dialog box.

9   In the Prints / Print dialog box, click Print if you wish to see these images printed, or Cancel to save your ink and paper for your own prints. On Mac OS, choose File > Close All.

Ordering professionally printed photos online

● **Note:** You need an active Internet connection to order prints online.

If you want high quality prints of your photos and photo projects—for yourself or to share with others—you can order professional prints from an online service.

On Windows, Photoshop Elements provides integrated links to online printing partners through the Organizer and the Create mode. In this exercise you'll learn how to order individual prints from the Organizer.

On Mac OS, you won't find the integrated links in Photoshop Elements, but you can sign up independently with an online printing service in your area, and then follow the online instructions. You can skim this exercise if you're interested in the basic process, or skip ahead to the next section: "Creating an Adobe ID."

1 In the Organizer, select one or more pictures that you would like to have printed professionally.

2 Choose File > Order Prints > Order Shutterfly Prints. In the Order Shutterfly Prints dialog box, do one of the following:

   • If you are already a Shutterfly member, click the "Already a member?" link, enter your name, e-mail address and password and click Sign In.

   • If you are not already a Shutterfly member, create a new account by entering your name, e-mail address, and a password of at least six characters. If you accept the Shutterfly Terms and Conditions, click the check box below the personal details fields, and then click Join Now.

Whether you choose to order prints from Shutterfly or Kodak, the experience is similar. Both services lead you through the ordering process in easy-to-follow steps.

3 In the first step—Size/Qty for Shutterfly, Customize for Kodak—you can customize your order by specifying print sizes and quantities for the photos in your order. Click Remove under a thumbnail image in the list on the left side of the dialog box to remove that photo from your order.

Alert icons beside the thumbnails let you know if your selected photos have a high enough resolution for high-quality prints at the sizes you've selected.

4 When you're done reviewing your order, click Next.

5 As you proceed with your order, you'll add the names and delivery addresses of recipients, review your order—making changes if necessary, provide your credit card details in the Payment / Billing dialog box, upload your images and confirm your order. For this exercise, click Cancel. A dialog box appears to ask if you want to stop using this service. Click OK.

Creating an Adobe ID

● **Note:** At this stage, Elements Membership services are available only to users in the United States.

Photoshop Elements users in the U.S. can create an Adobe ID to register their software and sign up for a free Photoshop.com account. If you're running Photoshop Elements on Windows you can register and sign in from within the application.

Creating an Adobe ID on Mac OS

On Mac OS you can create an Adobe ID and set up a Photoshop.com account from your Web browser independently if you wish to be part of the online Photoshop Elements community; however, you won't have access to the Inspiration Browser or other integrated Elements Membership services such as backup and sharing, which require the Organizer. To create an Adobe ID and a Photoshop.com account, point your Web browser to www.photoshop.com and click the Join button at the upper right of the page. You can skip the rest of this section and go on to "Creating a Web Photo Gallery on Mac OS" on page 186.

Creating an Adobe ID on Windows

On Windows, you can create an Adobe ID from within your Photoshop Elements software. Creating an Adobe ID enables Elements Membership services that are integrated with your software, giving you access to the Inspiration Browser as well as Organizer-based backup and sharing and other exciting Adobe-hosted services that extend the capabilities of your Photoshop Elements software.

Basic Elements Membership is free and gives you your own storage space and a personal Photoshop.com URL where you can not only share and showcase your images but also access your photos and videos anytime and from anywhere that you can connect to the Internet. You can also use your Photoshop.com account to back up your Photoshop Elements albums and even to synchronize albums on multiple computers. Basic membership also gives you access to the Inspiration Browser, with integrated tips, tricks and tutorials related to whatever you're currently working on, providing a powerful way to advance your skill set and helping you make the most out of your photos and creations.

You can upgrade to a Plus Membership to get more storage space as well as access to advanced tutorials. With Plus membership you also get regularly updated content such as project templates, themes, backgrounds, frames, and graphics delivered directly to your software to help you keep your projects fresh and appealing.

Signing up from the Welcome screen

1 Start Photoshop Elements.

2 In the Welcome screen, click Create Adobe ID. Enter your name, e-mail address and a password, type a name for your personal Photoshop.com URL, and then click Create Account.

3 An e-mail message will be sent to you to confirm the creation of your account. Follow the instructions in the e-mail to activate your account.

Signing up from the Organizer or Editor

1 In the Organizer or Editor, click the Create New Adobe ID link in the menu bar.

▶ **Tip:** You don't have use the link in the Welcome screen to create an Adobe ID. Links for registering and signing in are conveniently located throughout the Photoshop Elements workspace.

2 Enter out your personal details in the Create Your Adobe ID dialog box, and then click Create Account.

Signing in to your Photoshop.com account

1 Make sure, your computer is connected to the Internet, and then start Adobe Photoshop Elements.

2 In the Welcome screen, enter your Adobe ID and password, and click Sign In.

If you didn't sign in at the Welcome screen, you can always click the Sign In link at the top of either the Organizer or Editor workspace.

About sharing

In Lesson 1 (Windows) / Lesson 3 (Mac OS) you learned how to use the E-mail Attachments feature to create copies of your photos optimized as e-mail attachments. Another option is to use the Photo Mail feature, which embeds your photographs in the body of an e-mail within a colorful custom layout. To share items other than photos—such as slide shows, photo collages, or flipbooks—you are offered a choice of output options during the creation process.

● **Note:** The Photo Mail feature is not available on Mac OS. If you're running Photoshop Elements on Mac OS you can skip to the next section, "Creating a Web Photo Gallery on Mac OS" on page 186.

Using Photo Mail

1 In the Organizer, select one or more photos in the Media browser and click the Photo Mail button in the Share panel.

If this is the first time you have accessed an e-mail feature in Photoshop Elements you will be presented with the E-mail dialog box. Choose your e-mail service from the menu, enter your name and e-mail address, and then click Continue. You can review or change your settings later by choosing Edit > Preferences > Sharing.

2   Activate the Include Captions option beside Items, and then click Next.

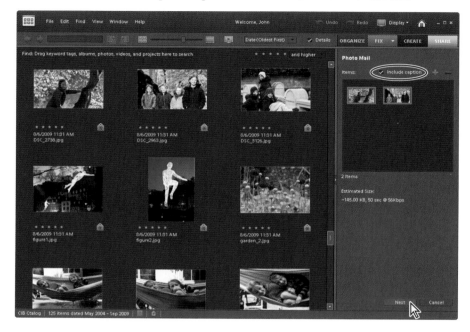

3   In the Message text box, delete the default text "Here are the photos…" and type a message of your own.

4   Select a recipient for your Photo Mail from the list in the Select Recipients pane. If you didn't work through Lesson 1 and your recipient list is still empty, click the Edit Recipients In Contact Book button (⬛) and create a new entry in the Contact Book dialog box.

5   Click Next. The Stationery & Layouts Wizard dialog box opens.

6   In the Stationery & Layouts Wizard dialog box, click each category in the list at the left of the dialog box to see the range of designs available. (*See the illustration on the next page.*) Choose a stationery style appropriate to your selected photos. A preview of your photo Photo Mail will appear on the right side of the dialog box.

7   Click Next Step.

8   Customize the layout by choosing from the Photo Size and Layout options. Choose a font from the menu under Text. Click the color swatch beside the font menu and choose a text color from the color palette. To edit the message text, click the message in the preview to make it active, and then edit the text as you would usually do. Use the same technique to edit the caption text.

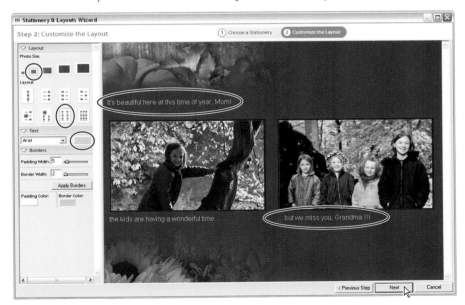

9   Click Next.

Photoshop Elements opens your default e-mail application and creates an e-mail message with your design embedded in the body of the message.

10 Switch back to the Photoshop Elements Organizer.

Creating a Web Photo Gallery on Mac OS

A Web Photo Gallery makes a great way to share and showcase your photos. You can choose from a variety of interactive layout templates that are optimized for viewing photos on the Web.

1 In Photoshop Elements, choose File > Open. In the Open dialog box navigate to and open your PSE8CIB > Lessons > Lesson07 folder. Select the four files 5_winter1.jpg through 5_winter4.jpg and click Open.

2 Click the green Share tab above the Panel Bin, and then click the Web Photo Gallery button at the top of the Share panel.

Bridge opens in Output mode. The Content panel has shrunk to a "filmstrip" at the bottom of the workspace, displaying thumbnails of the files in your Lesson07 folder, with the four winter photos selected. The Preview panel now occupies center stage.

3 Hide the Folders and Favorites panels by dragging the divider bar at the left of the Preview panel all the way to the left of the workspace.

4 To change the order in which the photos will appear in the Web Photo Gallery, drag the thumbnails to rearrange them in the Content panel, making sure to select all four images once more before you go on to the next step.

5 Drag the divider at the bottom of the Preview panel downwards to hide the Content panel.

6 At the top of the Output panel, choose Lightroom Flash Gallery from the Template menu and The Blues from the Style menu; then click the Refresh Preview button.

7 Working your way down the Output panel, review the options in the Site Info pane. For this exercise, leave the default text in the Site Title, Collection Title, Collection Description, Contact Info and E-mail Or Web Address text boxes. Collapse the Site Info pane by clicking the triangle at the left of the header bar.

Note: In the Bridge Preview panel, you can preview a maximum of ten images in a Web Photo Gallery preview; however, if you have included more than ten images they will all appear when you save or upload your gallery.

8 Review the options in the Color Palette pane below the Site Info pane. Here you can edit the color for every element that makes up this web gallery design. Click the Background color box. In the color picker, drag the slider at the right about one-third of the way towards the bottom of its range to set a darker blue for the background behind the main image. Click OK, and then click the Refresh Preview button to see the change applied in the Preview panel. Collapse the Color Palette pane by clicking the small triangle at the left of the header bar.

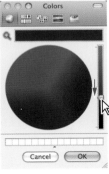

9 Try the various options for Layout, Preview Size, and Thumbnail Size in the Appearance pane, clicking the Refresh Preview button to see the effect of each change you make, and then collapse the Appearance pane.

Note: For some gallery templates the Appearance pane also includes a Transitions menu. For this Flash gallery the transitions cannot be edited.

10 The last pane in the Output panel is the Create Gallery pane. You can choose to save your gallery to disk or if you already have your own website you can enter the details and click Upload. For now, you can ignore these settings.

If you save the gallery to a folder on your hard disk, Bridge creates an HTML home page for your gallery (named index.htm or index.html), separate subfolders for JPEG images and thumbnails, and a content subfolder containing HTML pages. You can open the HTML home page file in any web browser to preview your gallery.

11 Click the Preview In Browser button in the top section of the Output panel. Click past any security alert messages from your browser.

12 Try the View Slideshow button and navigation controls below the main image. Click the thumbnails to change the main image.

13 When you're done previewing your gallery, close the browser window and click Essentials at the top of the Bridge application window to return the workspace to the previous mode. Choose File > Return To Adobe Photoshop Elements.

14 In Photoshop Elements, choose File > Close All.

To see a video with more detail on creating web galleries in Adobe Bridge, go to www.adobe.com/go/lrvid4014_bri.

The next few sections are specific to the Windows version of Photoshop Elements; you can skip to the section "About exporting" on page 197.

Creating an Online Album on Windows

A great way to share and showcase your photos is by creating an Online Album. You can choose from a variety of interactive layout templates that are optimized for viewing photos on the Web. Photoshop Elements guides you through the process of adding and arranging photos, applying templates, and sharing your files.

1   In the Organizer, click Show All if it's visible above the Media Browser. Choose View > Show File Names, if necessary, to see the file names below the thumbnails. Type **winter** in the Text Search box at the upper left of the workspace, and then press Enter on your keyboard to find the images for this exercise. The Media browser shows four photos named "5_winter1.jpg" to "5_winter4.jpg."

2   In the Media Browser, Ctrl-click to select the first two photos, and then click the green Share tab above the Task Pane.

3   In the Share panel, click the Online Album button. The Share panel presents you with a choice of options.

4   Activate Create New Album at the top of the panel, select Photoshop.com from the Share To options, and then click Next. The two selected photos are added to the new album and their thumbnails are displayed in the Content pane.

5   Under Album Details, type **Winter Walk** in the Album Name text box.

Adding photos to your Online Album

1   In the Media Browser, select the third photo, and then click the Add Items Selected In Media browser button (➕) below the Content pane. The selected photo is added to the album and now appears in the Content pane.

2   Drag the last of the four images in the Media Browser directly into the Content pane. All four photos are now included in the Winter Walk album.

Changing the order of photos in an Online Album

To change the order in which the photos will be displayed, simply drag the thumbnails to rearrange them in the Content pane.

1   Rearrange the order of the images so that the photos of the deer alternate with the photos showing blue sky.

Note: You can only share your album to Photoshop.com if you are a U.S. resident and have already signed up for Photoshop.com membership.
For information on the other album sharing options, Export To CD / DVD, Export To FTP, and Export To Hard Disk, please refer to Photoshop Elements Help.

2 Click the Sharing tab at the top of the Content pane. The Sharing pane presents a range of sharing options and the four photos are displayed in an interactive Online Album preview, using the default template. A filmstrip-style menu across the top of the preview pane displays thumbnails of template options. To see the name of a template, together with a brief description, hold the pointer above its thumbnail.

3 Double click the Classic template—the fourth template from the left in the filmstrip menu. The preview is updated to reflect your choice. A semi-transparent floating Slideshow Settings panel appears on the preview. The Slideshow Settings panel becomes opaque as you move the pointer over it. For now, hide the floating panel by clicking the Show / Hide Slideshow Settings button above the Templates menu.

4 In the Sharing pane at the right, activate the option Share To Photoshop.com. Activate Display In My Gallery if you wish to share your album publicly. Leave this option disabled if you wish to share your album only with those friends to whom you choose to send an invitation.

5 Type a message to be e-mailed with your invitation in the Message text box.

● **Note:** The View Online button in the Sharing pane will not become active until online sharing has been initiated and the upload is complete.

6 Under Send E-mail To, click the checkbox beside the name of any contact in the list to send an automatically generated e-mail inviting them to view your new Online Album. You can add more recipients to the list by clicking the Edit Recipients In Contact Book button () and creating new entries in the Contact Book dialog box.

7   Specify whether you wish to allow viewers to download photos or order prints, and then click Done.

8   Click the Organize tab above the Task Pane to return to the Organizer. In in the Albums palette, the Winter Walk album is now marked with an Online Album icon (). The Stop Sharing button () to the right of its name indicates that the Winter Walk album is currently being shared.

In the Media browser, the thumbnails of the four photos in your new album now display numbers in their upper left corners indicating their order in the album. Below each thumbnail there is now an Album icon () indicating that the photo is part of an album and a Backup/Synchronization icon () indicting that the image has been uploaded to Photoshop.com.

Sharing an existing album online

If you have a Photoshop.com account it's easy to convert any Photoshop Elements album into an Online Album. This can be demonstrated quite simply using the album you just created.

1   In the Albums panel, click the Stop Sharing button () to turn off sharing for the Winter Walk album. Click OK in the Stop Sharing This Album dialog box.

2   In the Organizer, click Show All above the Media Browser. Press Ctrl+Shift+A to make certain you have no files selected, and then click the green Share tab above the Task Pane.

3   In the Share panel, click the Online Album button. In the Online Album sharing options, the Winter Walk album is listed in the Albums pane and the options Share Existing Album and Share To Photoshop.com are already activated.

4   Click to select the Winter Walk album, and then click Next.

5 The Online Album preview appears, displaying the images in your Winter Walk album in the Classic template you selected earlier. In the Sharing pane at the right, activate the option Share To Photoshop.com and set the other options as you did in steps 4 to 7 of the previous exercise.

6 Click Done, and then click the Organize tab above the Task Pane to return to the Organizer. In in the Albums palette, the Winter Walk album is once again marked with the Online Album icon (🖼). The Stop Sharing button (🔄) indicates that the Winter Walk album is currently being shared.

Backing up and synchronizing media files

⬤ **Note:** This feature is currently only available to Photoshop Elements users in the U.S. who have signed up for Elements Membership and a Photoshop.com account.

If you have signed up for Elements Membership and activated your Photoshop.com account, you can choose to synchronize the files in your Photoshop Elements catalog and your Photoshop.com account, making your photos and videos available to you from any web browser through Photoshop.com and Photoshop Express.

You can manage your media from any web browser: add, delete, edit, or re-organize items at home or on the road. Any changes you make online will be synchronized back to Photoshop Elements on your desktop. Don't worry; the Synchronization feature will not overwrite anything on your base computer—Photoshop Elements creates a Version Set on your computer, so you will still have the original. If you delete something online, a copy is kept on your computer unless you confirm that you really do want it deleted from your Photoshop Elements Catalog.

In previous versions of Photoshop Elements only Albums could be backed up and synchronized in this way, but in Photoshop Elements 8 you can now choose to backup your entire catalog, making it even easier to protect your precious files.

Another exciting new feature in Photoshop Elements 8 is Multi Machine Sync. If you have separate installations of Photoshop Elements on more than one computer—perhaps on desktop computers at home and at the office, as well as the laptop you use when you travel—you can now synchronize them all to your Photoshop.com account. Any changes you make in your Photoshop Elements catalog on one computer, such as adding, deleting, editing or reorganizing images or albums, will be replicated on your other computers.

In Photoshop Elements 8 it's easier than ever to manage and monitor backup and synchronization—simply click the Backup/Synchronization Agent icon (📋), either at the bottom of the Organizer workspace or in the Windows System Tray (XP) or Notification Area (Vista).

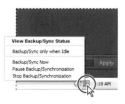

Setting backup and synchronization options

1   In the Organizer, click the Backup/Synchronization Agent icon (▓) at the bottom of the Organizer workspace and choose Open Backup/Synchronization Preferences. In the Backup/Synchronization Preferences dialog box, click the triangle beside Advanced Backup/Sync Options.

2   At a glance, you can find out everything there is to know about the current Backup and Synchronization status:

   - Backup and Synchronization is activated. The status bar shows how much of your online storage space is being used and how much free space you have.

   - New albums are set to backup and synchronize by default, and by default you will be asked for confirmation before files deleted online are deleted from your computer as part of the synchronization process.

   - Conflicts between the data in your catalog and your backed-up data online will not be resolved without a decision on your part, and there is currently no restriction on backup for large (time- and CPU-intensive) files.

   - All supported media file types are enabled for synchronization.

   - In the table below the preferences settings, you can see that synchronization is not enabled for media that is not included in any album, and that the album Winter Walk is enabled for backup and synchronization. The Online Album icon (▓) indicates that the Winter Walk album is currently being shared and the dimmed check-mark in the Sync column reflects the fact that backup and synchronization cannot be disabled for a shared album. To change this setting you would first need to stop sharing the album.

In the Backup/Synchronization Preferences dialog box you will also find a button for upgrading your Elements Membership to increase your online storage space at Photoshop.com, a setting for specifying a folder for downloads, and a button to enable backup and synchronization of your entire catalog.

3   Click OK to close the Backup/Synchronization Preferences dialog box.

You will also find a status bar indicating your online space usage—together with a link to your Backup/Synchronization Preferences—in the Welcome Screen once you've logged in to your Elements Membership account. For more detailed information on backup and synchronization options, please refer to Photoshop Elements Help.

Checking backup and synchronization status

The Backup/Synchronization Agent (⬛) at the bottom of the Organizer workspace and in the Windows System Tray (XP) or Notification Area (Vista) makes it easy to check on backup and synchronization status for your files without needing to open the preferences dialog box, and also offers additional commands that can be accessed without interrupting your workflow.

1   In the Organizer, click Show All if it's visible above the Media Browser.

2   Click the Backup/Synchronization Agent icon (⬛) at the bottom of the Organizer workspace and choose View Backed Up/Synchronized Files. The media Browser displays the photos from your Winter Walk album.

3   Repeat step 2 for the other two View commands at the top of the menu.

4   Click the Backup/Synchronization Agent icon in the Organizer just once more and choose View Backup/Synchronization Status. The Elements Backup/ Synchronization Status dialog box shows that (within the parameters set in the preferences) your catalog is currently in sync with your online account.

When backup and synchronization is in progress the Backup/Synchronization Status dialog box shows the real-time transfer of data from your Photoshop Elements catalog to your storage space at Photoshop.com.

5   Right-click the Backup/Synchronization Agent (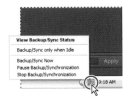) in the Windows System Tray (XP) or the Notification Area (Vista). Here you'll find some commands that can also be accessed from the agent in the Organizer and others which cannot, such as Backup/Sync Only When Idle and Stop Backup/Synchronization.

You can also double-click the Backup/Synchronization Agent icon to call up the Elements Backup/Synchronization Status dialog box.

Synchronizing separate computers

To synchronize your Photoshop Elements catalog across multiple computers, first connect each machine to the same Photoshop.com account by signing in from your Photoshop Elements installation on that machine. It's not necessary that you do this at the same time.

On each computer, turn on Backup/Sync in Photoshop Elements Preferences, and enable Backup/Sync for your entire catalog. Once a couple of synchronization cycles have run, all machines should have identical catalogs, with exactly the same Albums, keyword tags, image captions, and so on.

Don't attempt to aid the process; for example, by deliberately recreating a new album on your laptop to match the one you created on your desktop computer. In fact, Photoshop Elements would consider these to be two different files and you would end up with multiple copies on each machine. Simply make your changes on whichever computer you're working on and Photoshop Elements will update the other copies of your catalog.

The exception to this rule is that Photoshop Elements will not synchronize Stacks and Version Sets across multiple computers. The images inside your Stacks will be synchronised, but you'll need to recreate the stacking on each machine. For Version Sets, the top-most version—your edited version—will be synchronized.

If you're working on one computer and wish to make sure that the changes you make are synchronized to your other machines before you need to work with them, call up the Elements Backup/Synchronization Status dialog box from the Backup/Synchronization Agent and click the Sync Now button, and then do the same when you get to the next machine.

Using an online sharing service

From within Photoshop Elements you can use Adobe Photoshop Services to upload your images and creations to online sharing service providers. You can also use these services to download photos.

1   In the Organizer, select the photos you wish to share in the Media Browser.

2 Click the Share tab above the Task Pane. In the Share panel, click the white arrows to open the More Options menu and choose Share With Kodak Easyshare Gallery.

3 If the Welcome to Adobe Photoshop Services dialog box appears, do one of the following:

● **Note:** If you are still signed in to Adobe Photoshop Services from the exercise on ordering prints online, you don't need to sign in again. Just click Next to continue.

- If you are already an Ofoto or EasyShare Gallery member, click Sign In, and then use the e-mail address and password associated with your existing online account to sign in.

- Create a new account by entering your first name, e-mail address, and a password of at least six characters. If you agree with the Terms of Service, select the respective check box under Create Account, and then click Next.

4 In the Share Online dialog box, click Add New Address.

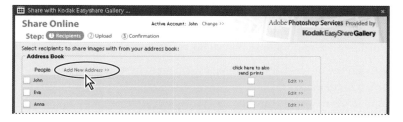

5 In the Add Address dialog box, complete the address information for the person with whom you wish to share your photos, and then click Next.

6 In the Share Online dialog box, click the check box for the newly added address. Under Message, type **Photos** in the subject field and **Enjoy!** in the message field; then, click Next and your photos will be uploaded.

7 In the Share Online Confirmation dialog box, click Done. Alternatively, if you wish to purchase prints of your photos click Order Prints, and then follow the on-screen directions.

An e-mail will be sent to the recipient you specified in step 6, containing a Web link to the photos which can be viewed as an online slide show.

About exporting

Even though Photoshop Elements offers a variety of ways to share your photos and creations, there may be situations where you wish to export copies of your files for use in another application. In the following exercises you'll copy your files to CD or DVD and export photos optimized for use in a web page design application.

Burning photos to CD or DVD

You might wish to copy a set of photos to a CD or DVD or to a removable storage device in order to share a large number of photos at full size with a friend, or as a means of backing up a selection of images.

Burning a CD or DVD on Windows

To prepare for this exercise, make sure you have a blank writable disc in the CD or DVD drive connected to your computer.

1 In the Media Browser, select the files you want to burn to CD or DVD, and then choose File > Burn Data CD/DVD or click the Burn Data CD/DVD button in the Share panel.

2 In the Burn Data CD/DVD dialog box, select a destination drive, and then click OK. If you'd prefer to stop now, without copying any files, click Cancel.

> **Note:** If you don't select any files before invoking the Burn Data CD/DVD command, you'll see a dialog box asking whether you want to copy all the files currently visible in the Media browser.

3 In the Media Browser, select the items you want to copy or move, and then choose File > Copy/Move To Removable Disk. The Copy/Move To Removable Disk wizard appears.

4 Under Offline Media, make sure that the Move Files option is disabled.

The Move Files option deletes the original files from your hard disk after they are copied to the new location, storing only a smaller low-resolution proxy file and a reference to the new location of the original file in your catalog. This option can be useful if you need to access the original files only occasionally and wish to save hard disk space on your computer

5 Under Stacks and Version Sets, you have the option to copy/move only the topmost file or all the files in a stack or version set. If there are no stacks or version sets in your selection, these options are dimmed.

6 Click Next. Select a destination drive in the Destination Settings dialog box. If you want to specify a target folder, click Browse and select the folder in the Browse For Folder dialog box.

7 Click Done to copy your files to the target location or Cancel to exit the Copy/ Move To Removable Disk wizard without copying or moving any files.

The File > Export > As New File(s) command gives you the option to export your photos in file formats other than the original. You can choose between JPEG, PNG, TIFF, or PSD file formats and specify image sizes, location, and custom filenames.

An alternative to burning a CD or DVD would be to use the File > Copy/Move to Removable Disk command to copy or move photos to any removable storage device connected to your computer—an external hard disk, USB memory stick, network drive, or CD/DVD writer.

Burning a CD or DVD on Mac OS

● **Note:** If you wish to burn a large selection of files to CD or DVD, it may be better to work from Bridge rather than first opening all the files in Photoshop Elements. For information on burning files to CD or DVD from Bridge, please refer to Adobe Bridge Help.

On Mac OS, you have the alternative options of choosing the Burn CD/DVD, Move To and Copy To commands from the File menu in Bridge, but for this exercise we'll look at burning a CD or DVD from within Photoshop Elements.

1 Make sure you have a writable disc in your computer's CD or DVD drive; then select the files you want to burn to CD or DVD in the Bridge Content panel. Right-click / Control-click a selected file and choose Open With > Adobe Photoshop Elements 8.

2 Select all the open files in the Project Bin; then click the Share tab above the Panel Bin and click the CD/DVD button in the Share panel. The Burn Disc dialog box appears.

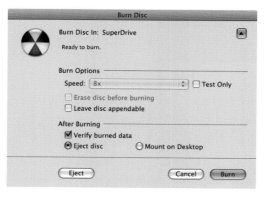

3 It's that simple! If you'd prefer not to actually copy any files, click Cancel.

Saving copies of your images for use on the Web

As a final exercise in this lesson you'll convert a file to JPEG format and optimize it for use on the Web. The JPEG file format reduces the file size and can be displayed by web browsers such as Internet Explorer. If your file contains multiple layers, the conversion to the JPEG file format will flatten them into one layer.

For this operation you'll use the Save For Web feature, which enables you to tweak the export settings while comparing the original image file with the proposed web-ready version of the image.

1   In the Media Browser / Bridge Content panel, select a photo you want to export for use on the Web.

2   Do one of the following:

   • On Windows, click the arrow on the orange Fix tab above the Task Pane and choose any of the three Edit modes—the Save For Web command is available from anywhere in the Editor.

   • On Mac OS, right-click / Control-click the selected file and choose Open With > Adobe Photoshop Elements 8.

3   In the Editor / Photoshop Elements, choose File > Save For Web.

4   In the Save For Web dialog box, choose Fit On Screen from the Zoom menu in the lower left corner of the dialog box.

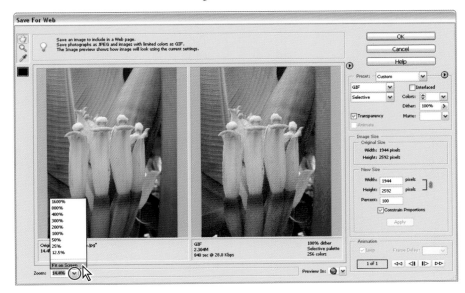

Note: While you're previewing photos in the Save For Web dialog box, you can magnify an image by clicking with the Zoom tool (🔍) from the toolbox in the upper left corner of the dialog box. Alt-click / Option-click with the zoom tool to zoom out. While you're zoomed in, you can drag either image with the Hand tool (✋) to move both images in unison so that you see the same portion of the image in both views.

5   Notice the file-size information under each view of the image. The view on the left displays the file size of the original document.

Note: If you need to further reduce the file size, choose the JPEG Low setting, which reduces the file size by discarding more image data and further compressing the image. You can specify intermediate levels between these options by tweaking the Quality setting, either by typing a new value or by clicking the arrow and dragging the slider.

6   On the right side of the dialog box, select JPEG Medium from the Preset menu. Notice the change in file size for the JPEG image on the right.

7   Under New Size, select Constrain Proportions and type **300** in the Width field. The Height is adjusted automatically to retain the image's original proportions. Click the Apply button. Once again, notice the change in the file size displayed beneath the JPEG view of the image. If necessary, choose Fit On Screen from the Zoom menu.

8   Click OK. Navigate to the My CIB Work folder in the Save Optimized As dialog box, add **_Work** to the end of the file name, and then click Save.

The JPEG format reduces the file size by using JPEG compression, which discards some of the data. The amount of data lost, and the resulting image quality, will vary depending on the image you're working with and the settings you choose.

9   In the Editor, choose File > Close, without saving changes.

Congratulations! You've completed this lesson and should now have a working understanding of the basics of printing, sharing, and exporting. You've learned how to set up single or multiple images for printing at home, how to order professional prints online and how to share photos in Photo Mail or to an online sharing service. You've created on Online Album and exported photos for use on the Web. Before you move on to the next lesson, take a few moments to work through the following review.

Review questions

1   What is Photo Mail? (Windows)

2   What is a Picture Package?

3   How can you fine-tune the composition of a photo for printing?

4   What are the advantages of backing up synchronizing your catalog to your Photoshop.com account? (Windows)

5   Is the Save For Web command only available in Full Edit mode?

Review answers

1   The Photo Mail feature embeds selected photos in the body of an e-mail within a colorful custom layout. You can tweak the layout and image size, choose backgrounds, frames, and effects, and add text messages and captions. You can send Photo Mail through Outlook Express, Outlook, or Adobe E-mail Service.

2   A Picture Package lets you print a photo repeated at a choice of sizes on the same page. You can choose from a variety of layout options with a range of image sizes to customize your picture package print.

3   You can now fine-tune the placement of each image within its own print well frame in the print preview, enabling you to get the image placed just right for printing without first editing it. Zoom or rotate an image with the controls beneath the print preview and drag to reposition it in the frame.

4   Backing up and synchronizing your catalog to your Photoshop.com account means that you can manage your media from any web browser—and any changes made to your catalog online will be synchronized back to Photoshop Elements on your desktop. Furthermore, with Multi Machine Sync you can now even synchronize your files across separate computers. Any changes you make to your catalog on one computer, such as adding, deleting, editing or reorganizing images or albums, will be replicated on your other machines. The capability to backup and synchronize your entire catalog now makes it even easier to manage and protect your precious files.

5   The Save For Web command is available in all three Edit modes: Full Edit, Quick Edit and Guided Edit.

8 ADJUSTING COLOR IN IMAGES

Lesson Overview

Photoshop Elements delivers a broad range of tools and options for working with color. Whether you want to make corrections for unusual lighting conditions, remove red eye effects, or brighten a smile, you'll find a range of solutions from one-click Auto Fixes to options that give you precise control of the adjustments you apply.

This lesson introduces you to a variety of tools and techniques for fixing color problems in your photos:

- Correcting color in Guided Edit mode
- Auto-correcting in Quick Fix and Full Edit mode
- Using automatic options to improve images
- Adjusting skin tones
- Correcting an image using Smart Fix
- Using Color Variations to correct color balance
- Whitening teeth and removing red eyes effects
- Selecting and saving selections
- Adjusting color selectively in defined areas
- Troubleshooting color printing
- Working with color management

 You'll probably need about two hours to complete this lesson.

Explore the many powerful and versatile tools and options available in Photoshop Elements for correcting color problems in your photos. Start with a few of the easy-to-use, one-step image correction features, and then experiment with some of the more advanced features and adjustment techniques that can be mastered easily.

Getting started

Before you start working on the exercises in this lesson, make sure that you have installed the software on your computer from the application CD (see the Photoshop Elements 8 documentation) and that you have correctly copied the Lessons folder from the CD in the back of this book onto your computer's hard disk. (See "Copying the Classroom in a Book files" on page 2.)

Setting up on Windows

For the exercises in this lesson you'll be working with images from the CIB Catalog that you created in the "Getting Started" section at the beginning of this book.

1   Start Photoshop Elements and click the Organize button in the Welcome Screen. Check the name of the currently active catalog, which is displayed in the lower left corner of the Organizer window.

2   If your CIB Catalog is not already open, choose File > Catalog, select the CIB Catalog in the Catalog Manager dialog box, and then click Open. If you don't see the CIB Catalog file listed, see "Creating a catalog" on page 3.

3   Once you have loaded your CIB Catalog, click the small arrow on the orange Fix tab above the Task Pane and choose Full Photo Edit.

Now you're ready for the first exercise, which begins at the bottom of this page.

Setting up on Mac OS

For the exercises in this lesson, you'll be working with the image files in the PSE8CIB > Lessons > Lesson08 folder that you copied to your hard disk in the section "Copying the Classroom in a Book files" at the beginning of this book.

For the first exercise you'll access the lesson file directly from Photoshop Elements, rather than browsing with Bridge.

1   Start Photoshop Elements.

2   Click the Close button in the upper right corner of the Welcome Screen and you're ready to begin.

Getting to know the Edit modes

In the course of this lesson you'll learn how to correct color problems in all three of the Photoshop Elements editing modes: Full Edit, Quick Edit, and Guided Edit.

Before you begin the exercises, you can take a moment to familiarize yourself with switching between the three modes and with the different editing workspaces.

1 In Full Edit mode, choose Window > Reset Panels or click the Reset Panels button () at the top of the workspace.

- By default, the Effects and Layers panels are open in the Panel Bin.

- Open other panels from the Window menu.

- Drag any panel by its header bar to float it wherever you like in the workspace.

- Click the header bar to collapse or expand a panel.

- Collapse a panel to an icon by clicking the double-arrow button in the header bar.

- To close a panel, first drag it out of the Panel Bin, and then click the Close button (x) in the header bar.

2 When you're done exploring, click the Reset Panels button (), and then click the arrow on the orange Edit tab above the Panel Bin and choose Edit Quick.

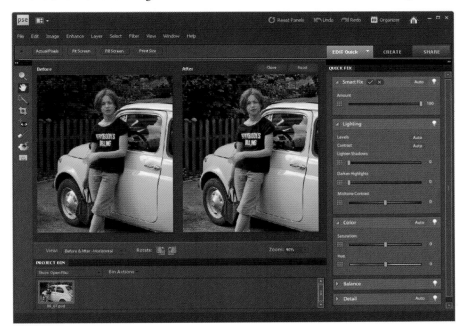

Each Edit mode offers a different set of tools, controls and views.

In Quick Edit mode, the Panel Bin displays the Quick Fix panel, with panes for the Smart Fix, Lighting, Color, Balance and Detail controls.

Collapse or expand any of these panes by clicking the triangle beside the name in the header.

In Quick Edit mode you cannot add, remove or float panels. To clear extra screen space, collapse the Project Bin by clicking its header bar and collapse the Quick Fix panel to an icon.

3 Click the Reset Panels button (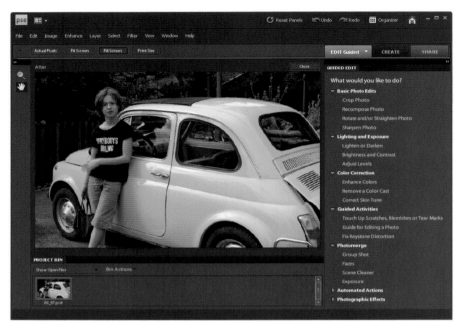), and then click the arrow on the orange Edit tab above the Panel Bin and choose Edit Guided.

In Guided Edit mode the Panel Bin displays only the Guided Edit panel, with grouped listings for a range of common image editing tasks. Click any listing for simple instructions and to find the tools or you'll need for that task. Collapse or expand any of the groups by clicking the triangle beside the group's name. In Guided Edit mode you cannot add, remove or float panels, or float your image window. To clear extra screen space, collapse the Project Bin by clicking its header bar and collapse the Guided Edit panel to an icon.

Correcting color problems

Many of the photographs used for the lessons in this book were chosen to illustrate common image faults—the kind of challenges that people face every day as they try to make the most of their photographs. Artificial light sources, unusual shooting conditions, and incorrect camera exposure settings can all result in tonal imbalances and unwelcome color casts in an image. In the following exercises we'll look at some of the ways Photoshop Elements can help you correct such problems.

You can make quick adjustments using the simple controls in Quick Edit mode or be stepped through a wide range of editing tasks in Guided Edit mode. You can have Photoshop Elements apply corrections automatically, processing your photos in batches, or work in Full Edit mode to perform sophisticated edits selectively.

Fixing files automatically in batches

Photoshop Elements allows you to fix multiple photographs with a single command by processing them as a batch. In this exercise, you'll apply automatic fixes to all the image files used in this lesson. You'll save the auto-adjusted files as copies so that at the end of each project you can compare these automatic results to the edits you have made to the original files using various other techniques.

1 Make sure you are in Full Edit mode; then choose File > Process Multiple Files.

2 In the Process Multiple Files dialog box, set the source and destination folders as follows:

- Choose Folder from the Process Files From menu.

- Under Source, click the Browse button. Find and select the Lesson08 folder in the Lessons folder. Click OK to close the Browse For Folder dialog box.

- Under Destination, click Browse. Then, find and select the My CIB Work folder that you created at the start of the book. Click OK to close the Browse For Folder dialog box.

3 Under File Naming, select Rename Files. Select Document Name from the menu on the left and type _**Autofix** in the second field. This adds the appendix "_Autofix" to the existing document name as the files are saved.

4 Under Quick Fix on the right side of the dialog box, click the checkboxes to activate all four options: Auto Levels, Auto Contrast, Auto Color, and Sharpen.

5 Review the settings in the dialog box, comparing them to the illustration below. Make sure that the Resize Images and Convert Files options are disabled. When you are sure that the settings are correct, click OK.

Note: For Windows users; if an error message appears after you click OK in the Process Multiple Files dialog box warning that some files couldn't be processed, you can ignore it. This error is often caused by a hidden file that is not an image, so it has no effect on the success of your project.

Note: An error message warning that files are missing indicates that your Lessons folder has been moved or was not expanded correctly. See "Copying the Classroom in a Book files" on page 2 and redo that procedure, following the instructions exactly.

Photoshop Elements goes to work, automatically opening and closing image windows. All you need to do is sit back and wait for the process to finish. The newly copied files are automatically tagged with the same keywords as the source files.

Adding the auto-corrected files to the Organizer (Windows)

For most files modified in the Editor, the Include In Organizer option is activated in the Save, Save As, and Save Optimized As dialog boxes by default.

However, when you batch-edit files with the Process Multiple Files feature, this option isn't part of the process—you must add the edited files to the Organizer manually.

1   In the Editor, click the Organizer button (▦) to switch to the Organizer.

2   In the Organizer, choose File > Get Photos And Videos > From Files And Folders.

3   In the Get Photos From Files And Folders dialog box, locate and open your My CIB Work folder, and then Ctrl-click or marquee-select all seven files with the prefix 08 and the suffix _Autofix.

4   Activate the Automatically Fix Red Eyes option, disable the Automatically Suggest Photo Stacks option, and then click Get Media.

5   The Import Attached Keyword Tags dialog box opens. Click Select All, and then click OK.

6   If the Auto Red Eye Fix Complete dialog box appears, click OK. If a message appears reminding you that only the new photos will appear in the Media browser, click OK.

The files are imported to your CIB Catalog and the Organizer displays thumbnails of the newly added images in the Media Browser.

Using Guided Edit

● **Note:** As you try more advanced tasks in Photoshop Elements 8, you may find that you need more information to solve any problems you encounter. For help with some common problems you might have while working through the lessons in this book, see the section "Why won't Photoshop Elements do what I tell it to do?" later in this lesson.

In the last exercise you saw how easy it is to have Photoshop Elements apply multiple Quick Fix corrections to a batch of image files automatically. In the next exercises you'll explore some different methods for correcting color.

If you are a newcomer to digital image editing, the Guided Edit mode in Photoshop Elements is a great place to start in order to learn how to solve many common image problems.

Click any of the wide range of editing tasks listed in the Guided Edit panel and you'll find easy to follow steps and instructions together with any tools and controls you'll need for that procedure.

Even more experienced users can enjoy the ease and simplicity of performing editing tasks using Guided Edit mode, and may just pick up some new tricks!

Correcting color in Guided Edit mode

One of the images in the Lesson08 folder, a photo of three glass vases, shows a very obvious color cast: the result of inadequate artificial lighting. In the next exercise, you'll correct this problem in Guided Edit mode.

Locating the lesson file on Windows

1   If you are not already in the Organizer, switch to it now by clicking the Organizer button (▦) at the top right of the Editor window.

2   In the Organizer, click the Find box beside the Lesson 8 tag in the Keyword Tags panel. The Image Browser is updated to show fourteen images tagged with the Lesson 8 keyword: the seven original photos from the Lesson08 folder and the automatically edited copies from your My CIB Work folder.

3   Select the original photo of the three vases, 08_01.jpg, making sure not to confuse the original file with the edited copy 08_01_Autofix.jpg.

4   Click the small arrow on the orange Fix tab at the top of the Task Pane and choose Guided Photo Edit from the menu; then wait while the image opens in the Editor.

Now you're ready for the exercise, which begins on the next page.

Locating the lesson file on Mac OS

1   Start Photoshop Elements if it's not already running. Either click Browse With Adobe Bridge in the Welcome Screen or chose File > Browse With Bridge.

2   In Bridge, click the link to your PSE8CIB folder, and then choose Edit > Find or press Command+F. In the Find dialog box your PSE8CIB folder is already selected in the Look In menu. Under Criteria, choose Keywords from the first menu, choose Equals from the second menu, and then type **lesson 8** in the text box. Activate the Include All Subfolders option and click Find.

3   The Bridge Content panel is updated to display fourteen images tagged with the Lesson 8 keyword: the seven original photos from the Lesson08 folder and the automatically edited copies from your My CIB Work folder. Right-click / Control-click the original photo of the three vases, 08_01.jpg, making sure not to confuse the original file with the edited copy 08_01_Autofix.jpg. Choose Open With > Adobe Photoshop Elements 8 from the context menu.

4   In Photoshop Elements, click the arrow on the orange Edit tab above the Panel Bin and choose Edit Guided.

Removing a color cast using Guided Edit

Unwelcome color casts are a very common problem in digital images. Fortunately, in Guided Edit you can correct the color in just one step!

1   If necessary, click the triangle beside the Color Correction entry in the Guided Edit panel so that you can see the nested options. Choose Remove A Color Cast from the Color Correction submenu.

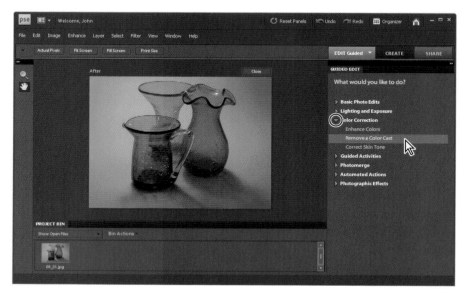

2   Click the display mode button near the bottom of the Guided Edit panel to change the display to the Before & After - Horizontal view.

3   Read the instructions under Correct Color Cast.
    Then, using the Color Cast Eyedropper tool, click near the top left corner of the Before image to remove the color cast. Notice the change in the After image.

4 If you're not satisfied with the result, click the Undo button () at the top of the workspace, and then click a different area in the Before image with the Color Cast Eyedropper tool. To clear the Undo/Redo history and start over with the original un-edited image, click the Reset button in the Guided Edit panel.

5 When you're satisfied with what you see in the After image, click Done.

Adjusting lighting using Guided Edit

As is often the case with poorly exposed photos, this image has more than just one problem. After the color cast has been removed, it's obvious that the image would benefit from some lighting adjustments.

1 If necessary, click the triangle beside the Lighting And Exposure entry in the guided tasks menu so that you can see the nested options, and then choose Lighten Or Darken from the submenu of Lighting And Exposure tasks.

2 When the Lighten Or Darken A Photo panel opens, click the Auto button. Notice the substantial improvement in the appearance of the image.

3 Use the Lighten Shadows, Darken Highlights, and Midtone Contrast sliders to fine-tune the lighting for this image. We set a value of 30 for Lighten Shadows, left the Darken Highlights slider at 0, and set the Midtone Contrast to a value of 35. Your choices may differ, depending on the results of your color correction in the previous exercise and your preferences for the look of the final image.

Note: To be able to recognize and avoid the image artifacts that can result from over-sharpening, sharpening is best applied at a magnification of 100%. Use the display mode button near the bottom of the Guided Edit panel to change the display to the After Only view, and then choose View > Actual Pixels.

4   When you're satisfied with the results of the lighting adjustment displayed in the After image, click Done.

5   In the guided tasks menu, choose Sharpen Photo from the Basic Photo Edits submenu. Click the Auto button near the top of the Sharpen Photo panel. Use the slider to fine-tune the sharpening to your liking, and then click Done.

6   Choose File > Save As. In the Save As dialog box, navigate to and open your My CIB Work folder. Leaving the JPEG file format selected, name the file **08_01_Guided**. On Windows, activate Include In The Organizer and disable Save In Version Set With Original.

7   Click Save. In the JPEG Options dialog box, click OK without making changes.

8   Choose File > Close, and then switch back to the Organizer.

With just a few clicks you have improved the appearance of the photo dramatically. You don't need to have prior experience using an image editor to get good results in Guided Edit mode.

Try the Guided Activities ("Touch Up Scratches, Blemishes Or Tear Marks," "Guide For Editing A Photo," and "Fix Keystone Distortion") each of which will step you through several image editing tasks in the recommended order to get professional results. In the exercise to follow, you'll move on to the next level of editing—working in the Quick Fix mode.

Using Quick Edit mode

In Quick Edit mode, Photoshop Elements conveniently assembles many of the basic photo fixing tools so that they're all at your fingertips in the Quick Fix panel.

If you find that one control doesn't work for your image, click the Reset button and try another. Whether or not you've used the Quick Fix panel before, the intuitive slider controls make adjusting your image easy.

Applying automatic adjustments separately

When you apply a combination of automatic fixes to a set of images using the Process Multiple Files feature, the process happens too fast for you to see the changes made to each image at each stage of processing.

In this exercise, you'll apply some of the same automatic fix options one at a time. This will enable you to see how each editing step affects an image and give you the opportunity to fine-tune the default settings for the best results.

Opening an image for Quick Fix editing

Once again, you can use the Lesson 8 Keyword Tags to find the sample image you want, and then open it in Quick Edit mode.

Locating the lesson file on Windows

1   If you already have the Lesson 8 files isolated in the Organizer from the last exercise, switch to the Organizer now, and then skip to step 4.

2   Start Photoshop Elements if it's not already running and open the Organizer. Check the lower left corner of the workspace to make sure that your CIB Catalog is loaded; if not, choose File Catalog and load the CIB Catalog now.

3   In the Organizer, click the Find box beside the Lesson 8 tag in the Keyword Tags panel.

4   Select the original photo of the three vases, 08_01.jpg, making sure not to confuse the original file with the edited copies.

5   Click the small arrow on the orange Fix tab at the top of the Task Pane and choose Quick Photo Edit. Wait while the image opens in the Editor.

Now you're ready for the exercise, which begins on the next page.

Locating the lesson file on Mac OS

1   If you already have the Lesson 8 files isolated in Bridge from the last exercise, switch to Bridge now, and then skip to step 4.

2   Start Photoshop Elements if it's not already running. Either click Browse With Adobe Bridge in the Welcome Screen or chose File > Browse With Bridge.

3   In Bridge, click your Favorites link to the PSE8CIB folder, and then choose Edit > Find or press Command+F. In the Find dialog box your PSE8CIB folder is already selected in the Look In menu. Under Criteria, choose Keywords from the first menu, choose Equals from the second menu, and then type **lesson 8** in the text box. Activate the Include All Subfolders option and click Find.

4   The Bridge Content panel displays all images tagged with the Lesson 8 keyword: the seven original photos from the Lesson08 folder and the automatically edited copies from your My CIB Work folder. Right-click / Control-click the original photo of the three vases, 08_01.jpg—making sure not to confuse the original file with the edited copies—and choose Open With > Adobe Photoshop Elements 8 from the context menu.

5   In Photoshop Elements, click the arrow on the orange Edit tab above the Panel Bin and choose Edit Quick.

Using Smart Fix

In the Quick Edit workspace the Quick Fix panel at the right contains five adjustment panes—Smart Fix, Lighting, Color, Balance, and Detail. The Smart Fix feature is actually a combination of several adjustments applied at once; it corrects overall color balance and improves shadow and highlight detail in your image. As with the other editing options in Quick Edit mode, you can either click the Auto button to apply the correction automatically or you can use the slider controls to fine-tune the adjustment. You can also combine these methods, as you will in this exercise.

1   Choose Before & After - Horizontal from the View menu in the lower left corner of the image window. If you prefer the before and after images one above the other rather than side-by-side, choose the Before & After - Vertical view.

2   In the Quick Fix panel, click the Smart Fix Auto button in the Smart Fix pane. Notice the immediate effect on the image.

3   Now, move the Smart Fix Amount slider to change the color balance and the highlight and shadow settings for your image. Experiment to find the setting you prefer. We set the Smart Fix Amount to a value of 40.

4   Click the Commit button () in the title bar of the Smart Fix pane to commit the changes.

Remember that whenever you make an adjustment to a setting in the Quick Fix panel, you need to click the Commit or Cancel button in the title bar of the relevant task pane to accept or discard the changes.

Applying other automatic fixes

Four more automatic Quick Fix adjustments are available in the Lighting, Color, and Detail panes.

1   In the Lighting panel, click the Auto button for the Levels feature.

You may or may not see a significant shift in the tonal balance of this image, depending on the adjustment you made to the Smart Fix edit.

2   Click the Auto buttons for Contrast, Color, and Sharpen in turn, noticing the effects of each of these adjustments on the After image.

3   In the Quick Fix Color pane, click the small grid icon beside the Saturation slider.

A grid of nine preview thumbnails is displayed, showing the full range of variation possible with the Saturation slider. A white border highlights the preview that represents the current saturation setting.

4   Move the pointer slowly over each preview thumbnail in the grid to see that level of saturation applied temporarily to your image.

Clicking any of the thumbnails will apply the respective level of adjustment. You can also click and hold the mouse button down, and then drag left or right to fine-tune the adjustment using the preview you clicked as a starting point

The Quick Fix previews—new in Photoshop Elements 8—not only provide a very intuitive interface for editing an image but also make a great way to learn about the effects of the adjustment controls as you work with them.

5   Experiment with the slider controls and Quick Fix preview grids in each pane of the Quick Fix panel. When you're satisfied with an adjustment, click the Commit button (✔) in the title bar of that pane to accept the changes.

6   If you wish to undo your modifications and start again with the original version of the image, click the Reset button above the After view.

7   When you've achieved the results you want, choose File > Save As. In the Save As dialog box, navigate to and open your My CIB Work folder, rename the file **08_01_Quick** and select the JPEG format. On Windows, activate Include In The Organizer and disable Save In Version Set With Original.

8   Click Save. When the JPEG Options dialog box appears, choose High from the Quality menu, and then click OK.

9   Choose File > Close.

Using the Touch Up tools

If you're familiar with the previous version of Photoshop Elements, you may expect to find the Touch Up pane in the Quick Fix panel. In Photoshop Elements 8, the familiar Touch Up tools are located in the toolbox at the left of the workspace.

All four Quick Edit Touch Up tools enable you to apply corrections and adjustments selectively to specific parts of an image:

● **Note:** The Whiten Teeth, Blue Sky, and Black And White - High Contrast tools in Quick Edit mode are all variants on the Smart Brush tool in Full Edit mode. For more detailed information on the Smart Brush, see "Using the Smart Brush" later in this lesson or refer to Photoshop Elements Help.

• The Red Eye Removal tool removes red eye effects in flash photos of people and red, green, or white eye effects in flash photos of pets.

• The Whiten Teeth tool brightens smiles.

• The Blue Sky tool can bring new life to a dull image.

• The Black And White - High Contrast tool simulates the high-contrast image effects that black and white film photographers produce by placing a red filter over the camera lens.

Except for Red Eye Removal, all Touch Up tool adjustments are applied on separate adjustment layers; they do not discard or permanently edit any information on the image layer. The adjustments remain "live"; you can return and modify the settings at any time, without degrading the original image.

Brightening a smile

We'll be looking closer at the Red Eye Removal feature in a later exercise. For now, let's try the Whiten Teeth tool.

Locating the lesson file on Windows

1 If you already have the Lesson 8 files isolated in the Organizer from the last exercise, switch to the Organizer now, and then skip to step 4.

2 Start Photoshop Elements if it's not already running and open the Organizer. Check the lower left corner of the workspace to make sure that your CIB Catalog is loaded; if not, choose File Catalog and load the CIB Catalog now.

3 In the Organizer, click the Find box beside the Lesson 8 tag in the Keyword Tags panel.

4 In the Media Browser, click to select the image 08_02.jpg, a photo of a woman's face—making sure not to confuse the original file with the Autofix copy.

5 Click the small arrow on the orange Fix tab at the top of the Task Pane and choose Quick Photo Edit. Wait while the image opens in the Editor.

Now you're ready for the exercise, which begins on the next page.

Locating the lesson file on Mac OS

1 If you already have the Lesson 8 files isolated in Bridge from the last exercise, switch to Bridge now, and then skip to step 4.

2 Start Photoshop Elements if it's not already running. Either click Browse With Adobe Bridge in the Welcome Screen or chose File > Browse With Bridge.

3 In Bridge, click your Favorites link to the PSE8CIB folder, and then choose Edit > Find or press Command+F. In the Find dialog box your PSE8CIB folder is already selected in the Look In menu. Under Criteria, choose Keywords from the first menu, choose Equals from the second menu, and then type **lesson 8** in the text box. Activate the Include All Subfolders option and click Find.

4 The Bridge Content panel displays all images tagged with the Lesson 8 keyword: the seven original photos from the Lesson08 folder and the edited copies from your My CIB Work folder. Right-click / Control-click the image 08_02.jpg, a photo of a woman's face—making sure not to confuse the original file with the Autofix copy—and choose Open With > Adobe Photoshop Elements 8 from the context menu.

5 In Photoshop Elements, click the arrow on the orange Edit tab above the Panel Bin and choose Edit Quick.

Setting up the Quick Edit workspace

You can prepare for the exercise by customizing the Quick Edit workspace.

1 Hide the Project Bin by clicking its header bar, and then click the black bar at the top of the Panel Bin to collapse the Quick Fix panel to an icon.

2 From the View menu below the Edit pane, choose Before & After - Vertical.

3 Use both the Hand tool and the Zoom slider below the After image to position the photo so that you have the closest possible view of the woman's mouth. You can drag either the Before or After view with the Hand tool—the two images will move in unison.

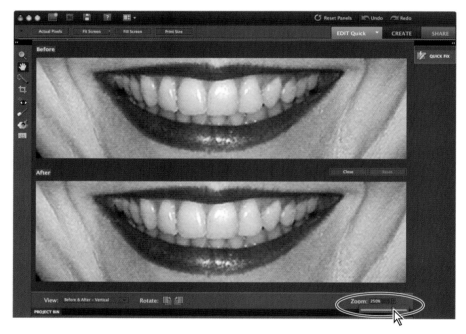

Using the Whiten Teeth tool

Now it's time for a little dental magic. With the Whiten Teeth tool, as with the other Touch Up tools, you'll work directly into the After image—these tools have no effect on the Before image.

1 Click to select the Whiten Teeth tool ( ) in the toolbox.

2 Notice that once the Whiten Teeth tool is active, settings and variants for the tool become available in the tool options bar right above the toolbox.

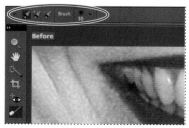

3 In the Whiten Teeth tool settings, click the triangle to open the Brush picker. As the image you're using for this exercise is of a fairly low resolution, you'll need a small brush—set the Diameter to 5 px. Set the Hardness value to 50%, and then click the triangle again to close the Brush picker.

4 Move the pointer over the After image. A small cross-hair cursor indicates the brush size set for the Whiten Teeth tool: Notice that in the tool settings at the top left of the Editor window, the brush icon on the left is highlighted to indicate that the tool is in New Selection mode. Drag the cross-hair across half of the upper teeth as shown below, and then release the mouse button.

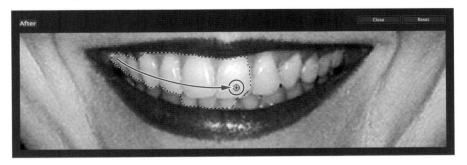

Adding to and subtracting from an adjustment selection

The Whiten Teeth tool, like the Blue Sky and Black And White Touch Up tools, is both a selection tool and an image adjustment tool. You have just used the tool to create a selection through which the tooth whitening adjustment is applied once. While this selection is active, you can still add to it or subtract from it, without re-applying the adjustment.

The Whiten Teeth selection and adjustment is being made on a new layer separate from the original image in the background layer. The edit remains active on its own adjustment layer—so you can return to alter the selection area or the way the adjustment is being applied at any time without degrading the original image.

1 Notice that in the tool options bar the brush icon in the center is now highlighted. Now that there is already an active selection, the brush has switched from the default New Selection mode to the Add To Selection mode automatically.

2 To add the rest of the upper teeth to the selection, drag with the Add To Selection brush as shown below, and then release the mouse button. You don't need to drag all the way to the last tooth on the right; the selection will expand automatically. Don't worry if the gums and parts of the lips are also selected— you'll deal with that in step 4.

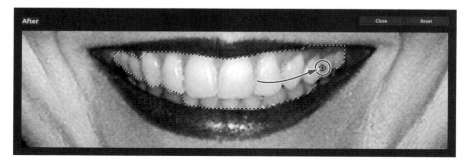

3 Carefully add the shaded lower teeth at both sides of the mouth to the selection by making two short, slow strokes as shown below—overlapping the cross-hairs cursor on the flashing border of the existing selection. If your selection expands too far, press Ctrl+Z / Command+Z to undo the last action and try again.

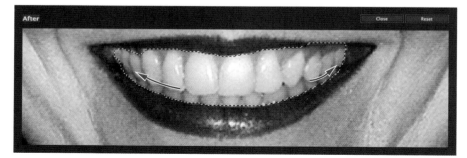

4 Hold down the Alt / Option key. The cursor changes to that of the Subtract From Selection brush—the cross-hairs become a minus sign. Notice that in the tool options bar the brush icon on the right is now highlighted. Holding down the Alt key, carefully drag with the Subtract From Selection brush to remove the lip and gum areas from the adjustment selection as shown below.

▶ **Tip:** Use very short strokes, slowly working the cursor towards the line you want. If you're not happy with the results that you're seeing, try altering the direction of your strokes, or even just clicking rather than dragging.

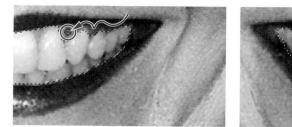
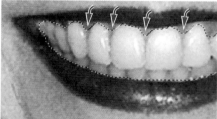

5 Release the Alt / Option key. The brush returns to Add To Selection mode. Look for any areas that still need to be added to the selection or that you may have removed from the selection by mistake in the last step. Drag very short strokes or simply click with the Add To Selection brush to pick up these areas.

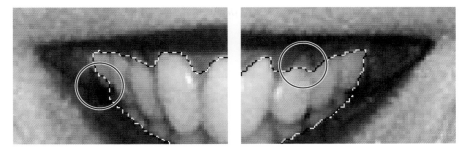

The selection is complete. The Whiten Teeth adjustment has been applied to the selected area on its own adjustment layer separate from the original image. Although the adjustment has had a noticeable effect, you can improve the image further by using the Whiten Teeth tool again.

6 Keeping the Whiten Teeth tool active, choose Select > Deselect to deselect the current adjustment. Using the Whiten Teeth tool again now, with no selection active, will create a new selection on a new adjustment layer—applying a second instance of the Whiten Teeth adjustment.

7 Use the brush picker to change the Hardness of the brush to 10%. Alternate between the Add To Selection and Subtract From Selection brushes to create an irregular selection area including only the brighter areas of the smile as shown in the illustration below. Avoid the most shadowed teeth—the whitening will look unnatural if applied too evenly. Teeth near the edges of the selection, and the naturally shaded lower teeth should only be partially selected.

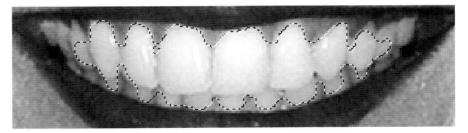

The Whiten Teeth adjustment is applied a second time through the new selection. Both the irregular selection and the softer brush setting help to create a more natural effect than re-applying the adjustment to the entire smile. You'll add some finishing touches to your dental work in the next exercise by tweaking the adjustments that you've already applied with the Whiten Teeth tool.

8 Choose Select > Deselect to deselect your last adjustment.

Modifying the Touch Up adjustment

Each time you applied The Whiten Teeth tool a separate adjustment layer was created in the image. Each edit remains active on its adjustment layer—you can still alter both the selection area and the way the adjustment is applied for each layer.

1   Click the small arrow on the orange Edit tab above the collapsed Panel Bin and choose Edit Full to switch to Full Edit mode.

2   In Full Edit mode, click the Reset Panels button () at the top of the workspace. Hide the Effects panel in the Panel Bin by clicking its header bar.

3   Notice that in the Layers panel there are two adjustment layers stacked above the original image in the Background layer. The layer Pearly Whites 2 with your last adjustment is highlighted, indicating that it's the active layer.

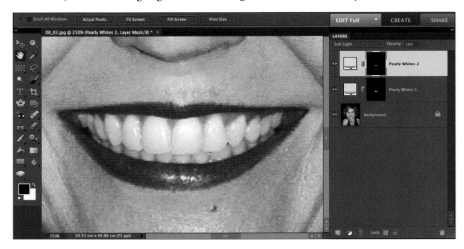

4   Choose Select > Deselect, and then choose View > Actual Pixels or double-click the Zoom tool in the toolbox to see more of the woman's face.

5   To judge how effective your adjustments have been, click the eye icons beside each adjustment layer in turn to toggle the layer's visibility, noticing the effect in the image window.

6   For the Whiten Teeth tool, Soft Light is the preset blending mode and the default opacity for each layer is 50%. Use the menu and slider at the top of the Layers panel to experiment with the Blending Mode and the Opacity value for each layer in turn.

7 When you're done experimenting, reset the Blending Mode for both adjustment layers to Soft Light. Increase the Opacity value for the layer Pearly Whites 1 to 80% and for the layer Pearly Whites 2 to 60%.

8 Double-click the colored layer thumbnail for the layer Pearly Whites 2 to open the color picker.

The Whiten Teeth tool applies a fill of an "ivory" color. You can brighten the effect, while still maintaining realism, by reducing the Saturation (S) value for that color.

9 Type in the text box to reduce the Saturation value from 20 to 10; then click OK.

10 Repeat step 9 for the adjustment layer Pearly Whites 1.

11 Choose File > Save As. Save the edited file to your My CIB Work folder as **08_02_Dental** in Photoshop (.PSD, .PDD) format; then choose File > Close.

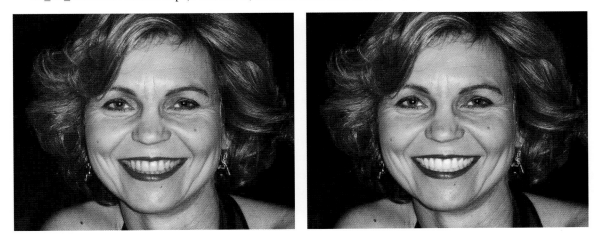

For many photographs, you will probably find that you can achieve satisfactory results with the Whiten Teeth tool in fewer steps, but the concepts and techniques you've learned in this lesson are equally applicable to any of the other Smart Brush adjustments, some of which you'll explore in the next two exercises.

Using the Smart Brush tool

The Whiten Teeth, Blue Sky, and Black And White - High Contrast tools in the Quick Fix mode toolbox are all variants on the Smart Brush tool in Full Edit mode. The Smart Brush is both a selection tool and an image adjustment tool; it creates a selection based on similarity of color and texture through which a your choice of preset edit is applied. While the selection is active, you can add to or subtract from it, without re-applying the adjustment. Each Smart Brush edit is made on its own adjustment layer and does not affect the original image. The Smart Brush edit remains active on the adjustment layer, so you can return at any time to alter the selection area or change the way the adjustment is being applied—or even delete the adjustment layer entirely—without degrading the original image.

Locating the lesson file on Windows

1   If you already have the Lesson 8 files isolated in the Organizer from the last exercise, switch to the Organizer now, and then skip to step 4.

2   Start Photoshop Elements if it's not already running and open the Organizer. Make sure that your CIB Catalog is loaded.

3   In the Keyword Tags panel, click the Find box beside the Lesson 8 tag.

4   In the Media Browser, click to select the image 08_03.jpg, a photo of a row of houses—making sure not to confuse the original file with the Autofix copy.

5   Click the small arrow on the orange Fix tab at the top of the Task Pane and choose Full Photo Edit. Wait while the image opens in the Editor.

Now you're ready for the exercise, which begins on the next page.

Locating the lesson file on Mac OS

1   If you already have the Lesson 8 files isolated in Bridge from the last exercise, switch to Bridge now, and then skip to step 4.

2   Start Photoshop Elements if it's not already running. Either click Browse With Adobe Bridge in the Welcome Screen or chose File > Browse With Bridge.

3   In Bridge, click your Favorites link to the PSE8CIB folder, and then choose Edit > Find or press Command+F. In the Find dialog box your PSE8CIB folder is already selected in the Look In menu. Under Criteria, choose Keywords from the first menu, choose Equals from the second menu, and then type **lesson 8** in the text box. Activate the Include All Subfolders option and click Find.

4   In the Bridge Content panel, right-click / Control-click the image 08_03.jpg, making sure not to confuse the original file with the Autofix copy—and choose Open With > Adobe Photoshop Elements 8 from the context menu.

5   In Photoshop Elements, click the arrow on the orange Edit tab above the Panel Bin and choose Edit Full.

Applying a Smart Brush adjustment

In this exercise and the next you'll use the Smart Brush to liven up defined areas of a photograph selectively.

1   In Full Edit mode, click the Reset Panels button (⟳) at the top of the workspace, and then hide the Effects panel and the Project Bin by clicking their header bars. Choose Window > Images > Consolidate All To Tabs to dock the floating image window in the Edit pane, and then choose View > Fit On Screen.

2   Select the Smart Brush (🖌) from the toolbox, and then drag the Smart Brush adjustment presets picker from the tool options bar to a convenient position.

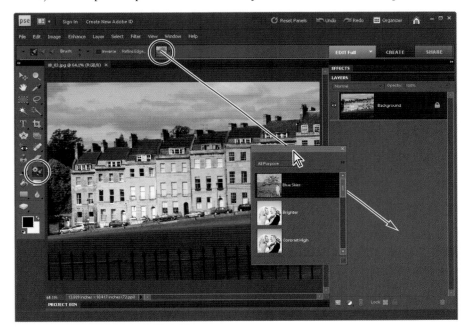

3   Click the categories menu at the top of the moveable Smart Brush presets picker and choose the category Nature. Scroll down through the options in the Nature category and select Greenery. Click the Close button (x) in the header bar of the Smart Brush presets picker.

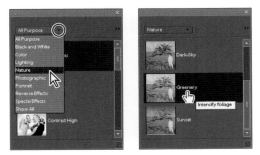

Tip: To close the Brush Picker, click anywhere in the options bar press the Esc key on your keyboard.

4 In the tool options bar, open the Brush Picker and set the brush diameter to 30 px (pixels). Drag about half-way across the lawn in the foreground, and then release the mouse button. Don't worry about selecting the fence as well.

Tweaking a Smart Paint adjustment

The Greenery brush has not made a very effective difference to the image. Let's try some methods for modifying the adjustment to boost the effect.

1 The adjustment you just applied shows a pin—a colored marker that identifies a Smart Brush edit when the Smart Brush tool is active—at the point in the image where you began applying the Smart Brush. Right-click / Control-click the pin and choose Change Adjustment Settings from the menu.

Note: Invoking the Change Adjustment Settings command will call up different controls for different Smart Brush presets, depending on the combination of adjustments that make up each preset.

2 The Adjustments panel opens in the Panel Bin. Experiment with the sliders, noting the changes in the image. When you're done experimenting, click the Reset button at the bottom of the Adjustments panel to return the settings to the defaults for the Greenery preset; you'll be looking at another way to modify the effects of this Smart Brush adjustment yet.

3 Hide the Adjustments panel by clicking its header bar.

4 In the Layers panel, the new adjustment layer, Greenery 1, is the active layer. Set the Opacity value for the new layer to 50% and the Blending Mode to Overlay.

This modification is much more effective, intensifying the colors in the lawn area and increasing the dramatic effect created by the contrast between the shaded foreground and the sunlit facades of the buildings.

5 Paint over the rest of the lawn with the new Greenery adjustment settings, and then choose Select > Deselect Layers.

Applying multiple Smart Paint adjustments

You can use the Smart Brush on the same area as many times as you wish. If you re-apply the same adjustment preset the effects are usually cumulative, though the results will depend on the layer blending mode for that preset. You can also apply different Smart Brush presets to the same image area, combining their effects.

1 With the Smart Brush tool still selected in the toolbox, click the thumbnail in the tool options bar to open the Smart Brush adjustment presets picker. Drag the adjustment presets picker to a convenient position clear of the image.

2 In the presets picker, choose the Nature category; then select the Blue Skies preset. Drag across the sky from a point at the lower left, just above the trees. In the Layers panel, change the Blending mode for the new layer Blue Skies 1 from the preset Color Burn to Soft Light and increase the Opacity value from 75% to 100%. Choose Select > Deselect Layers to deactivate the new adjustment.

3 In the presets picker, select Cloud Contrast; then drag left all the way across the sky from the top right corner of the image. There are now two Smart Brush pins on the image. Change the Blending mode for the new layer Cloud Contrast 1 from Normal to Overlay and reduce the Opacity value from 100% to 40%. Choose Select > Deselect Layers to make the new adjustment inactive.

4 Choose the Dark Sky preset and drag across the sky from the upper left. Change the layer Opacity to 75% and choose Select > Deselect Layers. There are now three Smart Brush pins on the image, and three new layers in the Layers panel.

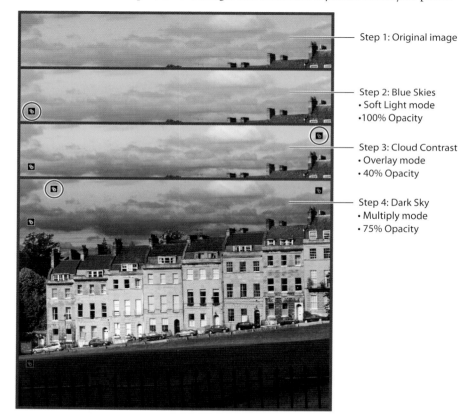

Step 1: Original image

Step 2: Blue Skies
• Soft Light mode
•100% Opacity

Step 3: Cloud Contrast
• Overlay mode
• 40% Opacity

Step 4: Dark Sky
• Multiply mode
• 75% Opacity

5 Chose File > Save As. Name the file **08_03_SmartBrush** and save it to your My CIB Work folder in Photoshop (.PSD, .PDD) format with Layers activated. Before you close the file, experiment more with the adjustment layers, and then right-click / Control-click the adjustment pins to explore the settings.

Comparing methods of fixing color

The automatic correction features in Photoshop Elements do an excellent job of bringing out the best in most photographs, but each image—and each image problem—is unique. Some photographs don't respond well to automatic fixes and require a more hands-on approach to color correction.

Photoshop Elements offers many ways to deal with color correction. The more techniques you master, the more likely you'll be able meet the challenge of fixing a difficult photograph. In this section, you'll study three different methods for correcting a color problem, and then compare the results.

Creating extra working copies of an image

In the following exercises you'll compare three different approaches to correcting the same color problem, so you'll need three copies of the same photograph.

1   In the Organizer / Bridge, use the Lesson 8 keyword tag to locate the file 08_04.jpg. Take care not to confuse the original file with the Autofix copy.

2   Do one of the following:

- On Windows, select the file in the Media Browser; then click the small arrow on the orange Fix tab above the Task Pane and choose Quick Photo Edit.

- On Mac OS, right-click / Control-click the image in the Bridge Content panel and choose Open With > Adobe Photoshop Elements 8 from the context menu. In Photoshop Elements, click the arrow on the orange Edit tab above the Panel Bin and choose Edit Quick.

3   Click the Reset Panels button (⟳) at the top of the Quick Edit workspace and then double-click the Hand tool in the toolbox or choose View > Fit On Screen.

4   Choose File > Duplicate. In the Duplicate Image dialog box, click OK to accept the default name 08_04 copy.jpg. Repeat the process to create a second duplicate, 08_04 copy 2.jpg.

Leave all three copies of the image file open for the next exercises. You can tell at a glance that the files are open because their thumbnails appear in the Project Bin. The image file names appear as Tooltips when you hold the pointer over each thumbnail in the Project Bin. Alternatively, right-click / Control-click anywhere inside the Project Bin and choose Show File Names from the context menu.

● **Note:** By now, you should be familiar with the technique of using keyword tags to locate the files you need. For the remainder of this chapter, the instructions for finding the lesson files will be summarized rather than stepped through in detail. If you need to refresh your memory, please refer to the steps at the start of any of the previous exercises in this chapter.

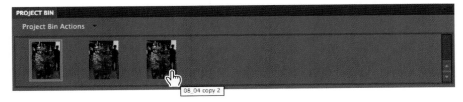

Correcting color automatically

At the start of this lesson, you applied all four automatic Quick Fix options to all of the images in the Lesson08 folder when you processed the files as a batch. In this exercise, you'll apply just one Quick Fix adjustment.

1 In the Project Bin, double-click the original image—08_04.jpg—to make it the active file.

2 Choose Before & After - Horizontal from the View menu below the Edit pane.

3 In the Quick Fix panel, click the Auto button in the Color pane to auto-correct just the color. Compare the Before and After views.

There is a marked improvement in the image; the Auto Color fix has corrected most of the blue-green color cast resulting from fluorescent lighting. The skin tones are somewhat warmer, but the contrast has suffered and the tonal range is still flat.

4 Choose File > Save. Save the file to your My CIB Work folder in JPEG format, changing the name to **08_04_Work**. On Windows, make sure that the Save In Version Set With Original option is disabled. Click Save, leaving all the other options unchanged in the Save dialog box and the JPEG Options dialog box.

Adjusting the results of an automatic fix manually

An automatic fix can serve as a good starting point for some manual fine-tuning.

1 In the Project Bin, double-click the image 08_04 copy.jpg to make it active.

2 In the Quick Fix panel, click the Auto button in the Color pane.

3 The image still has a slight blue-green cast. This can be seen clearly in the white wall showing at the top right of the frame. In the Balance pane, increase the Temperature and Tint values to 53 and 3 respectively to make the color warmer.

4 In the Lighting pane, click the Auto Contrast button; then set the Lighten Shadows value to 5 and the Midtone Contrast value to 15. Click the Commit button () at the top of the Lighting pane.

► Tip: When you are making multiple Quick Fix adjustments it's not necessary to click the Commit button for each edit. The current adjustment is committed automatically when you change another setting in the Quick Fix panel.

The contrast has improved, the color is intensified and the skin tones have lost the greyish look caused by the fluorescent lighting, but the image is still under-exposed. Once again, this is quite evident in the tone of the white wall in the background.

5 Choose Enhance > Adjust Lighting > Levels. In the Levels dialog, move the white slider—the highlights slider—to the left to a value of 200; then click OK.

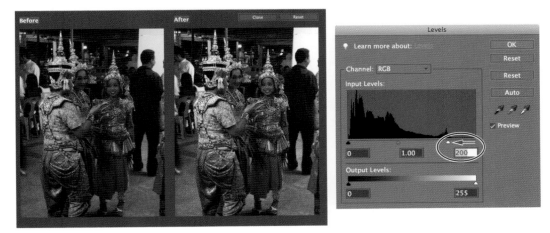

6 Choose File > Save. Save the file to your My CIB Work folder in JPEG format, changing the name to **08_04 copy_Work**. Click Save, leaving the other options unchanged in both the Save dialog box and the JPEG Options dialog box.

Tweaking results from an automatic fix

The top five commands in the Enhance menu apply the same image adjustments as the various Auto buttons in the Quick Fix panel. Enhance menu commands are available in both the Quick Fix and Full Edit modes, but not in Guided Edit.

Both the Quick Fix and Full Edit modes also offer other methods of enhancing color that allow you greater control over the results. These are the commands in the lower half of the Enhance menu. In this exercise, you'll use one of these options to tweak the adjustments applied by the Auto Color fix button.

1   In the Project bin, double-click the image 08_04 copy 2 to make it the active file.

2   In the Color pane, click Auto to apply the Quick Fix color correction.

3   Choose Enhance > Adjust Color > Color Variations. The Color Variations dialog box appears.

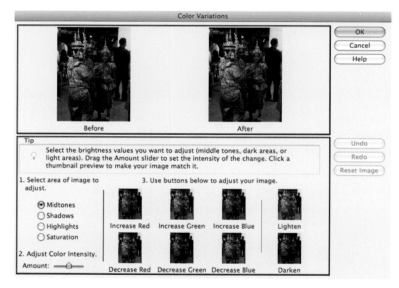

4   In the lower left area of the Color Variations dialog box, make sure that Midtones is selected, and then move the Amount slider down one stop to the one-third position. Click the Increase Red thumbnail once.

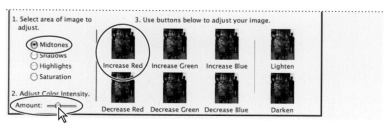

5 Still in the Color Variations dialog box, select Highlights and move the Amount slider up to the two-thirds position. Click the Decrease Green thumbnail twice and the Decrease Blue and Lighten thumbnails three times each; then click OK.

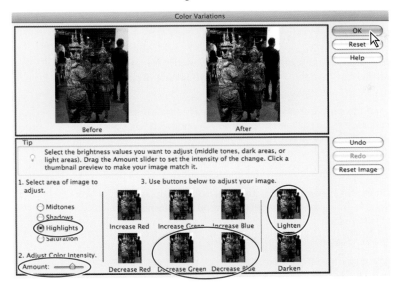

The Color Variations adjustments have made the colors warmer and more vivid, reducing the blue-green color cast and improving the tonal range. If you wish to try again, using a smaller Amount value or a different combination of adjustments, click the Reset button above the After image and start again from Step 3.

6 Choose File > Save As, and navigate to your My CIB Work folder. Rename the file **08_04 copy 2_Work**, and select the JPEG format. Click Save, leaving the other options in the Save and JPEG Options dialog boxes unchanged.

About viewing modes and image window arrangements

When you work in Quick Edit or Guided Edit modes, only one image—the active file—appears in the work area, regardless of how many files are open. Files that are open but inactive appear only as thumbnails in the Project bin.

Working in Full Edit mode, other arrangements are possible. You can usually adjust the size and placement of image windows in the work area. If you can't arrange individual windows freely, your view is probably set to Maximize Mode. If opening or closing a file sometimes causes unexpected rearrangements of image windows, your view is probably set to Tile.

Maximize Mode (below, left) fills the work area with the active image window.

Tile (below, center) re-sizes and arranges all open images so that the image windows cover the work area. If Tile mode is active when you close an image file or open a new one, Photoshop Elements will rearrange the image windows in tile formation.

Cascade (below, right) enables you to resize, arrange, or minimize files.

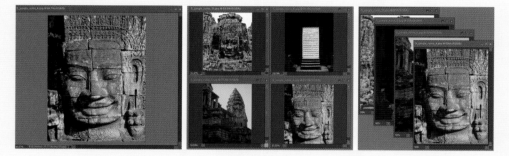

There are two ways to switch from one mode to another:

- Use the Window > Images menu and choose Maximize Mode, Tile, or Cascade. If there is a check mark on the Maximize Mode command, choose Maximize Mode again to disable it and switch to the mode you were using previously.

- Use the buttons on the far right end of the window title bar. The available buttons vary, depending on which viewing mode is active, and on the size of the work area on your monitor. If the work area is reduced, these buttons may not appear.

For more information on working with image windows, see Adobe Photoshop Elements Help.

Comparing results

As you can tell by checking the Project bin, all three of your saved work files are still open in the Editor. Let's compare them to the autofix file from the batch process at the beginning of this lesson.

1   Choose File > Open. Locate and open your My CIB Work folder. Select the file 08_04_Autofix, and then click Open.

2   At the top of the Panel Bin, click the orange Edit tab and choose Edit Full.

3   In Full Edit mode, hide the Project Bin by clicking its header bar; then choose Window > Images > Tile.

4   Use the Zoom tool and the Hand tool to see an area of interest in one of the images, and then choose Window > Images > Match Zoom and Windows > Images > Match Location. These commands are also accessible by clicking the Arrange button (⬚) at the top of the workspace and choosing from the menu.

● **Note:** At any given time there is only one active image window. Look at the text in the title bars of the open image windows; the file name and image details are dimmed in the title bars of all but the active image window.

5   In the toolbox, select the Hand tool (🖑). In the tool options bar, activate the Scroll All Windows option. Drag in the active window to see different areas of the image. Compare the four images and decide which looks best. Make your choice the active window and choose Window > Images > Float In Window.

6   Choose View > Fit On Screen to enlarge the image so it fits in the window. You can cycle through all open windows by pressing Ctrl-Tab or Ctrl-Shift-Tab.

7   Choose File > Close All. If the Save dialog box appears, click Don't Save.

Adjusting skin tones

Photoshop Elements offers another unique solution to color cast problems that is available in both the Full Edit and Quick Fix modes.

1   Choose File > Open. Navigate to and open your Lesson08 folder; then select the image 08_04.jpg and click Open. Use the Zoom and hand tools to position the image so that you can focus on the faces and hands of the three dancers.

2   Choose Enhance > Adjust Color > Adjust Color For Skin Tone. In the Adjust Color For Skin Tone dialog box, make sure the Preview option is activated. As you move the pointer over the image, the cursor changes to an eyedropper tool.

Consider the peculiarities of the image at hand. Be aware of strongly colored lighting or other factors apart from the color cast that might produce unrealistic skin tones. In this case, the dancers' faces are heavily made-up for a stage performance.

▶ **Tip:** Even while the Adjust Color For Skin Tone dialog box is open, you can still use keyboard commands to change the zoom level. or press the space bar to call up the Hand tool and move the image if you wish to focus on a different area.

3   Look for the lightest part of the raised hand of the dancer on the left—just above the wrist— and click with the eyedropper tool. The color balance for the entire photo is adjusted using the sampled skin tone as a reference.

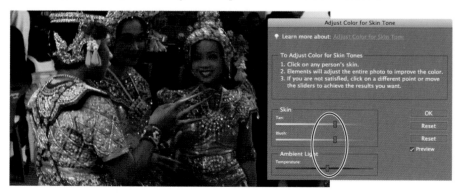

4   Move the Tan, Blush, and Temperature sliders to achieve the skin tones you want, and then choose File > Save As. Name the file 08_04_Skin and save it to your My CIB Work folder in JPEG format; then choose File > Close.

Working with red eye

The red eye effect occurs when a camera flash is reflected off the retina at the back of the eye so that the dark pupil looks bright red. In this lesson you'll learn two techniques for dealing with the problem.

1   In the Organizer / Bridge, use the Lesson 8 keyword tag to locate the file 08_05.jpg, taking care not to confuse the original file with the Autofix copy.

2   Do one of the following:

- On Windows, select the file in the Media Browser; then click the small arrow on the orange Fix tab above the Task Pane and choose Quick Photo Edit.

- On Mac OS, right-click / Control-click the image in the Bridge Content panel and choose Open With > Adobe Photoshop Elements 8 from the context menu. In Photoshop Elements, click the arrow on the orange Edit tab above the Panel Bin and choose Edit Quick.

Using automatic Red Eye Fix

In both Full Edit and Quick Edit mode, you can apply an automatic red eye correction with a single menu command.

1   Hide the Quick Fix panel by clicking the double-arrow at the top right of the Panel Bin header bar and the Project Bin by clicking its header bar. Choose Before & After - Horizontal from the View menu below the Edit pane. Use the Zoom and Hand tools to focus on the face of the girl in the middle.

2   Choose Enhance > Auto Red Eye Fix.

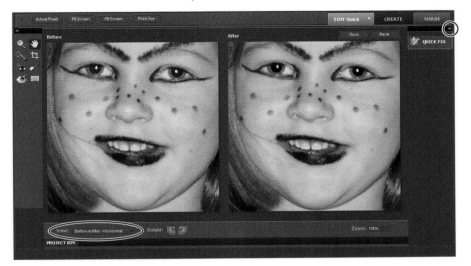

Note: By now, you should be familiar with the technique of using keyword tags to locate the files you need. For the remainder of this chapter, the instructions for finding the lesson files will be summarized rather than stepped through in detail. If you need to refresh your memory, please refer to the steps at the start of any of the first few exercises in this chapter.

Note: On Windows, you can choose to have Photoshop Elements apply the automatic red eye fix as your images are imported into the Organizer. Simply activate the Automatically Fix Red Eyes option in the Get Photos dialog box when you're importing your photos (see the "Automatically fixing red eyes during import" side-bar in Lesson 2).

As you can see, automatic red eye correction does a great job for this little girl. Unfortunately, it hasn't worked for her sisters.

3 Use the Zoom and Hand tools to check the eyes of the other two girls.

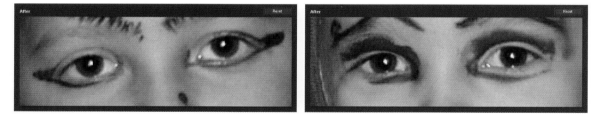

The automatic adjustment had no discernible effect for the girls at either side of the photo. Admittedly, the red eye effect is less pronounced in both cases, but it is also more complex and difficult to remove. The pupils of the girl in the center are crisply defined against her blue irises while there is less contrast in the hazel irises of the other girls.

4 Click the Reset button above the After image to clear the Auto Red Eye Fix.

The automatic red eye removal feature works well for most images, but when you want more control you need to use the Red Eye Removal tool.

Using the Red Eye Removal tool

For stubborn red eye problems that don't respond well to the automatic fix, the Red Eye Removal tool (⬛), which can be found in both the Full Edit and Quick Edit toolbox, is an easy-to-use and efficient solution.

In this exercise you'll now learn how to customize the Red Eye Removal tool to deal with difficult cases.

1 If the image 08_05.jpg is not already open in Quick Edit mode—and reverted to its original state—from the last exercise, open it now in Quick Edit mode.

2 From the View menu below the Edit pane, choose Before And After - Vertical.

3 Zoom and position the image so that you can focus on the eyes of the girl on the left of the photo.

4 Select the Red Eye Removal tool (⬛) from the toolbox.

5 In the Red Eye Removal tool settings in the tool options bar, change the Pupil Size value to 10% and the Darken Amount to 50%. You can either use the slider controls, type the new values in the text fields, or simply drag left or right over the Pupil Size and Darken Amount text.

6 In the After image, click once in the reddest part of each pupil with the Red Eye Removal tool. If there is little effect, undo and click a slightly different spot.

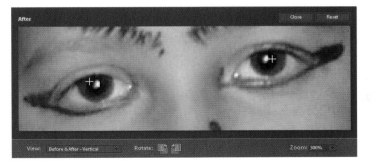

The red is removed from both eyes. The adjustment has also darkened the less defined parts of the irises, but we'll accept that for now.

7 Use the Zoom and Hand tools to position the image so that you can focus on the eyes of the girl on the right of the photo.

8 In the Red Eye Removal tool settings in the tool options bar, change the Pupil Size value to 100% and the Darken Amount to 75%.

9 With the Red Eye Removal tool still selected, drag a marquee rectangle around each eye in turn.

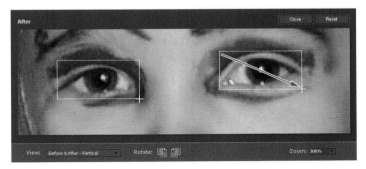

You may need to experiment with the size and positioning of the rectangle you drag around an eye to get the best results. If you're not satisfied, just undo and try again.

10 Finally, you can re-instate the Auto Red Eye Fix for the little girl in the middle. Zoom out just enough so that you can see all three faces, and then choose Enhance > Auto Red Eye Fix.

11 Choose File > Save As and navigate to the My CIB Work folder. Rename the file **08_05_Work** and select the JPEG format. On Windows, disable the Save In Version Set With Original option.

12 Click Save, leaving all other options in the Save and JPEG Options dialog boxes unchanged.

Making selections

By default, the entire area of an image or image layer is active: any adjustments you make are applied across the whole photo. If you want to make changes to a specific area or object within an image, you first need to make a selection. Once you have made a selection it becomes the only active area of the image—the rest of the image layer is protected or masked from the effects of your edits.

Typically, the boundaries of a selection are indicated by a selection marquee—a flashing border of dashed black and white lines. You can save a selection and re-use it at a later time. This can be a terrific time-saver when you need to use the same selection several times.

You can use several different tools to create selections; you'll get experience with most of them in the course of the lessons in this book. Selections can be geometric in shape or free form, and they can have crisp or soft edges. Selections can be created manually with the mouse pointer, or calculated by Photoshop Elements based on similarities of color and texture within the image.

Perhaps the simplest, most effective way to create a selection is to paint it onto an image. This exercise focuses on the use of two selection tools in Photoshop Elements, the Selection Brush tool and the Quick Selection tool.

● **Note:** By now, you should be familiar with the technique of using keyword tags to locate the files you need. For the remainder of this chapter, the instructions for finding the lesson files will be summarized rather than stepped through in detail. If you need to refresh your memory, please refer to the steps at the start of any of the first few exercises in this chapter.

1 In the Organizer / Bridge, use the Lesson 8 keyword tag to locate the file 08_06.psd, taking care not to confuse the original file with the Autofix copy.

2 Do one of the following:

- On Windows, select the file in the Media Browser; then click the small arrow on the orange Fix tab above the Task Pane and choose Full Photo Edit.

- On Mac OS, right-click / Control-click the image in the Bridge Content panel and choose Open With > Adobe Photoshop Elements 8 from the context menu. In Photoshop Elements, click the arrow on the orange Edit tab above the Panel Bin and choose Edit Full.

3 Hide the Panel Bin by clicking the double-arrow at the top right of the header bar and the Project Bin by clicking its header bar.

4 Choose Window > Images > Consolidate All To Tabs, and then double-click the Hand tool or choose View > Fit On Screen.

Notice that this file has been saved as a Photoshop file and not as a JPEG file. The Photoshop file format can store additional information along with the image data. In this case, a portion of the flower has previously been selected and the selection has been saved in the file.

5 Choose Select > Load Selection. In the Load Selection dialog box, choose "petals" from the Source menu. In the Operation options, activate New Selection, and then click OK.

The saved selection "petals" is loaded. Most of the lotus flower is now surrounded by a flashing selection marquee, indicating that it has become the active portion of the image.

The four lowest petals need to be added to make the selection complete. In the next exercise, you'll add the missing petals and modify the saved selection.

6 Choose Select > Deselect to clear the current selection.

7 In the toolbox, select the Selection Brush tool, which is grouped with the Quick Selection tool.

Using the Selection Brush tool

The Selection Brush tool makes selections in either of two ways. In Selection mode, you simply paint over the area you want to select. In Mask mode you paint a semi-opaque overlay over areas you don't want selected.

1 In the tool options bar, set the Selection Brush controls to match the illustration below. Click the Add To Selection button at the far left; then set the brush Size to 60 px (pixels), choose Selection from the Mode menu, and set the brush Hardness value to 100%.

2 Drag with the Selection Brush to paint over the interior of the lowest four petals. Don't try to paint to the edges; you'll do that in the next step.

Notice that you're actually painting a live selection onto the image, surrounded by a flashing selection marquee. Release the mouse button every second or two so that you don't have to repeat too much work if you need to undo a stroke.

Now you need to reduce your brush size to paint around the edges of the petals, adding to your selection.

You could move the Size slider to change your brush size, but while you're working it's far more convenient to press the open bracket key ([) to reduce the brush size in increments and the close bracket key (]) to enlarge it.

3 Press the left bracket key ([) to reduce the Selection Brush size to 15 pixels.

4 Drag with the Selection Brush to paint the selection to the edges of the petals. Use the bracket keys to change the brush size as needed, until the selection outline completely surrounds all four petals.

▶ **Tip:** Use the Zoom tool to magnify the area of interest in the photo when you need to make a detailed selection.

▶ **Tip:** If you have accidentally selected an area you didn't want to select, use the buttons at the left of the tool options bar to switch the brush mode from Add To Selection to Subtract From Selection and paint back over the unwanted area.

If you found using the Selection Brush tool tedious, you'll appreciate learning about the Quick Selection tool later in this lesson. But first, you'll make use of your hard work and save the results.

Editing a saved selection

In this exercise you'll add your current selection to the "petals" selection that was saved with the file. You can modify saved selections by either replacing them, adding to them, or subtracting from them.

1 With your selection still active, choose Select > Load Selection.

2 In the Load Selection dialog box, choose the saved selection "petals" as the Source Selection. In the Operation options, activate the Add To Selection option; then click OK.

Note: The New Selection option replaces the saved selection with the current selection. The Subtract from Selection option subtracts the current selection from the saved selection. Intersect with Selection replaces the saved selection with the intersection between the current selection and the saved selection.

This setting will combine your current selection of the lowest petals with the saved selection of the rest of the flower.

You should now see the entire lotus flower outlined by the flashing selection border.

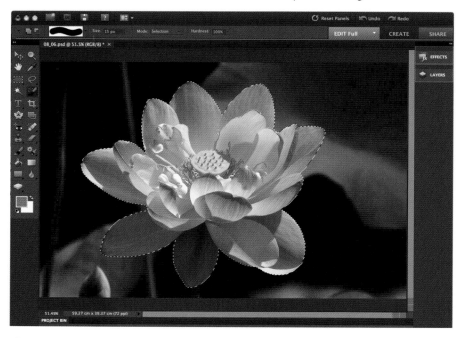

Note: Once you have loaded a saved selection you can also add to it or subtract from it by Shift-dragging or Alt-dragging with any of the selection tools.

If you've missed a spot, simply paint it in with the Selection Brush tool. If you've selected too much, switch to Subtract From Selection mode in the tool options bar, set an appropriate brush size, and then paint out your mistakes.

3   Choose Select > Save Selection. In the Save Selection dialog box, choose petals as the Selection name, activate Replace Selection in the Operation options, and then click OK.

4   Choose Select > Deselect.

Using the Quick Selection tool

The Quick Selection tool enables you to select an area in the image by simply drawing, scribbling, or clicking on the area you want to select. You don't need to be precise, because while you're drawing, Photoshop Elements expands the selection border based on color and texture similarity.

In this exercise, you'll use the Quick Selection tool to select everything but the lotus flower, and then switch the selected and un-selected areas in the photo to establish the selection you want. This technique can be a real time-saver in situations where it proves difficult to select a complex object directly.

1   In the toolbox, select the Quick Selection tool (✎). The Quick Selection tool is grouped in the toolbox with the Selection Brush you used earlier.

2 In the tool options bar, make sure the New Selection mode button on the far left is activated. Set a brush diameter in the Brush picker. For the purposes of this exercise, you can use the default brush diameter of 30 px (pixels).

3 Scribble over the area around the lotus flower, making sure to touch some of the yellow, green, and black areas as shown in the illustration below. Release the pointer to see the result. As you draw, Photoshop elements automatically expands the selection based on similarity of color and texture.

▶ **Tip:** If you want to simply scribble-select an area in the image, you can use a larger brush. If you need more control to draw a more precise outline, choose a smaller brush size.

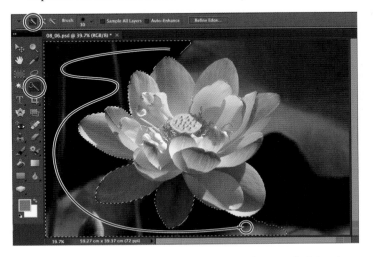

4 With an active selection already in place, the Quick Selection tool defaults to Add To Selection mode. Scribble over, or click into, un-selected areas around the lotus flower until everything is selected but the flower itself.

5 Finally, turn the selection inside out by choosing Select > Inverse, thereby masking the background and selecting the flower—ready for the next exercise.

Working with selections

Now that you have an active selection outline around the lotus flower, you can apply any adjustment you like and only the flower will be affected.

1   With the flower still selected, click the orange Edit tab at the top of the Panel Bin and switch to Quick Edit mode.

2   To make comparison more convenient, choose Before & After - Horizontal from the View menu at the left below the Edit pane.

3   In the Quick Fix Color pane on the right, click and drag the Hue slider to the left or right to change the color of the lotus flower.

Notice that the lotus changes color, but the background does not. Only the pixels inside a live selection are affected by edits or adjustments.

4   Click the Cancel button (x) in the Color panel to undo your changes.

You could also invert the selection to apply changes to the background instead of the water lily.

5   Click the Edit tab at the top of the Panel Bin and switch to Full Edit mode.

6   With the lotus flower still selected, choose Select > Inverse.

7   Choose Enhance > Convert To Black And White.

8   Under Select A Style in the Convert To Black And White dialog box, choose Urban/Snapshots.

9 Experiment with the different styles to see the effects on the image. Use the Adjustment Intensity sliders to vary the amount of change for red, green, blue, and contrast. Click Undo if you make adjustments you don't like.

10 Click OK to close the Convert To Black And White dialog box.

11 Choose Select > Deselect.

12 Choose File > Save As and save the file in the My CIB Work folder. In the File Name text box, type **08_06_Work**. Make sure that the Format setting is Photoshop (.PSD, .PDD). On Windows, disable the option Save In Version Set With Original.

13 Choose File > Save, and then choose File > Close.

Congratulations, you've completed another exercise. You've learned how to use the Selection Brush tool and the Quick Selection tool to isolate areas of an image. You've also learned to mask out areas to which you don't want changes applied and how to add a new selection to existing, saved selection. These techniques will be invaluable as you learn to use other selection tools.

Why won't Photoshop Elements do what I tell it to do?

In some situations, the changes you try to apply to an image may not seem to work. You may hear a beep, indicating that you're trying to do something that's not allowed. The following list offers explanations and solutions for common issues that might be blocking your progress.

Commit is required

Several tools, including the Type tool require you to click the Commit button before you can move on to another task. The same is true when you crop with the Crop tool or resize a layer or selection with the Move tool.

Cancel is required

The Undo command isn't available while you have uncommitted changes made with some tools—for example, the Type tool, Move tool, and Crop tool. If you want to undo these edits, click the Cancel button instead of using the Undo command or shortcut.

Edits are restricted by an active selection

When you create a selection (using a marquee tool, the Quick Selection tool, or the Selection Brush tool, for example), you limit the active area of the image. Any edits you make will apply only within the selected area. If you try to make changes to an area outside the selection, nothing happens. Edits are restricted by an active selection. If you want to deactivate a selection, choose Select > Deselect, and then you can work on any area of the image.

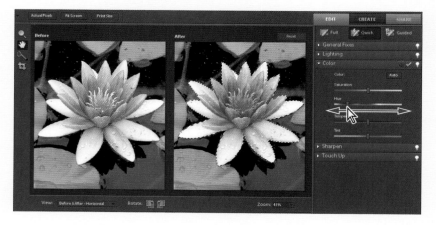

Move tool is required

If you drag a selection, the selection marquee moves, not the image within the selection marquee. If you want to move a selected part of the image or an entire layer, use the Move tool .

Why won't Photoshop Elements do what I tell it to do? *(continued)*

Background layer is selected

Many changes cannot be applied to the Background layer. For example, you can't erase, delete, change the opacity, or drag the Background layer to a higher level in the layer stack. If you need to apply changes to the Background layer, double-click it and rename it (or accept the default name, Layer 0).

Active layer is hidden

In most cases, the edits you make apply to only the currently selected layer—the one highlighted in the Layers palette. If an eye icon does not appear beside that layer in the Layers palette, then the layer is hidden and you cannot edit it. Or, if the image on the selected layer is not visible because it is blocked by an opaque upper layer, you will actually be changing that layer, but you won't see the changes in the image window.

The active layer is hidden, the view is blocked by an opaque upper layer, or the active layer is locked.

Active layer is locked

If you lock a layer by selecting the layer and then clicking the Lock in the Layers palette, the lock prevents the layer from changing. To unlock a layer, select the layer, and then click the Lock at the bottom of the Layers palette to remove the Lock.

Wrong layer is selected (for editing text)

If you want to make changes to a text layer, be sure that layer is selected in the Layers palette before you start. If a non-text layer is selected when you click the Type tool in the image window, Photoshop Elements creates a new text layer instead of placing the cursor in the existing text layer.

Replacing the color of a pictured object

Photoshop Elements offers two methods for switching a color in a photo: the Color Replacement tool and the Replace Color dialog box. The Color Replacement tool is grouped in the toolbox with the Brush tool, the Impressionist Brush tool, and the Pencil tool and enables you to replace specific colors in your image by painting over a targeted color with another. You can also use the Color Replacement tool for color correction.

Using the Replace Color dialog box is faster and more automated than using the Color Replacement tool, but it doesn't work well for all images. This method is most effective when the color of the object you want to change is not found in other areas of the image. The photograph of a yellow car used for the following exercises is a good candidate for this approach as there is very little yellow elsewhere in the image.

Replacing a color throughout the image

In this exercise, you'll repaint a yellow car. You'll make your changes on a duplicate of the Background layer, which will make it easy to compare the finished project to the original picture.

Though it's quick and easy to apply, the Replace Color feature can produce quite spectacular results. You'll do this exercise twice. First, you'll work on the entire image area, which will give you an indication of where and how much the color change will affect the rest of the image. For the second part of the exercise you'll use a selection to restrict the changes to just the car.

● **Note:** By now, you should be familiar with the technique of using keyword tags to locate the files you need. For the remainder of this chapter, the instructions for finding the lesson files will be summarized rather than stepped through in detail. If you need to refresh your memory, please refer to the steps at the start of any of the first few exercises in this chapter.

1 In the Organizer / Bridge, use the Lesson 8 keyword tag to locate the file 08_07.psd, taking care not to confuse the original file with the Autofix copy.

2 Do one of the following:

- On Windows, select the file in the Media Browser; then click the small arrow on the orange Fix tab above the Task Pane and choose Full Photo Edit.

- On Mac OS, right-click / Control-click the image in the Bridge Content panel and choose Open With > Adobe Photoshop Elements 8 from the context menu. In Photoshop Elements, click the arrow on the orange Edit tab above the Panel Bin and choose Edit Full.

3 Choose Window > Reset Panels or click the Reset Panels button (🔁) at the top of the workspace. Hide the Effects panel and the Project Bin by clicking their header bars.

4 Choose Window > Images > Consolidate All To Tabs, and then double-click the Hand tool or choose View > Fit On Screen.

5 In the Editor, choose Layer > Duplicate Layer and accept the default name. Alternatively, you can drag the Background layer to the New Layer button () at the bottom of the Layers panel. By duplicating the layer, you have an original to fall back on should you need it.

6 With the Background copy layer still selected in the Layers panel, choose Enhance > Adjust Color > Replace Color.

7 In the Replace Color dialog box, make sure the Eyedropper tool—the left-most of the three eyedropper buttons—is activated, and then activate the Image option below the preview thumbnail so that you can see a color preview of the photo. Click with the Eyedropper tool to sample the yellow paint of the car.

8 Below the thumbnail preview in the Replace Color dialog box, change the Selection option from Image to Selection, so that you see the extent of the color selection indicated in white on a black background.

9 Drag the Hue slider (and optionally the Saturation and Lightness sliders) to change the color of the selected area. For example, set the Hue value to –140 to change the yellow to light blue.

10 To adjust the area of selected color—or color-application area—start by clicking the second of the three eyedropper buttons to activate the Add To Sample mode for the Eyedropper tool, and then click in the edit window in areas where the paint on the car still appears yellow.

11 Drag the Fuzziness slider left or right until you find an acceptable compromise between full coverage on the car and the effect on other areas in the image. Refer to the selection preview and try to avoid picking up too much color in the girl's skin.

12 When you're satisfied that you've done the best you can, click OK to close the Replace Color dialog box.

Depending on what color and color characteristics you used to replace the yellow, you probably can see some shift in color in the garden in the background. The plastic tail-light lens has also been affected. You may be able to live with that, but unfortunately it's very difficult to achieve good coverage on the car without the new color also creeping into the tones of the young girl's hair and skin. In the next exercise you'll find a way to do just that.

Replacing a color in a limited area of the image

In this exercise you'll repeat the previous procedure, but this time you'll limit the color change to a selected area of the photograph.

1 Choose Edit > Undo Replace Color, or select the step before Replace Color in the Undo History panel (Window > Undo History).

2 In the toolbox, select the Lasso tool and draw a rough selection marquee around the car. It's OK if a little of the background is included in the selection. Don't be concerned about the girl as yet.

● **Note:** The Lasso tool is grouped in the toolbox with the Magnetic Lasso tool and the Polygonal Lasso tool. To switch from one lasso tool to another, click the tool in the toolbox and hold the mouse button down until a menu appears. Choose the desired tool from the menu.

3 In the toolbox, select the Quick Selection tool (🖌). In the tool options bar, click the tool variant at the right to set the Quick Selection tool to Subtract From Selection mode. In the Brush picker, set the brush diameter to 10 pixels.

4 Using the Quick Selection tool in Subtract From Selection mode, remove the figure of the girl from the selection. Hold down the Shift key to switch to Add To Selection mode. Use the open bracket key ([) to reduce the brush size and the close bracket key (]) to enlarge it. Use the same techniques to remove the tail-light assembly from the selection to protect it from the color change.

▶ **Tip:** There's no need to be concerned with removing the girl's blurred left hand from the selection. Just as the original yellow color shows through the blur, so will the new color.

5 Choose Enhance > Adjust Color > Replace Color. Using the same techniques and settings you used in steps 4 to 8 of the previous exercise, make adjustments in the Replace Color dialog box to change the color of the car.

6   When you're satisfied with the results, click OK to close the Replace Color dialog box; then choose Select > Deselect, or press Ctrl+D / Command+D.

7   Choose File > Save As and save the file to your My CIB Work folder. Name the file **08_07_Work** and chose the Photoshop (.PSD, .PDD) format. On Windows, disable Save In Version Set With Original.

8   Click Save, and then choose File > Close.

Take a bow—you've finished all the exercises in this lesson. In the last exercise, you learned how to make a selection with the Lasso tool and then edit the selection with another tool. You replaced one color with another using the Replace Color dialog box and in the process you were introduced to the Undo History panel.

About printing color pictures

Color problems in your photos can result from a variety of causes, such as incorrect exposure, the quality of the camera, or the conditions under which a photograph was taken. If an image is flawed, you can usually improve it by editing it with Photoshop Elements, as you did with the images in this lesson.

Sometimes, pictures that look great on your computer don't turn out so well when you print them. There are things you can do to make sure that what you get from the printer is closer to what you see on screen.

It's important that you calibrate your monitor regularly so that it's set to display the range of color in your photographs as accurately as possible.

Your prints may also look bad if your color printer interprets color information differently from your computer. You can correct that by activating the appropriate type of color management.

Working with color management

Moving a photo from your camera to your monitor and from there to a printer shifts the colors in the image. This shift occurs because every device has a different color gamut or color space—the range of colors that the device is capable of interpreting and producing. To achieve consistent color between digital cameras, scanners, computer monitors, and printers, you need to use color management.

Color management software acts as a color interpreter, translating the image colors so that each device can reproduce them in the same way. This software knows how each device and program understands color, and adjusts colors so that those you see on your monitor are similar to the colors in your printed image. It should be noted, however, that not all colors may match exactly.

Color management is achieved through the use of profiles, or mathematical descriptions of each device's color space. If these profiles are compliant with the standards of the ICC (International Color Consortium), they help you maintain consistent color. When you save a file, select ICC Profile in the Save As dialog box.

Photoshop Elements' color management controls are located in the Edit menu.

Setting up color management

1   Choose Edit > Color Settings. On Windows, you'll need to be in the Editor.

2   Select one of these color management options:

- **No Color Management** uses your monitor profile as the working color space. It removes any embedded profiles when opening images, and does not apply a profile when saving.

- **Always Optimize Colors For Computer Screens** uses sRGB as the working color space, preserves embedded profiles, and assigns sRGB when opening untagged files.

- **Always Optimize For Printing** uses Adobe RGB as the working color space, preserves embedded profiles, and assigns Adobe RGB when opening untagged files.

- **Allow Me To Choose** lets you choose to assign sRGB (the default) or Adobe RGB when opening untagged files.

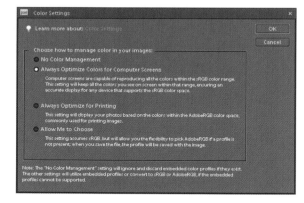

3   Click OK to close the Color Settings dialog box.

Further information on color management, including monitor calibration, can be found in a series of topics in Help. To access this information, choose Help > Photoshop Elements Help and search for these subjects.

Review questions

1 What are the key differences between adjusting images in Full Edit mode, Quick Edit mode and Guided Edit mode?

2 Can you apply automatic fixes when you are in Full Edit mode?

3 What tools can you use to fix the red-eye phenomenon created by some flash cameras?

4 What makes selections so important for adjusting color?

5 Name at least two selection tools and describe how they work.

Review answers

1 Full Edit provides a more flexible and powerful image correction environment. Full Edit offers lighting and color correction commands, tools for fixing image defects, making selections, adding text, and painting on your images. Quick Fix provides easy access to a range of basic image editing controls for quickly making common adjustments and corrections. If you are new to digital photography, Guided Edit is the best place to start. Guided Edit steps you through each procedure to help you get professional results.

2 Yes. The Enhance menu contains commands that are equivalent to the Auto buttons in the Quick Fix panel: Auto Smart Fix, Auto Levels, Auto Contrast, Auto Color Correction, as well as Auto Red Eye Fix. The Enhance menu also provides an Adjust Smart Fix command, which opens a dialog box in which you can specify settings for automatic adjustments.

3 In both the Full Edit and Quick Edit mode you can fix red eye effects automatically by choosing Enhance > Auto Red Eye Fix. The Red Eye Removal tool located in the toolbox enables you to specify the tool settings to deal with difficult cases. On Windows, you can fix red eye automatically during the process of importing photos or choose Edit > Auto Red Eye Fix after the photos have been imported to the Organizer.

4 You use a selection to define an area as the only part of a layer that can be altered. The areas outside the selection are protected from change for as long as the selection is active. This aids greatly in image correction, as it enables you make adjustments selectively, targeting specific areas or objects in an image.

(*continued on next page*)

5 The first tool you used in this lesson to make selections is the Selection Brush tool, which works like a paintbrush. The Quick Selection tool is similar to the Selection Brush tool, but is in most cases a faster, more flexible option. The Lasso tool creates free-form selections. There are more selection tools than are discussed in this lesson: The Magic Wand tool selects all the areas with the same color as the color on which you click. The Rectangular Marquee tool and the Elliptical Marquee tool make selections of fixed geometric shape. The Magnetic Lasso tool helps to draw selections along even irregular object edges, while the Polygonal Lasso tool restricts drawing to straight lines, making it the tool of choice for selecting straight-sided objects.

9 FIXING EXPOSURE PROBLEMS

Lesson Overview

Photoshop Elements makes it easy to fix images that are too dark or too light and rescue photos that are dull, flat, or simply fading away.

Start with Quick Fix and Guided Edit and work up to Full Edit as you learn how to make the most of poorly exposed images, retrieve detail from photos that are too dark and liven up images that look flat and washed-out. Photoshop elements delivers powerful, easy-to-use tools for correcting exposure and lighting problems in all three Edit modes.

In this lesson you'll be introduced to a variety of techniques for dealing with a range of common exposure problems:

- Brightening underexposed photographs
- Correcting parts of an image selectively
- Saving selection shapes to reuse in later sessions
- Working with adjustment layers
- Choosing layer blending modes
- Using layer opacity settings
- Adjusting lighting controls manually
- Enhancing overexposed and faded photographs

 You'll probably need between one and two hours to complete this lesson.

Learn how to make the most of images that were captured in unusual lighting conditions, retrieving detail from overly dark photos and putting the spark back into images that look dull and washed-out. Find out how Photoshop Elements can help you save those faded memories—no matter what your level of experience—with a suite of powerful, easy-to-use tools and the versatility of three Edit modes.

261

Getting started

Before you start working on the exercises in this lesson, make sure that you have installed the software on your computer from the application CD (see the Photoshop Elements 8 documentation) and that you have correctly copied the Lessons folder from the CD in the back of this book onto your computer's hard disk. (See "Copying the Classroom in a Book files" on page 2.)

This lesson builds on the skills and concepts covered in the earlier chapters and assumes that you are already familiar with the main features of the Photoshop Elements workspace. Should you need to brush up on the basic concepts see Lesson 1, "A Quick Tour of Photoshop Elements" and Photoshop Elements Help.

Setting up on Windows

For the exercises in this lesson you'll be working with images from the CIB Catalog that you created in the "Getting Started" section at the beginning of this book.

1   Start Photoshop Elements and click the Organize button in the Welcome Screen. Check the name of the currently active catalog, which is displayed in the lower left corner of the Organizer window.

2   If your CIB Catalog is not already open choose File > Catalog, select the CIB Catalog in the Catalog Manager dialog box, and then click Open. If you don't see the CIB Catalog file listed, see "Creating a catalog file" on page 3.

3   Once you have loaded your CIB Catalog, click the small arrow on the orange Fix tab above the Task Pane and choose Full Photo Edit, without selecting any images in the Media Browser.

Setting up on Mac OS

For the exercises in this lesson, you'll be working with the image files in the PSE8CIB > Lessons > Lesson09 folder that you copied to your hard disk in the section "Copying the Classroom in a Book files" at the beginning of this book.

For the first set of exercises you'll access a lesson file directly from Photoshop Elements, rather than browsing with Bridge.

1   Start Photoshop Elements.

2   Click the Close button in the upper right corner of the Welcome Screen and you're ready to begin.

Correcting images automatically in batches

You'll start this lesson in the same way that you began your work in Lesson 8—by batch-processing the lesson images and applying the Photoshop Elements automatic fix adjustments. Later you can compare the results of the automated adjustments to the outcomes of the techniques you'll learn in the exercises to follow.

1 Choose File > Process Multiple Files.

2 In the Process Multiple Files dialog box, set the source and destination folders as follows:

   • From the Process Files From menu, choose Folder.

   • Under Source, click the Browse button. Find and select the Lesson09 folder in your Lessons folder. Click OK / Choose to close the Browse For Folder / Choose A Folder dialog box.

   • Under Destination, click Browse, and then select the My CIB Work folder that you created inside your Lessons folder at the start of the book. Click OK / Choose.

3 Under File Naming, click the check box to activate the Rename Files option, and then choose Document Name from the menu on the left. Choose None from the menu on the right; then type **_Autofix** in the text box. This adds the appendix "_Autofix" to the existing document names as the files are saved.

4 Under Quick Fix on the right side of the dialog box, activate all four options: Auto Levels, Auto Contrast, Auto Color, and Sharpen.

5 Review the Source, Destination and File Naming settings in the Process Multiple Files dialog box, comparing them to the illustration below. Make sure that the Resize Images and Convert Files options are disabled, and then, click OK.

Photoshop Elements takes a few seconds to process the files. Image windows will open and close automatically as the adjustments are applied. There's nothing else you need to do. If any alerts or warnings appear, click OK.

At the end of this lesson, you can compare the results of these basic, automatic fixes with the results you achieve by applying the manual techniques you'll learn as you work through the exercises. In some cases, the automatic method of fixing images may be sufficient to meet your needs.

Brightening an underexposed image

Slightly underexposed photographs tend to look dull and flat, or too dark. While the auto-fix lighting feature does a terrific job of brightening up many of these photos, in this exercise you'll learn some different methods for adjusting exposure.

Applying the Quick Fix

The first technique you'll learn makes use of the Quick Edit mode. On Windows, make sure that you're still in the Editor before beginning the exercise; if not, switch to the Editor now.

1   Choose File > Open. Navigate to and open the Lesson09 folder inside your Lessons folder. Select the file kat_and_kind.jpg, and then click Open.

2   Click the small arrow on the orange Edit tab above the Panel Bin and choose Edit Quick from the menu.

3   Click the Smart Fix Auto button at the top of the Quick Fix panel. The photo becomes a little brighter but the skin tones remain quite dark.

4 In the Lighting pane, drag both the Lighten Shadows and Midtone Contrast sliders to the right to set values of 27 and 25 respectively.

The image is substantially improved, though the skin tones are still a little cool.

5 In the Balance and Color panes, drag both the Temperature and Hue sliders just fractionally to the right. Take care not to make the sky too pink or overly yellow; we set Temperature and Hue values of 52 and 4 respectively.

6 When you're satisfied with the result, commit the changes by clicking the Commit button (✓) in the header bar of the pane in which you made your last adjustment.

Original image   Auto Smart Fix and Lighting sliders   Temperature and Hue tweaked

7 Choose File > Save As. In the Save As dialog box, navigate to and open your My CIB Work folder, rename the file kat_and_kind_Quick and choose the JPEG format. On Windows, make sure that the option Save In Version Set With Original is disabled.

8 Click Save. In the JPEG Options dialog box, choose High from the Quality menu, and then click OK.

9 Choose File > Close or click Close above the edited image in the Edit pane.

Without much effort you improved the image significantly. Let's try some other methods to adjust the lighting in the image and you can compare the results later.

Exploring Guided Edit

In Guided Edit mode Photoshop Elements offers a wide range of commonly performed image correction and editing tasks presented in a way that makes it easy for even a novice to get great results. Easy-to-follow prompts and instructions and simple controls enable you to edit your photos quickly as you learn concepts and techniques you can apply even in Full Edit mode.

1 Click the small arrow on the orange Edit tab above the Panel Bin and choose Edit Guided from the menu.

2 Choose File > Open and navigate to your Lesson09 folder; then select the same under-exposed image you used for the last exercise and click Open.

3 In the guided tasks menu, click the orange triangle beside Lighting and Exposure if necessary to see the options, and then click Lighten Or Darken.

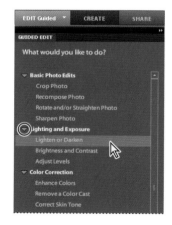

4 The Lighten Or Darken A Photo panel opens. Click the Auto button near the top right corner of the panel. For this image, the result is not quite as good as we might wish. Click the Reset button below the slider controls, or choose Edit > Undo Auto Levels to revert the image to its original state.

5   Use the sliders to adjust the lighting in the image manually. Drag the Lighten
    Shadows slider to set a value of 50 and set the Midtone Contrast to a value of
    20; then click Done.

6   Choose File > Save As. In the Save As dialog box, navigate to and open your
    My CIB Work folder, rename the file kat_and_kind_Guided and choose the
    JPEG format. On Windows, disable Save In Version Set With Original.

7   Click Save. In the JPEG Options dialog box, choose High from the Quality
    menu, and then click OK. Choose File > Close or click Close in the Edit pane.

Again, the adjusted image looks considerably better than the original; however, it
would be ideal if the mother and child could be treated separately from the background of sea and sky.

Fixing an image in Full Edit mode

Underexposure problems are very often caused when your camera automatically
cuts down exposure to compensate for backlighting. In the case of our example
image, the large area of relatively light sea and sky may contribute to the problem in
this way, compounded by the fact that the lighting on our subjects is low and indi-
rect. Perhaps the camera's exposure settings were also incorrect. If your photo is
a particularly difficult case, more elaborate methods than those you've used in the
Quick Fix and Guided Edit modes might be necessary to achieve the best results.

In the Full Edit mode you can work with layers and blending modes and make selections to isolate specific parts of an image for special treatment.

Using blending modes

In an image file with multiple layers, each layer has its own blending mode that defines the way it will effect the layer or layers below it in the stacking order. By default, a new layer has a Normal blending mode: it will not blend with the layer below except where it contains transparency or when the opacity for the layer is set to less than 100%. The Darken and Lighten blending modes will blend a layer with the layer below it only where the result will darken or lighten the lower layer. Other blending modes produce more complex results.

If a photo is too dark, duplicating the background layer and applying the Screen blending mode to the new layer may correct the problem. If this technique produces too strong an affect, you can use the layer opacity setting to tone it down. Inversely, if your photo is overexposed—too light—duplicating the background layer and applying the Multiply blending mode may be a solution.

1 Click the small arrow on the orange Edit tab above the Panel Bin and choose Edit Full from the menu.

2 If you don't see the Layers panel in the Panel Bin, click the Reset Panels button in the menu bar (Windows) / application window header bar (Mac OS). For this exercise you can hide the Project Bin by clicking in its header bar.

3 Choose File > Open and navigate to your Lesson09 folder; then select the same under-exposed image you used for the last two exercises and click Open. In the Layers panel you can see that the image has only one layer: the Background.

4 Duplicate the Background layer by doing any one of the following:

- Right-click the Background layer in the Layers panel and choose Duplicate Layer from the context menu. Click OK in the Duplicate Layer dialog box, accepting the default name.

- With the Background layer selected in the Layers panel, choose Layer > Duplicate Layer, and then click OK in the Duplicate Layer dialog box, accepting the default name.

- Drag and drop the Background layer onto the New Layer button ( ) at the bottom of the Layers panel.

The new Background copy layer is highlighted in the Layers panel, indicating that it is the selected (active) layer.

5 With the Background copy layer selected in the Layers panel, choose Screen from the layer blending mode menu. Notice how the image becomes brighter.

● **Note:** If the layer blending mode menu is disabled, make sure that the copy layer, not the original Background layer, is selected in the Layers panel.

6 Choose File > Save As.

7 In the Save As dialog box, name the file **kat_and_kind_Screen**, choose Photoshop (PSD) from the Format menu, and make sure the Layers option is activated. Save the file to your My CIB Work folder. On Windows, disable Save In Version Set With Original. Click Save. If the Photoshop Elements Format Options dialog box appears, activate Maximize Compatibility and click OK.

8 In the Layers panel, click the eye icon beside the layer name to toggle the visibility of the Background Copy layer so that you can compare the original to the adjusted image. When you're done, close the file without saving.

In this exercise you've seen how using a blending mode can brighten up a dull image. However, you should be careful about applying a blending mode over an entire image, as it can sometimes adversely affect parts of the photos that were OK to begin with. In this example, the sky is now overexposed and some subtle color detail has been lost. In the following exercises, you'll use other blending modes that are useful for correcting a wide range of image problems.

Adjusting color curves

Using the Adjust Color Curves command is a great way to fix common exposure problems, from photos that are too dark as a result of backlighting to images that appear washed-out due to overly harsh lighting. You can choose one of the preset adjustment styles as a solution or as a useful starting point—or improve color tones by adjusting the highlights, mid-tones, and shadows separately.

Experiment with color curve adjustments on a duplicate layer to preserve your original. In the Adjust Color Curves dialog box, you can see the results of each preset in the before and after preview, and then use the sliders to fine-tune the adjustment.

Choose Enhance > Adjust Color > Adjust Color Curves to open the Adjust Color Curves dialog box. To adjust only a specific area of the image, first select it with one of the selection tools before you open the Color Curves dialog box.

For the example shown below, the Lighten Shadows adjustment preset made a good starting-point for some manual fine-tuning of the shadows and mid-tones.

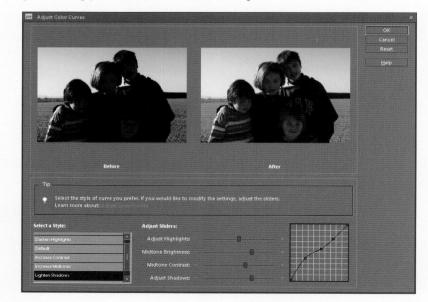

Adding adjustment layers

Sometimes you need to go back and tweak an adjustment after you've had time to assess your first efforts. You may even want to alter your settings during a much later work session—perhaps to fit the image to a particular purpose for a project or presentation. This is when you'll really appreciate the power and versatility of adjustment layers and fill layers.

An adjustment layer is like a overlay or lens over the underlying layers, perhaps darkening the photo, perhaps making it appear pale and faded or intensifying its hues—but remaining separate from the image data. Any effects applied on an adjustment layer can be easily revised, because the pixels of the image are not permanently modified. This is an appreciable advantage, especially when you wish to apply the same changes to several images. You can either copy the adjustment layer and place it on top of the layers in another photo, or use the Process Multiple files command (for more information please refer to Photoshop Elements Help).

Creating adjustment layers for lighting

In this next exercise, we'll stay in Full Edit mode and use the same underexposed image to explore the possibility of making improvements using an adjustment layer.

1   Choose File > Open. Navigate to your Lesson09 folder, select the image file kat_and_kind.jpg, and then click Open.

2   With the Background layer selected in the Layers panel, click the Create Adjustment Layer button () and choose Brightness/Contrast from the menu. The Adjustments panel opens automatically.

3   In the Adjustments panel, drag the sliders to set Brightness and Contrast values of +80 and +25 respectively.

4   Click the Create Adjustment Layer button again, but this time choose Levels (instead of Brightness/Contrast) from the menu. Levels is an effective tonal and color adjustment tool. Notice the additional layer created in the Layers panel.

5 In the Levels dialog box, drag the black, gray, and white arrows (assigned to shadows, mid-tones and highlights respectively) under the tonal distribution graph to the left or right until the balance of dark and light areas looks right to you. We used values of 11, 1.2, and 250.

6 Choose File > Save As. In the Save As dialog box, name the new file **kat_and_kind_Adjustment**; then choose the Photoshop (PSD) format and make sure the Layers option is activated. Save the file to your My CIB Work folder. On Windows, disable Save In Version Set With Original. Click Save. If the Photoshop Elements Format Options dialog box appears, activate Maximize Compatibility and click OK.

7 Close the file.

The beauty of adjustment layers is that you can always return to adjust your settings, even in future work sessions—as long as you have saved the file in the Photoshop (PSD) format, preserving the layers (the default). If you reopen the file that you just closed and click the Brightness/Contrast layer, the Adjustments panel will show the Brightness and Contrast sliders as you set them: +80 and +25. The adjustment is still live and can be refined; if necessary, you could even revert to the original, uncorrected image by either hiding or deleting the adjustment layers.

Correcting parts of an image

Although the adjustment layers did a lot to help bring out the color and image detail from our dark original photo, the background is now overexposed. So far in this lesson, all the corrections you've made to the photo have been applied to the image as a whole. In the next exercise you'll apply adjustments selectively to just part of the image.

Creating a selection

In this exercise you'll divide the image into two parts: our subjects in the foreground, and the sea and sky in the background. You'll start by selecting the silhouette of the mother and child and saving the selection.

There are various ways of making a selection—you've already explored some of them in Lesson 8. The choice of selection tool depends largely on the picture. For this exercise, we'll start with the Quick Selection tool, which makes a selection based on similarity in color and texture. Just scribble inside a pictured object and the Quick Selection tool automatically determines the selection borders for you.

1 Open the original image file kat_and_kind.jpg once again.

2 In the toolbox, select the Quick Selection tool (⚡), which is grouped with the Selection Brush tool.

3 Make sure the New Selection mode is selected for the Quick Selection tool in the tool options bar. A brush size of 20 to 30 px diameter will be fine.

4 Place the cursor at the lower right corner of the woman and slowly drag a line to the top of her head and then down across the child's face and body. Notice that the active selection automatically expands to create a border around the silhouette of our subjects. Not bad at all for a quick first pass.

Next you need to refine the border a little to capture the silhouette as closely as possible. You'll need to deselect the small area of background between the child's shoulder and her mother's chin and pay attention to hair and highlight areas. To refine your selection, you'll alternate between the Quick Selection tool's Add To Selection (🖫) and Subtract From Selection (🖫) modes. Buttons for these modes are located beside the New Selection mode button in the tool options bar.

Tip: You can use the left and right bracket keys ([,])on your keyboard to reduce or increase the brush size as you work—without stopping to open the Brush Picker.

5   Choose the Subtract From Selection (🖫) mode for the Quick Selection tool from the tool options bar. Reduce the brush size if you wish.

6   With the Subtract From Selection tool, click in the space between the girl's shoulder and her mother's chin. The selection contracts to exclude this background area.

7   Keeping the Quick Selection tool active, press Ctrl+= (equal sign) to zoom in to the image, and hold the spacebar for the Hand tool to move the image as required. Press the left bracket key '[' on your keyboard repeatedly to reduce the brush size for the Quick Selection tool. Alternate between the Add To Selection (🖫) and Subtract From Selection (🖫) modes and use a combination of clicks and very short strokes to modify the selection border around the area you deselected in step 6, paying attention to the hair and the small spaces in-between.

8 Without being overly fussy, continue to refine the selection around the subjects' heads using the same technique. Your work will be much simpler if you use the keyboard shortcuts to navigate in the image and for the tool settings. Press Ctrl+= (equal) and Ctrl+- (minus) to zoom in and out. Hold the spacebar for the hand tool to move the image in the preview window. Increase and decrease the brush size by pressing the right and left bracket keys: ']' and '['. With the Quick Selection tool in New Selection mode, you can switch temporarily to Add To Selection mode by holding the Shift key, and to Subtract From Selection mode by holding the Alt key.

9 Finally, pay attention to the brightly highlighted area that runs from the little girl's right cheek down her arm and includes a portion of her mother's fingers. You should end up with a tight flashing selection outline around the silhouettes of both of the subjects.

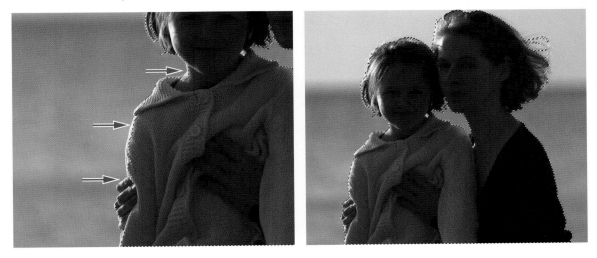

10 To soften the hard edges of the selection, you can smooth and feather the outline. Click Refine Edge in the tool options bar.

11 In the Refine Edge dialog box, type a value of **2** for Smooth and **1** px (pixel) for Feather. These settings are quite low, but should be appropriate for our lesson image, which has a relatively low resolution. Notice that the Refine Edge dialog box has its own Zoom and Hand tools to help you get a better view of the details of your selection. Click OK.

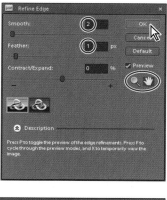

12 Choose Select > Save Selection. In the Save Selection dialog box, choose New from the Selection menu, type **Mother and Child** for the selection name, and then click OK. Once a selection is saved, you can always re-use it later—after assessing your adjustments you can reload the selection to modify them.

Using layers to isolate parts of an image

Now that you've created a selection that includes only the figures in the foreground of the photo, you can adjust the exposure and color for the subjects and the background independently. You can bring out the shaded detail in the faces without overexposing the sky, and accentuate the blues in the background without making the skin tones too cold.

The next step in this process is to use your selection to isolate the foreground and background areas on separate layers. To make the job easier, let's make sure that the layer thumbnails are of a satisfactory size.

1 Choose Panel Options from the Layers panel Options menu.

2 In the Layers Panel Options dialog box, select either the large or medium thumbnail option. Any thumbnail size will work, just as long as you don't choose None—seeing the layer thumbnails can help you visualize the layers you're working with. Click OK.

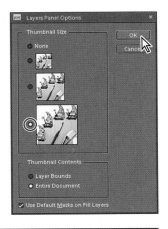

3 Choose View > Fit On Screen or, if the Zoom tool is active, click the Fit Screen button in the tool options bar so that you can see the entire image.

4 Do one of the following:

- If the selection you made in the previous exercise is still active, choose Select > Inverse, and then go on to Step 5.

- If the selection is not still active, choose Select > Load Selection. Choose Mother And Child from the Source Selection menu, click the check box to activate the Invert option and choose New Selection under Operation; then click OK.

5 Choose Edit > Copy to copy the selected area, and then choose Edit > Paste. The copied area is pasted onto a new layer, named *Layer 1* by default.

You can see the new layer in the Layers panel, already selected. In the image window the selection is no longer active.

6 In the Layers panel, select the Background layer. Choose Select > Load Selection. Under Source, choose Mother And Child from the Selection menu, but this time do not activate the Invert option. Click OK.

7 Choose Edit > Copy, and then, keeping the Background layer selected, choose Edit > Paste.

You now have three layers: Layer 1 with the sea and sky, Layer 2 with the figures in the foreground, and the Background layer with the entire image.

● Note: A new layer, whether it's created by pasting into the image, clicking the new layer button or using a menu command—appears immediately above the selected layer. The checker-board pattern in layers 1 and 2 indicates transparent areas.

8 You'll find it much easier to work with the Layers panel if you give your layers descriptive names—especially when you're working with many layers. Double-click the name of Layer 2. The pointer changes to a text entry cursor and the name text is selected. Type **Figures** as the new name for the layer. Change the name of Layer 1 to **Sea & Sky**.

Now you're ready to work on the separated layers to improve the photo as a whole.

Correcting underexposed areas

We can now apply the most effective technique from the earlier exercises to the subjects of our photo selectively, and then fine-tune the result.

1 In the Layers panel, select the Figures layer and choose Screen from the blending menu. The figures are brighter and clearer, while the Sea & Sky layer remains unchanged.

2 Choose Enhance > Adjust Color > Adjust Color For Skin Tone. The pointer becomes an eyedropper. Sample a neutral skin area such as the center of the child's forehead, and then click OK.

Adding more intensity

Now that the figures in the foreground look so much better, the sea and sky behind them need to be adjusted to appear less dull and murky.

1   In the Layers panel, select the Sea & Sky layer.

2   Choose Enhance > Auto Levels. The sea and sky look blue again—and far more vibrant—and we have also recovered a lot of textural detail in the background. However, the effect is too strong to sit well with the subdued late-afternoon light on our subjects.

3   Change the opacity of the Sea & Sky layer to 60% by dragging the Opacity slider or typing the new value into the text box.

With these few adjustments to the separate layers, the photograph now looks far more lively. There are still possibilities that you could play around with to improve different areas of the image; for example you could separate the sky onto a new layer and intensify the cloud contrast. There is also more you could do with blending modes and layer opacity—you'll learn more about those techniques later in this lesson and as you work further through this book.

4   Choose File > Save As. In the Save As dialog box, name the file **kat_and_kind_ Layers** to be saved to your My CIB Work folder, in Photoshop (PSD) format with the Layers option activated. On Windows, the option Save In Version Set With Original should be disabled. If the Photoshop Elements Format Options dialog box appears, keep Maximize Compatibility selected and click OK.

5 Close the file.

In Lesson 8 you learned how you can tile the image windows to best compare the results of your different methods for adjusting an image. It's a good idea to make use of that technique now to compare the six adjusted and saved versions of this photograph before moving on to the next exercise.

Improving faded or overexposed images

In this exercise, you'll work with the scan of an old photograph that has faded badly and is in danger of being lost forever—a photo of a beloved grandmother and her twin sister as babies. Such a photo may not be an award-winning image, but it could represent a valuable and treasured record of personal history, which you might want to preserve for future generations.

The automatic fixes you applied to a copy of this image at the beginning of this lesson (see "Correcting images automatically in batches") improved the photograph markedly. In this project, you'll try to do even better using other techniques.

Setting up on Windows

1   If you're still in the Editor from the last exercise, switch to the Organizer now by clicking the Organizer button (▦) at the top right of the Editor window. If you're starting a new session, start Photoshop Elements, click the Organize button in the welcome screen, and then make sure your CIB Catalog is active.

2   In the Organizer, click the Find box beside the Lesson 9 tag in the Keyword Tags panel and select the image frida_and_mina.jpg in the Media Browser.

3   Click the small arrow on the orange Fix tab at the top of the Task Pane and choose Full Photo Edit from the menu; then wait while the image opens in the Editor.

Setting up on Mac OS

1   Start Photoshop Elements if it's not already running.

2   Click Browse With Adobe Bridge in the Welcome Screen or chose File > Browse With Bridge.

3   In Bridge, choose Edit > Find or press Command+F on your keyboard. In the Find dialog box choose Browse from the Look In menu under Source, and then locate your PSE8CIB folder. Under Criteria, choose Keywords from the first menu, choose Equals from the second menu, and then type **lesson 9** in the text box. Activate the Include All Subfolders option and click Find.

4   The search results are displayed in the Content panel. Right-click / Control-click the black and white image frida_and_mina.jpg and choose Open With > Adobe Photoshop Elements 8.

Creating a set of duplicate files

You'll compare a variety of editing techniques during the course of this set of exercises. You can begin by creating a separate file to test each method and naming each new file for the technique it will demonstrate.

1 If you don't see the Project Bin, click its header bar at the bottom of the Edit pane or choose Window > Project Bin. If you don't see the filename below the thumbnail in the Project Bin, right-click / Control-click the thumbnail and choose Show Filenames from the context menu. Choose View > Fit On Screen or click the Arrange button (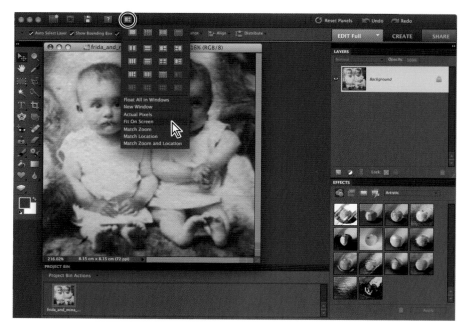) at the top of the workspace and choose Fit On Screen from the menu.

2 Choose File > Duplicate. In the Duplicate Image dialog box, type **frida_and_ mina_Shad_High**, and then click OK.

3 Perform Step 2 twice more, naming the duplicates **frida_and_mina_Bright_ Con** and **frida_and_mina_Levels**.

4 In the Project Bin, double-click the frida_and_mina.jpg thumbnail to make that image active. If you can't see the whole of a filename under a thumbnail in the Project Bin, hold the pointer over the thumbnail; the name of the file is displayed as a Tooltip.

5 Choose File > Save As. Type **frida_and_mina_Blend_Mode** in the Save As dialog box as the new filename and select Photoshop (PSD) from the Format menu. Select your My CIB Work folder as the Save In location. On Windows, disable Save In Version Set With Original.

6 Click Save. Click OK to accept the default settings in any dialog boxes or messages that appear. Leave all four images open for the rest of the project.

7 Choose Window > Images > Consolidate All To Tabs.

While you're working in the Editor, you can always tell which images you have open—even when a single active photo fills the edit window—by looking in the project bin. When you can see more than one photo in the edit window, you can identify the active image by the un-dimmed text in its title bar.

8 Choose Window > Images > Tile.

9 Make sure that frida_and_mina_Blend_Mode.psd is the active image, and then choose Window > Images > Match Zoom. Click the Arrange button (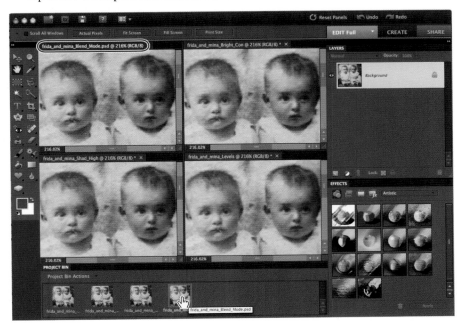) at the top of the workspace and choose Match Location.

Using blending modes to fix a faded image

A layer's blending mode can make the layer interact with those beneath it in a variety of ways. The Multiply mode intensifies or darkens pixels in an image. The Overlay mode tends to brighten an image while preserving its tonal range. For this project, you'll use the Overlay mode to add clarity and brilliance without canceling out the effect of the Multiply blending mode you'll use on the underlying layers.

1 Make sure that frida_and_mina_Blend_Mode.psd is still the active image. If necessary, double-click its thumbnail in the Project Bin to make it active.

2 In the Layers panel right-click / Control-click the Background layer and choose Duplicate Layer from the context menu. Click OK in the Duplicate Layer dialog box, accepting the default name "Background copy." Leave the Background copy layer selected in the Layers panel, ready for the next step.

3 In the Layers panel, choose Multiply from the layer blending mode menu.

4 Drag the Background copy layer with its Multiply blend mode onto the New Layer button ( ) at the bottom of the Layers panel to create a copy of the Background copy layer. Accept the default name, Background copy 2.

5 In the Layers panel, change the blending mode for the layer Background copy 2 from Multiply to Overlay. Set the layer's Opacity value to 50%, either by dragging the Opacity slider or by typing the new value in the text field.

The stacking order of the layers makes a difference to how blending modes affect an image. In our example, if you drag the layer with the Multiply blending mode to a position above the layer with the Overlay mode, you'll see slightly different results.

● **Note:** You cannot change the Opacity, the layer Blending mode or the stacking order of the Background layer, which is locked.

6 (Optional) Fine-tune the results by adjusting the Opacity settings for the two background copy layers until you achieve a pleasing balance.

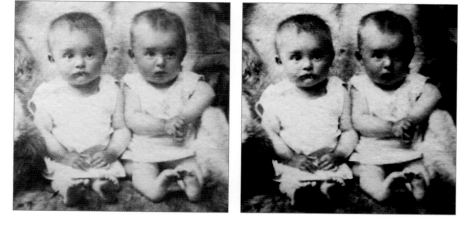

The Multiply blending mode made the image bolder and the Overlay blending mode brightened it considerably, but the contrast is still unimpressive.

7 Choose File > Save to save the file in your My CIB Work folder, leaving the file open. If a message appears about maximizing compatibility, click OK to close it, or follow the instructions in the message to prevent it from appearing again.

Adjusting shadows and highlights manually

Although both the Auto-fix and the technique using blending modes do a good job of correcting fading images, some of your own photos may be more challenging. You'll try three more techniques in the exercises to follow.

The first method involves making manual adjustments to the Shadows, Highlights, and Midtone Contrast of the image.

1   In the Project Bin, double-click the thumbnail for the image frida_and_mina_ Shad_High to make it the active window. Choose Window > Images > Float In Window; then click the Arrange button (⊞) at the top of the workspace and choose Fit On Screen.

2   Choose Enhance > Adjust Lighting > Shadows/Highlights.

3   Activate the Preview option in the Shadows/Highlights dialog box if it is not already active. If necessary, move the dialog box so that you can also see most of the frida_and_mina_Shad_High image window.

By default, the Lighten Shadows setting is 25%. You can see the effect on the image by toggling the Preview option on and off in the Shadows/Highlights dialog box.

4   In the Shadows/Highlights dialog box, set the Lighten Shadows value to 30%, the Darken Highlights value to 15%, and the Midtone Contrast value to +20%.

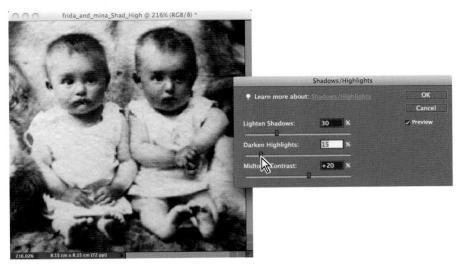

> **Tip:** The controls you are using to make the adjustments for this technique are also available in the Lighting panel in Quick Fix mode.

5   Adjust the three settings as needed until you think the image is as good as it can be. When you're done, click OK to close the Shadows/Highlights dialog box.

6   Choose File > Save and save the file as frida_and_mina_Shad_High to your My CIB Work folder, in JPEG format. Click OK to accept the default settings in the JPEG Options dialog box and leave the file open in the Edit pane. Choose Window > Images > Tile.

Adjusting brightness and contrast manually

The next approach you'll take to fixing an exposure problem makes use of another option from the Enhance > Adjust Lighting menu.

1   In the Project Bin, double-click the image frida_and_mina_Bright_Con to make it active. Choose Window > Images > Float In Window; then click the Arrange button (⊞) at the top of the workspace and choose Fit On Screen.

2   Choose Enhance > Adjust Lighting > Brightness/Contrast.

3   In the Brightness/Contrast dialog box, click the checkbox to activate Preview, if it is not already active. If necessary, drag the Brightness/Contrast dialog box aside so that you can see most of the frida_and_mina_Bright_Con image window.

4   Drag the Brightness slider to -20, or type **-20** in the text field, being careful to include the minus sign when you type. Set the Contrast to +60.

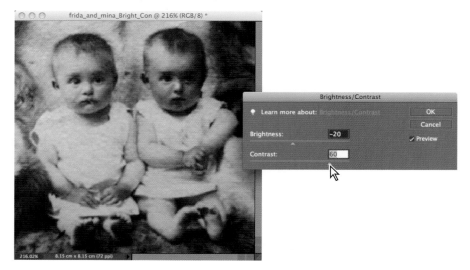

5   Adjust the Brightness and Contrast settings until you are happy with the quality of the image. Click OK to close the Brightness/Contrast dialog box.

6   Choose File > Save and save the file as frida_and_mina_Bright_Con to your My CIB Work folder, in JPEG format; then click OK to accept the default settings in the JPEG Options dialog box. Leave the file open in the Edit pane and choose Window > Images > Tile.

Adjusting levels

The Levels controls (again, available from the Enhance > Adjust Lighting menu) affect the range of tonal values in an image—the degree of darkness or lightness, regardless of color. In this exercise, you'll enhance the photograph by shifting the reference points that define the spread of those tonal values.

1 In the Project Bin, double-click the image frida_and_mina_Levels to make it active. Choose Window > Images > Float In Window; then click the Arrange button (⊞) at the top of the workspace and choose Fit On Screen.

2 Choose Enhance > Adjust Lighting > Levels. Activate the Preview option in the Levels dialog box, if it is not already active. If necessary, drag the Levels dialog box aside so that you can also see most of the image window.

The Levels graph represents the distribution of tonal values across all the pixels in the image, from darkest at the left to lightest at the right. A trough in the curve indicates that there are few pixels in that part of the range; a peak shows the opposite. As you can see from the graph, this image has no truly black pixels or completely white pixels. By dragging the end sliders inward to where the pixels start to register in the graph, you redefine which levels are calculated as black or white. This will enhance the contrast between the lightest and darkest tones in the image.

3 In the Levels dialog box, drag the black triangle below the left end of the graph to the right and position it under the point where the graphed curve begins to climb. The value in the first Input Levels box should be approximately 42.

4 Drag the white triangle from the right side of the graph until it reaches the end of the steepest part of the graphed curve. The value in the third Input Levels box should be approximately 225.

5 Drag the gray triangle below the center of the graph toward the right to set the mid-tone value to approximately 0.90. Click OK to close the Levels dialog box.

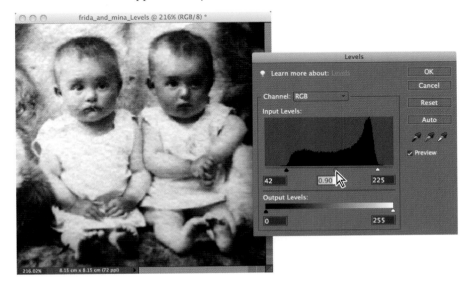

6 Choose File > Save and save the file to your My CIB Work folder in JPEG format as frida_and_mina_Levels. Click OK to accept the default settings in the JPEG Options dialog box and leave the file open. Choose Window > Images > Tile.

Comparing results

You can now compare the six versions of the image: the original file, the four files you saved showing the results of the preceding exercises, and the image that was fixed automatically as part of a batch process at the beginning of this lesson.

1 Choose File > Open. Locate and open the file frida_and_mina_ Autofix.jpg in the My CIB Work folder. If you don't see the file in the Open dialog box, make sure that All Formats / All Readable Documents is the active selection in the Files Of Type / Enable menu. Repeat the same process for the original file frida_and_mina.jpg in your Lesson09 folder.

2 Check the Project Bin to make sure that all of the six files for this project are open: the original image, frida_and_mina.jpg and five others with the appendixes _Blend_Mode.psd, _Shad_High.jpg, _Bright_Con.jpg, _Levels.jpg, and _Autofix.jpg. If you can't see the entire file name of an image, hold the pointer over the thumbnail in the Project Bin to see the file name in a Tooltip.

3 Choose Window > Images > Tile.

4 Now you'll set the zoom level for all the open windows. Select the Zoom tool; then, in the tool options bar, click the Zoom Out button and activate Zoom All Windows. Click in any of the image windows so that you can see enough of the photo to enable you to compare the different results. Zoom in to focus on details. Select an area of interest in any of the six windows, and then choose Window > Images > Match Zoom and Window > Images > Match Location. These commands are also accessible by clicking the Arrange button (▦) at the top of the Photoshop Elements workspace.

5 Compare the results and pick your favorite. The best method for fixing a file depends on the type of problem being addressed, the areas of the image that are affected, and how you intend to use the adjusted image. The requirements for an image to be used as a background behind text will be very different from those for a featured graphic.

6 Choose File > Close All. Save any changes to your CIB Work folder if you're prompted to do so.

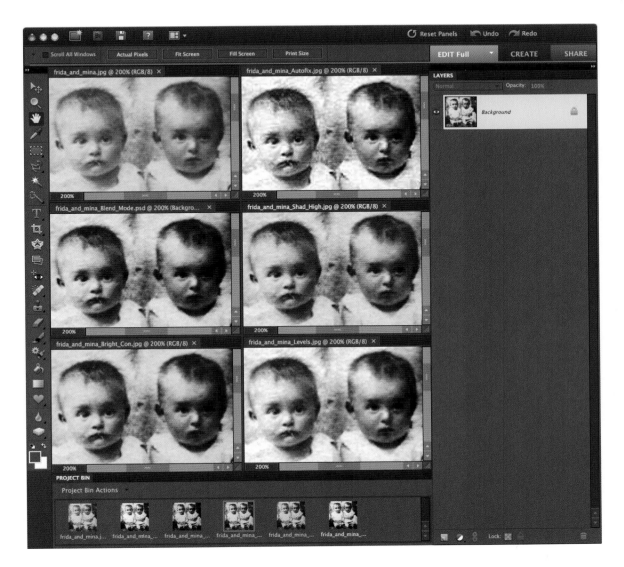

Congratulations! You've finished another lesson. In the exercises in this lesson you used a variety of both automatic and manual techniques for correcting exposure problems. You've tried auto-fixes, layer blending modes, and lighting adjustment controls. You've learned how to apply these different methods both separately and in combination to layers and selected areas to get the most from a problem image.

Before you move on to the next lesson, "Repairing, Retouching, and Recomposing Images," take a few moments to review what you've learned by reading through the questions and answers on the next page.

Review questions

1   How can you create an exact copy of an existing layer?

2   Where can you find the controls for adjusting the lighting in a photograph?

3   How do you change the arrangement of image windows in the work area?

4   What is an adjustment layer and what are its unique advantages?

Review answers

1   You must be in Full Edit mode to copy a layer. Select a layer in the Layers panel and choose Layer > Duplicate Layer. You can access the same command in the Layers panel Options menu or by right-clicking / Control-clicking the layer in the Layers panel. Alternatively, drag the layer to the New Layer button. Whichever method you use, you get two layers identical in all but their names, stacked one above the other.

2   You can adjust the lighting for a photo in Full Edit, Guided Edit, and Quick Edit mode. In Full Edit, you can use the Enhance > Adjust Lighting menu to open various dialog boxes that contain the controls. Alternatively, you can choose Enhance > Auto Levels, Enhance > Auto Contrast, or Enhance > Adjust Color > Adjust Color Curves. In Guided Edit mode, choose operations from the Lighting and Exposure pane. In Quick Edit mode, you can use the Lighting pane in the Quick Fix panel.

3   You cannot rearrange image windows in Quick Edit and Guided Edit modes, which display only one photograph at a time. In the Full Edit workspace, there are several ways you can arrange them. Choose Window > Images, and select one of the choices listed there—you can access the same options and more by clicking the Arrange button ( ). Another method is to drag the image window title bar to move an image window, and drag a corner to resize it (provided Maximize mode is not active).

4   An adjustment layer does not contain an image; instead, it modifies some quality of all the layers below it in the Layer panel. For example, a Brightness/Contrast layer will alter the brightness and contrast of any underlying layers. One advantage of using an adjustment layer instead of adjusting an existing layer directly is that adjustment layers can be easily modified or even removed. Toggle the eye icon for the adjustment layer to remove or restore the edit instantly. You can change a setting in an adjustment layer at any time—even after the file has been saved. An adjustment layer can also be copied and pasted into another image to apply the same settings there.

10 REPAIRING, RETOUCHING, AND RECOMPOSING IMAGES

Lesson Overview

For some images you'll need to deal with flaws other than color or exposure problems. A picture that was taken hurriedly might be spoiled by being tilted or poorly composed. Perhaps you have an antique photograph that is creased and worn or a scanned image marked by dust and scratches.

Sometimes the problem has nothing to do with the photograph itself, such as an extraneous object that clutters an otherwise striking composition or even just spots and blemishes on a portrait subject's skin.

In this lesson, you'll learn a range of techniques for restoring, retouching and rearranging the composition of such flawed images:

- Using the Straighten tool
- Improving the composition of an image with the Recompose tool
- Retouching skin with the Healing Brush tool
- Repairing creases with the Clone Stamp tool
- Working with opacity and blending modes in layers
- Using the Selection Brush tool
- Masking parts of an image

 You'll probably need between one and two hours to complete this lesson.

Not every image problem is a result of incorrect camera settings. Learn how to straighten a tilted photo, rearrange an image's composition, and retouch spots and blemishes on your subject's skin. The same tools, techniques and tricks used to remove spots or repair creases and tears when you're restoring a treasured keepsake can also be used creatively to manipulate reality and produce exactly the image you want.

293

Getting started

Before you start working on the exercises in this lesson, make sure that you have installed the software on your computer from the application CD (see the Photoshop Elements 8 documentation) and that you have correctly copied the Lessons folder from the CD in the back of this book onto your computer's hard disk. (See "Copying the Classroom in a Book files" on page 2.)

This lesson includes four independent exercises—you can either work straight through or complete them in separate sessions. The first three projects vary only slightly in length and complexity, while the forth is a little more involved.

Finding the lesson files on Windows

While you're working on the projects in this lesson, you'll use sample images from the CIB Catalog that you created in the "Getting Started" section at the beginning of this book. To open your CIB Catalog, follow these steps:

1 Start Photoshop Elements and click the Organize button in the Welcome Screen. Wait until the Organizer has finished opening.

2 Check the name of the currently active catalog, which is displayed in the lower left corner of the Organizer window. If your CIB Catalog is already open, you can go on to step 4.

3 If your CIB Catalog is not already open, choose File > Catalog; then select the CIB Catalog in the Catalog Manager dialog box and click Open. If you don't see the CIB Catalog file listed, see "Creating a catalog" on page 3.

4 Click Show All if it's visible above the Media Browser. In the Keyword Tags panel, expand the Imported Keyword Tags category, and then click the find box beside the Lesson 10 tag to isolate the images for the projects in this lesson.

5 Click to select the file 10_01.jpg in the Photo Browser. If you don't see the filenames below the thumbnails in the Photo Browser, choose View > Show File Names.

6 In the Organizer, click the small arrow on the orange Fix tab above the Task Pane and choose Full Photo Edit. When the Editor opens you're ready for the first exercise on the next page.

Finding the lesson files on Mac OS

For the projects in this lesson, you'll be working with the sample image files in the PSE8CIB > Lessons > Lesson10 folder that you copied to your hard disk in the section "Copying the Classroom in a Book files" at the beginning of this book.

1 Start Photoshop Elements and click Browse With Adobe Bridge in the Welcome Screen. If Photoshop Elements opens without displaying the Welcome Screen, choose File > Browse With Bridge. Wait until Bridge has finished launching.

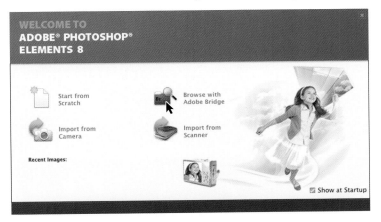

2 In Bridge, click Essentials in the row of workspace options across the top of the application window. Click your link to the PSE8CIB folder in the Favorites panel. If you don't see the Favorites panel, right-click / Option-click the header of any other panel and choose Favorites Panel from the context menu.

3 In Bridge, choose Edit > Find or press Command+F on your keyboard. Under Source in the Find dialog box, your PSE8CIB folder is already selected as the Look In folder. Under Criteria, choose Keywords from the first menu, choose Equals from the second menu, and then type lesson 10 in the text box. Activate the Include All Subfolders option and click Find.

4 The search results are displayed in the Content panel. Right-click / Ctrl-click the image 10_01.jpg and choose Open With > Adobe Photoshop Elements 8.

> **Note:** If you have not yet added the PSE8CIB folder to your Favorites in Bridge, locate the PSE8CIB folder inside your Documents folder and either drag it into the Favorites panel or choose File > Add To Favorites.

Using the Straighten tool

As you can see, the picture is not exactly horizontal. In this case, the photo was taken by a young child unused to handling the camera, but it's easy for any of us to be distracted by our live subjects or rushed by awkward shooting conditions and the result is often an image that would be just fine—if only it were straight!

With the Straighten tool you can manually specify a line in a tilted image to be used as either a horizontal or vertical reference in relation to which the image will be rotated. Assess your image first to identify which axis to use; in this photo there is no true vertical reference—the left side of the large painting frame is not suitable as the frame is hanging at an angle to the wall—so you'll specify a horizontal reference which is the default for the Straighten tool.

1 Hide the Project Bin by clicking its header bar or choose Window > Project Bin.

2 Click the double-arrow icon in the upper right corner of the Panel bin to collapse the open panels, and then choose Fit On Screen, either from the View menu or the menu on the Arrange button (▣) at the top of the workspace, giving you more room to work on the image.

3 Select the Straighten tool (▣). In the tool options bar across the top of the Edit pane, make sure that Canvas Options is set to Grow Or Shrink Canvas To Fit. With the Straighten tool, drag a line from the right-angled corner at the left end of the couch to the corresponding corner at the right end.

▶ **Tip:** To straighten an image around a vertical reference such as an architectural element or a signpost, hold down the Ctrl key (Windows) or Command key (Mac OS) on your keyboard as you drag with the Straighten tool. The image will be rotated so that your reference line becomes vertical.

4 When you release the mouse button, Photoshop Elements straightens the image relative to the line you've just drawn. Choose Fit On Screen from the View menu or the menu on the Arrange button () so that you can see all of the newly enlarged canvas surrounding the rotated image.

▶ **Tip:** For this image we chose the Straighten tool setting Grow Or Shrink Canvas To Fit because we wish to have manual control over cropping. When this is not an issue, try the options Crop To Remove Background and Crop To Original Size, which are also available from the Canvas Options menu in the tool options for the Straighten tool.

5 In the toolbox, select the Crop tool (⌗). Drag a cropping rectangle inside the image, which is now displayed at an angle—being careful not to include any of the blank area around the photo. When you're satisfied with the crop, click the green Commit button in the lower right corner of the cropping rectangle.

▶ **Tip:** In some cases, you can achieve good results by choosing Rotate > Straighten Image or Rotate > Straighten And Crop Image from the Image menu. Both of these commands perform straightening functions automatically.

6 The straightened and cropped image is much more comfortable to look at than the tilted original. Choose File > Save As. Name the file **10_01_Straight.jpg** to be saved to your My CIB Work folder in JPEG format. On Windows, disable the option Save In Version Set With Original.

7 Click Save; then click OK to accept the default JPEG Options settings.

8 Choose File > Close to close the file.

Improving the composition of an image

Have you ever wished you could convert a photo from landscape to portrait format without cropping off content at the sides? Do you have a group shot where you wish the group had stood a little closer together? Or a photo where a walk-on extra draws attention away from the stars and the main story? With the new Recompose tool you can fix these and other image composition problems in a few easy steps.

Essentially, the Recompose tool enables you to crop your photo from the *inside*, rather than at the edges. Whether you simply want to bring people closer together, fit a horizontal image to a vertical space, or remove extraneous objects that spoil the composition, the Recompose tool puts image editing magic at your fingertips.

As with the Healing brushes and the Clone Stamp tool that are covered later in this chapter—and the Photomerge tools you'll explore in Lesson 12—the Recompose tool is also a lot of fun to use creatively, making it possible to manipulate reality to produce exactly the image you want.

Setting up on Windows

1   If you're still in the Editor from the last exercise, switch to the Organizer now by clicking the Organizer button (▦) at the top right of the Editor window, and then go on to step 2. If you're beginning a new session, start Photoshop Elements, click the Organize button in the welcome screen, and then make sure your CIB Catalog is active.

2   In the Organizer, click the Find box beside the Lesson 10 tag in the Keyword Tags panel and select the image 10_02.jpg in the Media Browser.

3   Click the arrow on the orange Fix tab at the top of the Task Pane and choose Full Photo Edit from the menu.

Setting up on Mac OS

1   Start Photoshop Elements if it's not already running.

2   Click Browse With Adobe Bridge in the Welcome Screen or chose File > Browse With Bridge.

3   If you still have the lesson 10 files isolated in the Content panel, you can go on to step 4; otherwise, once Bridge opens choose Edit > Find or press Command+f on your keyboard. In the Find dialog box choose Browse from the Look In menu and locate your PSE8CIB folder. Under Criteria, choose Keywords from the first menu, choose Equals from the second menu, and then type **lesson 10** in the text box. Activate the Include All Subfolders option and click Find.

4   In the Content panel. Right-click / Ctrl-click the image 10_02.jpg and choose Open With > Adobe Photoshop Elements 8.

Recomposing a group photo

In this exercise, you'll use the Recompose tool to tighten the arrangement of this group portrait—creating a square composition.

1   Click the Crop tool and hold the mouse button down until the tool menu appears; then select the Recompose tool. A message appears with quick instructions on using the tool. For now, click OK to dismiss the message.

2   Make the image window a little larger so that you can see some gray space around the edge of the photo. The image is now surrounded by a live bounding box, with control handles at each corner and at the mid-point of each side.

For minor recomposing operations, all you need to do is drag the handles; the Recompose tool makes use of content-aware scaling technology that distinguishes people and other featured objects and attempts to prevent them being distorted as the background is compressed around them. For this example we'll use the special Recompose brushes instead, which generally produce better results.

3   In the Tool options bar across the top of the Edit pane, select the green Mark For Protection brush.
    Either type in the brush size text box or press the right bracket ( ]) key on your keyboard repeatedly to increase the brush size to 80 px.

As its name suggests, this brush enables you to define areas in the image that you want protected from any scaling operation.

4 Paint roughly over the figures in the photo. Paint a little extra space to the left of the little girl on the left of the picture and also mark the windows and the white shutter for protection. If you find that you've over-painted, use the green eraser beside the protection brush to modify your strokes. Press the left and right bracket keys ([,]) to decrease or increase the brush size as you work.

5 In the Tool options bar, select the red Mark For Removal brush.

You can use this brush to define any areas that you wish the Recompose tool to remove from the image. In this photo there is no extraneous object that we need to get rid of but you can mark parts of the stone wall and the Recompose tool will remove those areas before compressing others. This will help to retain the climbing roses against the wall and lessen possible distortion elsewhere.

6 Alternate between the red Mark For Removal brush and its associated eraser, using the bracket keys to re-size the brush if necessary as you work.

7 Now for the fun part! Move the pointer over the handle on the right side of the bounding box and when the double-arrow cursor appears, drag the handle slowly in towards the center of the photo. Watch as part of the image is removed and other areas are compressed and merged with their surroundings as you drag. As the proportions of the image become closer to a square, keep an eye on the width (W) and height (H) values in the Tool options bar; stop dragging and release the mouse button when the two values are equal.

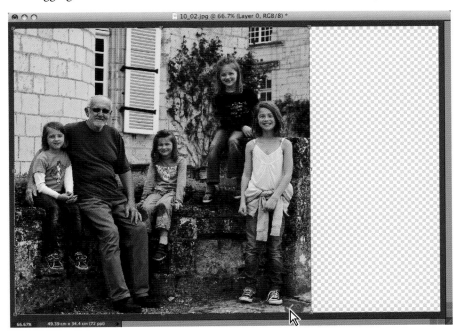

As this was a fairly extreme operation performed on an image of relatively low resolution, you may find some seam artifacts, especially near the edges of areas that were removed or protected. If these are noticeable enough to worry you, a few strokes with the Clone Stamp tool or the Healing Brush tool will fix the problem. You'll learn about using those tools later in this lesson. Use the Zoom tool to inspect the area between the shutter, which was protected and the leaves on the wall, which were compressed. Experiment with recomposing the original image in different ways; try removing a slice of the image through the rose plant instead of down the stone wall and compare the results.

8 Click the green Commit button at the lower right of the recomposed photo or press Enter / Return to accept and render the new composition.

9 Choose Image > Crop. A cropping box appears on the image; drag the handles to crop the file to the new square format, trimming away the transparent area. The edges of the cropping box snap to the edges of the image to make the operation very easy. Click the green Commit button or press Enter / Return.

10 Choose File > Save As. Name the new image **10_02_Recompose.jpg** to be saved to your My CIB Work folder in JPEG format. On Windows, disable the option Save In Version Set With Original.

11 Click Save; then click OK to accept the default JPEG Options settings.

12 Choose File > Close to close the file.

The Recompose tool is as easy to use as it is powerful—with possibilities that are virtually limitless. Play with as many pictures as you can; you'll learn what to expect from different images and textures as you have fun finding new ways to be creative.

Fixing blemishes

There are three main tools in Photoshop Elements for fixing flaws in your photos:

The Spot Healing Brush tool

The Spot Healing Brush is the easiest way to remove wrinkles in skin and other small imperfections in your photos. Either click once on a blemish or click and drag to smooth it away. By blending the information of the surrounding area into the problem spot, imperfections are made indistinguishable.

The Healing Brush tool

The Healing Brush can fix larger imperfections with ease. You can define one part of your photo as a source to be sampled and blended into another area. The Healing Brush is so flexible you can even remove large objects from a uniform background—such as a person in a wheat field.

The Clone Stamp tool

Rather than blending the source and target areas, the Clone Stamp tool paints directly with a sample of an image. You can use the Clone Stamp tool to remove or duplicate objects in your photo. This tool is great for getting rid of garbage, power lines, or a signpost that may be spoiling a view.

Removing wrinkles and spots

In this exercise, you'll explore several techniques for retouching skin flaws and blemishes to improve a portrait photograph. Retouching skin can be a real art, but luckily Photoshop Elements provides several tools that make it easy to smooth out lines and wrinkles, remove blemishes, and blend skin tones.

Setting up on Windows

1 If you're still in the Editor from the last exercise, switch to the Organizer now by clicking the Organizer button (▦) at the top right of the Editor window, and then go on to step 2. If you're beginning a new session, start Photoshop Elements, click the Organize button in the welcome screen, and then make sure your CIB Catalog is active.

2 In the Organizer, click the Find box beside the Lesson 10 tag in the Keyword Tags panel and select the image 10_03.jpg in the Media Browser.

3 Click the small arrow on the orange Fix tab at the top of the Task Pane and choose Full Photo Edit from the menu.

4 In the Editor, click the Reset Panels button at the top of the workspace. Hide the Project Bin and collapse the Effects panel by clicking their header bars.

Now you're ready to begin the first exercise which starts on the next page.

Setting up on Mac OS

1 Start Photoshop Elements if it's not already running.

2 Click Browse With Adobe Bridge in the Welcome Screen or chose File > Browse With Bridge.

3 If you still have the lesson 10 files isolated in the Content panel, you can go on to step 4; otherwise, once Bridge opens choose Edit > Find or press Command+f on your keyboard. In the Find dialog box choose Browse from the Look In menu and locate your PSE8CIB folder. Under Criteria, choose Keywords from the first menu, choose Equals from the second menu, and then type **lesson 10** in the text box. Activate the Include All Subfolders option and click Find.

4 In the Content panel. Right-click / Ctrl-click the image 10_03.jpg and choose Open With > Adobe Photoshop Elements 8.

5 In Photoshop Elements, click the Reset Panels button at the top of the workspace. Hide the Project Bin and collapse the Effects panel by clicking their header bars.

Preparing the file for editing

Before you start retouching, you'll need to set up two extra layers.

1 Drag the Background layer to the New Layer button (⬛) at the bottom of the Layers panel to create another layer, named "Background copy" by default.

2 Drag the Background copy layer to the New Layer button to create a third layer: Background copy 2.

Using the Healing Brush tool

You'll begin the retouching process using the Healing Brush tool.

1 Drag the toolbox and the Layers panel to float on top of the image so that you can make the image window as large as possible.

2 Use the Zoom tool to zoom in on the upper half of the photo, as you'll be retouching the skin around the woman's eyes first.

3   Make sure that the top layer, Background copy 2, is still active, and then select the Healing Brush tool () which is grouped together with the Spot Healing Brush tool in the toolbox.

4   In the tool options bar above the Edit pane, click the small arrow to open the Brush Picker. Set the Diameter to 20 px. Set the brush Mode to Normal and Source to Sampled. Disable the options Aligned and Sample All Layers.

5   Alt-click / Option-click a smooth area on the woman's right cheek to define the area sampled as a reference texture.
Note that if you switch to another tool and then back to the Healing Brush, you'll need to repeat this step.

6   Draw a short horizontal stroke under the left eye. As you drag, it looks as if you're creating a strange effect, but when you release the mouse button, the color is blended and natural skin tones fill the area.

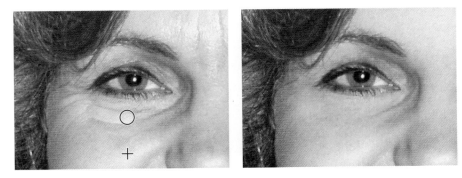

7   Continue to smooth the skin on the face and neck with the Healing Brush. Avoid the areas very close to the eyes, shadowed areas, and the hair-line. You can also reduce the worst of the shine caused by the harsh flash. As you work, re-establish the reference area occasionally by Alt / Option-clicking in new areas of the face to sample appropriate skin tone and texture. Press the left and right bracket keys ([,]) to decrease or increase the brush size as you work.

▶ **Tip:** Be careful to keep your brush strokes short. Try just clicking rather than dragging, but take care to overlap your clicks to avoid creating a spotty effect. Longer strokes may produce unacceptable results—especially near shaded areas as the darker tones may spread. If that happens, choose Edit > Undo Healing Brush, or use the Undo History panel to backtrack (see the next page). Also, make sure that the Aligned option is not activated in the tool options bar.

▶ Tip: The harsh flash lighting makes this photo quite a challenging candidate for retouching, causing strong reflections on the skin and difficult shading at the sides of the nose. If you're seeing results you don't like, try setting the brush size smaller or reversing the direction of your strokes. If the problem is related to the shadowed areas, try stroking towards rather than away from the shadows or temporarily changing the mode for the Healing Brush tool to Lighten in the tool options Mode menu.

8   Use the Undo History panel (Window > Undo History) to quickly undo a series of steps. Every action you perform is recorded in chronological order from top to bottom of the panel. To restore the file to an earlier state, simply select an earlier (higher) action in the Undo History panel.

If you change your mind before making any further changes to the file, you can still return the image to a later state by selecting a step lower in the list.

The Healing Brush tool copies *texture* from the source area, not color. It samples the colors in the target area—the area you're brushing—and arranges those colors according to the texture of the reference area. Consequently, the Healing Brush tool appears to be smoothing the skin. So far however, the results are not convincingly realistic—but you'll work on that in the next exercise.

Refining the healing brush results

In this exercise, you'll use layer opacity and another texture tool to finish your retouching work on this image.

1   Use the Navigator panel (Window > Navigator) to zoom in to the area of the woman's face around the eyes and mouth.

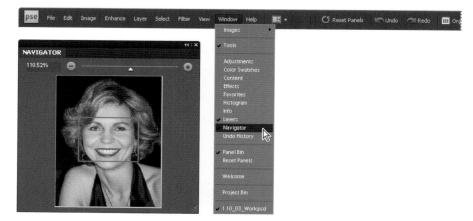

Extensive retouching can leave skin looking artificially smooth, like molded plastic. Reducing the opacity of the retouched layer gives the skin a more realistic look by allowing some of the wrinkles on the un-edited Background layer to show through.

2   In the Layers panel, change the Opacity of the layer "Background copy 2" to about 50%, using your own judgment to set the exact percentage.

We preferred quite a low setting, wishing a fairly natural look for this photo of a friend, but the opacity value you set will depend on the extent of your retouching and the purpose for which the edited image is intended.

The opacity change restores some realism, but three noticeable blemishes have also made a reappearance—one on each cheek and one just below the lower lip.

3   Select the layer "Background copy" to make it the active layer.

4   Set the brush size for the Healing Brush tool to 20 px and click once on each blemish. Gone!

5   In the toolbox, select the Blur tool (⬤). In the tool options bar, set the brush diameter to approximately 13 px and set the Blur tool's Strength to 50%.

6   With the layer "Background copy" still active, drag the Blur tool over some of the deeper lines around the eyes and brow. Use the Navigator panel to change the zoom level and shift the focus as needed. Reduce the Blur tool brush diameter to 7 px and smooth the lips a little, avoiding the edges.

▶ **Tip:** To remove spots and small blemishes in your photo, try the Spot Healing Brush as an alternative to the Healing Brush. You can either click or drag with the brush to smooth away imperfections without first setting a reference point.

Compare your results to those below—the original, the version retouched with the Healing Brush, and final refined version. Toggle the visibility of your retouched layers to compare the original image in your Background layer with the edited results.

Original   Healing Brush 100% Opacity   Healing Brush 50% Opacity over Blur tool

7   Choose File > Save As. Name the new image **10_03_Retouch** to be saved to your My CIB Work folder in Photoshop (PSD) format. On Windows, disable the option Save In Version Set With Original.

8   Make sure that the Layers option is activated, and then click Save.

9   Choose File > Close.

In this exercise, you've learned how to set an appropriate source for the Healing Brush tool, and to sample the texture of the source area to repair flaws in another part of the photograph. You also used the Blur tool to smooth textures, and an opacity change to achieve a more realistic look.

Restoring a damaged photograph

All sorts of nasty things can happen to precious old photographs—or precious new photographs, for that matter—and it is often impossible to locate the negative. For this series of exercises you'll work with an uncropped version of one of the photos you adjusted in the previous chapter.

The scanned image of an antique photograph that you'll use in this project is a challenging restoration job, because of large creases in the original print, among other flaws.

Unfortunately, there's no way to fix such significant damage in just one or two keystrokes but to rescue an important heirloom photograph like this one, a little effort is worthwhile and the results can be dramatic.

Photoshop Elements provides the tools you'll need to restore this picture convincingly to an approximation of its original condition. You'll repair creases, replace parts of the image that are actually missing, fix frayed edges and remove dust and scratches. You may be surprised to discover how easy it is to achieve impressive results.

Setting up on Windows

1 If you're still in the Editor from the last exercise, switch to the Organizer now by clicking the Organizer button (▦) at the top right of the Editor window, and then go on to step 2. If you're beginning a new session, start Photoshop Elements and click the Organize button in the welcome screen. In the Organizer, make sure your CIB Catalog is active.

2 Click the Find box beside the Lesson 10 tag in the Keyword Tags panel and select the image 10_04.psd—a scanned antique photo of twin babies—in the Media Browser.

3 Click the small arrow on the orange Fix tab at the top of the Task Pane and choose Full Photo Edit from the menu.

4 In the Editor, choose Window > Reset Panels or click the Reset Panels button at the top of the workspace. Hide the Project Bin and collapse the Effects panel by clicking their header bars.

Now you're ready to begin the first exercise which starts near the bottom of the next page.

Setting up on Mac OS

1 Start Photoshop Elements if it's not already running. Click Browse With Adobe Bridge in the Welcome Screen or chose File > Browse With Bridge.

2 If you still have the lesson 10 files isolated in the Content panel, you can go on to step 3; otherwise, once Bridge opens choose Edit > Find or press Command+f on your keyboard. In the Find dialog box choose Browse from the Look In menu and locate your PSE8CIB folder. Under Criteria, choose Keywords from the first menu, choose Equals from the second menu, and then type **lesson 10** in the text box. Activate the Include All Subfolders option and click Find.

3 In the Content panel. Right-click / Ctrl-click the image 10_04.psd and choose Open With > Adobe Photoshop Elements 8 from the context menu.

4 In Photoshop Elements, choose Window > Reset Panels or click the Reset Panels button at the top of the workspace. Hide the Project Bin and collapse the Effects panel by clicking their header bars.

Preparing a working copy of the image file

The first thing you need to do is to set up a work file with a duplicate layer.

1 Choose File > Save As. Name the new image **10_04_Repair**, to be saved to your My CIB Work folder in Photoshop (PSD) format. On Windows, disable the option Save In Version Set With Original.

2 Click Save.

3 Make a duplicate of the Background layer by doing one of the following:

- Choose Layer > Duplicate Layer.
- Choose Duplicate Layer from the Layers panel Options menu.
- Right-click / Ctrl-click the Background layer in the Layers panel and choose Duplicate Layer from the context menu.

4 In the Duplicate Layer dialog box, click OK to accept the default name: Background copy.

5 Click the Arrange button at the top of the workspace, and then click the Consolidate All button at the upper left of the Arrange menu to dock the floating image window in the Edit pane.

6 Choose Window > Navigator, and then arrange your workspace as shown in the illustration below by dragging the divider bar at the top of the Navigator panel upwards to make the preview as large as possible without losing sight of the two layers in the Layers panel.

You could also work with your image window and panels floating, but as you'll need to move around the image at high magnification this arrangement might be the most convenient.

Using the Clone Stamp tool to fill in missing areas

The first thing you'll do is to eliminate the creases using the Clone Stamp tool. The Clone Stamp tool paints with information sampled from another part of the image, which is perfect for both covering unwanted objects and replacing missing detail, as you'll be doing for the worn areas along the creases.

1   With the help of the Navigator panel or the Zoom tool, zoom in on the crease in the lower right corner.

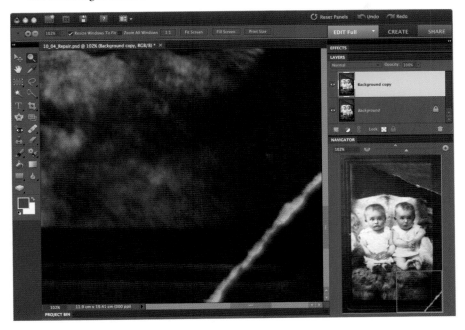

2   In the toolbox, select the Clone Stamp tool (🔨), which is grouped with the Pattern Stamp tool.

3   Click the triangle on the left end of the tool options bar and choose Reset Tool from the menu.

The Reset Tool command reinstates the default values for the Clone Stamp tool: Size: 21 px, Mode: Normal, Opacity: 100%, with the Aligned option activated.

4 In the tool options bar, open the Brush Picker. Choose Basic Brushes from the Brushes menu, and then select a hard mechanical brush with the size of 48 pixels. Set the Mode to Normal, the Opacity to 100%, and activate Aligned.

5 Move the Clone Stamp tool to the left of the crease at the bottom of the picture. Hold down the Alt / Option key and click to set the source point—the area to be sampled. Centering the source on a horizontal line makes it easier to align the brush for cloning. The tool duplicates the pixels from this point in your image as you paint elsewhere.

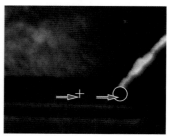

● **Note:** If necessary, you can reset the sample source at any time as you work by Alt / Option-clicking in a different location.

6 Position the brush over the damaged area so that it is aligned horizontally with the source reference point. Click and drag to the right over the crease to copy the source image over the damaged area. As you drag, cross-hairs appear, indicating the source—that is, the area that the Clone Stamp tool is sampling.

7 To repair the upper part of the crease, set the source position in the area above the crease and drag downwards. This will help you blend the repair with the vertical edges of the photograph's mount.

8 Continue to drag the brush over the creased, damaged area, resetting the source position as necessary, until the repair is complete.

The cross-hairs follow the movement of the brush. With the Aligned option activated in the tool options bar, the cross-hairs maintain the same position relative to the brush that was established when you made the first brush stroke. When the Aligned option is disabled, the cross-hairs return to their original position at the beginning of each new stroke, regardless of where it is made.

9 Now you'll smooth out the fold across the upper right corner. For this operation the Healing Brush tool () is the best choice, because the fold is quite severe and has caused significant variations in the background color as well as surface damage. The Healing brush set to a small brush size is also the right tool to deal with the large white speck on the ear of the baby on the right.

10 Choose File > Save to save your changes.

Using the Selection Brush tool

The next step in restoring this photo is to use the Dust & Scratches filter to remove the stray spots and scuffed edges from the scanned image. This filter smooths the pixels by blurring the image just slightly. This is fine for the background, but our subjects—the children—should be kept as detailed and sharp as possible. To do that, you'll need to create a selection that includes only the areas you want to blur. This is where the Selection Brush tool comes in very handy.

1 Select the Selection Brush tool ( ), grouped with the Quick Selection tool in the toolbox. Be careful not to select a painting brush tool by mistake.

2 In the tool options bar, select a round brush shape and set the brush size to about 60 px (pixels). Leave the other options at the default values: Mode should be set to Selection and Hardness should be set to 100%.

Tip: You can make a selection with the Quick Selection tool faster than is possible using the Selection Brush; however, the Quick Selection tool makes a selection based on similarities in color and texture automatically—giving you less control—so it's more effective in some cases than in others.

3 Drag the Selection Brush around the edges of the photograph first, and then work your way inward. Decrease or increase the brush size as needed, using the left and right bracket keys ([,]) on your keyboard, as you paint the selection to include everything but the children. Don't worry if some of your strokes overlap on the babies; you'll learn how to refine the selection in the next exercise.

4 Choose Select > Save Selection.

5 Type **Backdrop** as the name of the saved selection and click OK to close the Save Selection dialog box.

Painting with the Selection Brush tool is an very intuitive way to create a complex selection. In images like this one, where there are no distinct color blocks, few sharp boundaries between pictured items and few crisp geometric shapes, the Selection Brush tool is especially useful.

Another advantage of the Selection Brush tool is that it is very forgiving. You can hold down the Alt / Option key as you paint to remove an area from a selection. Alternatively, you can use the Selection Brush in Mask mode—another intuitive and natural-feeling way to refine the selection—as you'll do in the next exercise.

What is a mask?

A mask is simply the opposite of a selection. A selection is a defined area that you can modify; everything outside the selection is unaffected by the changes you make. A mask protects an area from changes, just like the solid areas of a stencil or the masking tape you'd put on window glass at home before you paint the frame.

Another difference between a mask and a selection is the way Photoshop Elements presents them visually. You're familiar with the flashing black and white dashed outline that indicates a selection marquee. A mask appears as a colored, semi-transparent overlay on the image. You can change the color and opacity of the mask overlay to make sure it contrasts with the image you're working on, or to see more of the detail hidden beneath it. The overlay color and opacity settings are accessible in the tool options bar when the Selection Brush tool is set to operate in Mask mode.

Refining a saved selection

As you progress through this book, you're gathering lots of experience with saving selections. In this procedure, you'll amend a saved selection and replace it with your improved version.

1 Make sure that your Backdrop selection is still active in the image window. If it's not still active, choose Select > Load Selection, choose the saved selection, and then click OK.

2 Make sure the Selection Brush tool ( ) is still selected in the toolbox.

3 In the tool options bar, select Mask from the brush Mode menu. You can see the mask as a semi-transparent colored overlay on the un-selected—or protected—areas of the image. In this mode, the Selection Brush tool paints a mask rather than a selection.

4 Examine the image, looking for unmasked areas with details that should be protected (places where the Selection Brush strokes overlapped onto the children) and parts of the backdrop that are masked and should not be.

Use the Navigator panel slider or the Zoom tool ( ) to adjust your view of the image, as necessary.

5 Reduce the brush size for the Selection Brush to about 30 pixels, and then paint out any areas that you want to mask. Press the Alt key while painting to erase part of the mask.

6 Switch back and forth between Selection and Mask modes, making corrections until you are satisfied with the selection (or the mask, if you like). Your goal is to make sure that fine details you want to preserve are masked.

7 Choose Select > Save Selection. In the Save Selection dialog box, choose Backdrop from the Selection menu. Under Operation, activate the Replace Selection option and click OK.

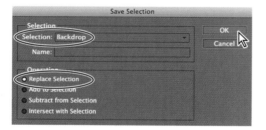

8 While the Selection Brush tool is still active, make sure that the Selection mode—not the Mask mode—is active in the Mode menu in the tool options bar. Keep the selection active for the next procedure.

Filtering flaws out of the backdrop area

Now that you've made your selection, you're ready to apply the filter that will soften the selected areas, reducing the tiny scratches and dust specks in the background of the image.

1 If the Backdrop selection is no longer active, choose Select > Load Selection and choose Backdrop before you click OK to close the dialog box.

2 Choose Filter > Noise > Dust & Scratches.

3 In the Dust & Scratches dialog box, make sure that Preview is selected, and then drag the Radius slider to 6 pixels and the Threshold slider to 10 levels. Move the dialog box so that you can see most of the image window, but don't close it yet.

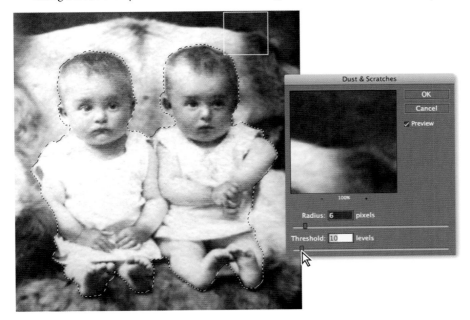

4 Examine the results in the image window. The scuffed edges of the image should be softened and the stray dust and tiny scratches eliminated. Move the cursor inside the magnified preview in the Dust & Scratches dialog box and drag with the hand tool to change the area of the image that is displayed.

5 Make adjustments to the Radius and Threshold values until you are satisfied with the results, and then click OK to close the Dust & Scratches dialog box.

6 Choose Select > Deselect, and then choose File > Save to save your work.

The Dust & Scratches filter does a good job of clearing away spots created by flaws on the negative or scan, without affecting the un-selected—or masked—areas.

Adding definition with the Smart Brush

The Smart Brush provides a quick and easy way to apply an adjustment to just part of a photo. Unfortunately, like the Quick Selection tool, the Smart Brush makes its selection based on similarities in color and texture in an image, which makes it a little difficult to use on an image such as our example. However, you have already spent time with the Selection Brush to create a selection that will isolate the subjects of the photo from the background; for this exercise you can use that saved selection to quickly tidy up any effect from the Smart brush that extends outside the area you intend to adjust.

1 In the Layers panel, select the layer Background copy and choose Layer > Duplicate Layer. In the Duplicate Layer dialog box, click OK to accept the default name for the new layer: Background copy 2.

2 Select the Smart Brush tool (🖌) in the toolbox. The floating Smart Paint panel appears. If the panel does not appear, you can open it by clicking the colored thumbnail in the tool options bar. Drag the Smart Paint panel aside so that you can see the two babies in the Edit window.

3 From the categories menu at the top of the Smart Paint panel, choose Lighting, and then select Darker from the list of Smart Paint adjustments.

4 In the tool options bar, open the Brush Picker and set the brush Diameter to 30 px and the Hardness to 75%.

5 Make sure the layer Background copy 2 is selected. With the Smart Brush, paint over the face of the baby on the left and over the arms and legs of both babies. You can hold down the Alt key as you paint to remove areas from the selection. Don't worry about the selection spilling over onto the background, but try to exclude the babies' clothes.

6 Choose Select > Deselect Layers to make the adjustment inactive.

7 From the categories menu at the top of the Smart Paint panel, choose Portrait, and then select Details from the list of Smart Paint adjustments.

8 With the Smart Brush, paint completely over both babies and their clothes. This time you can be even more casual with your brushwork; don't worry at all if the effect spills over onto the background—you'll tidy it up in a moment.

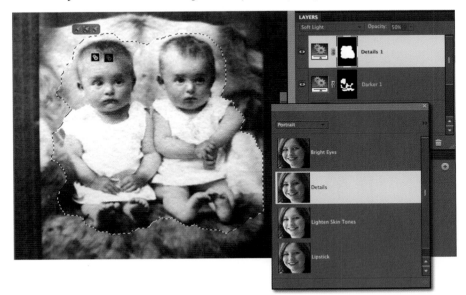

9 Choose Select > Deselect Layers to make the adjustment inactive and close the floating Smart Paint adjustments panel.

Merging layers

You'll now merge the two Smart Brush adjustment layers with the layer Background copy 2 beneath them.

1 In the Layers panel, Ctrl-click to select the top three layers: Background copy 2, Darker 1, and Details 1.

2 Choose Layer > Merge Layers. The three selected layers are merged into one. The new merged layer takes its name from the layer that was on top in the stacking order: Details 1. The Smart Brush adjustments are no longer "live" or able to be edited.

3 Make sure the new merged layer is still active in the Layers panel and choose Select > Load Selection.

4 In the Load Selection dialog box, choose the saved selection Backdrop from the Selection menu, and then click OK.

5 Choose Edit > Delete, and then Select > Deselect. The background is removed from around the two babies in the merged layer Details 1.

6 To see the effects of your Smart Brush adjustments, toggle the visibility of the layer Details 1 by clicking the eye icon beside its name in the Layers panel.

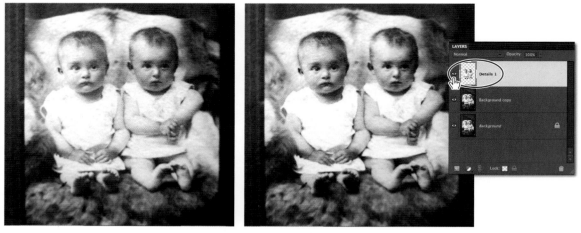

7 In the Layers panel, Ctrl-click to select the top two layers: Background copy and Details 1.

8 Choose Layer > Merge Layers. The two selected layers are merged into one. The new merged layer takes its name from the layer that was on top in the stacking order: Details 1.

Finishing up the project

Compared to the original condition of the photograph, the image is already vastly improved, but if you're in a perfectionist mood you can fix just a few more areas before saving your work.

1 Use the Zoom and Hand tools—or the Navigator panel—to examine the entire image, looking for dark or light flecks created by dust on the negative or the ravages of time, especially in the dark areas of the photograph.

2 In the toolbox, select the Blur tool ( ) and type **40 px** as the brush Size in the tool options bar.

3 Click or drag the tool over any dust spots you find, to blend them into the surrounding area.

4 Use the Clone Stamp tool to remove the pink smudge from the dress of the baby on the right and the Healing Brush to remove the black mark on the calf of the child on the left.

5 Choose File > Save, and then close the file.

Original   Retouched

Congratulations, you've finished this lesson on recomposing, repairing and retouching images. You've explored a variety of techniques for fixing visual flaws in your photos, from straightening an image to smoothing wrinkles from skin. You sampled one area of an image to repair another with both the Clone Stamp and the Healing Brush and worked with selections and masks. You learned how to reset a tool to its default settings and worked more with layers and the Smart Brush. You also learned how to crop an image from the inside, rearranging its composition and altering its proportions without trimming away important elements.

Take a moment to review the lesson by reading through the review on the next page before you move on to chapter 11, "Working with Text."

Review questions

1 What is the purpose of the Recompose brushes and erasers that appear in the tool options bar when you select the Recompose tool?

2 How can you quickly undo a whole series of edit steps at once?

3 What are the similarities and differences between the Healing Brush tool and the Spot Healing Brush tool for retouching photos?

4 Why was it necessary to make a selection before applying the Dust & Scratches filter to restore our damaged photograph?

5 What is the difference between a selection and a mask?

Review answers

1 The green Mark For Protection brush enables you to define areas in the image that you want protected from any scaling operation. The red Mark For Removal brush is used to define any areas that you wish the Recompose tool to remove from the image; great for taking extraneous objects out of an image. The Recompose tool will cut those areas marked for removal before compressing other areas. Each of the Recompose brushes has its own associated eraser.

2 Use the Undo History panel to quickly undo a series of steps at once. Every action performed on the file is recorded in chronological order in the Undo History panel. To restore the file to an earlier state, simply select an earlier action—higher in the list—in the Undo History panel. If you change your mind before making further changes to the file, you can still restore the image to a later state by selecting a step lower in the list.

3 Both the Healing Brush tool and the Spot Healing Brush tool blend pixels from one part of an image into another. The Spot Healing Brush tool, especially with the Proximity Match option selected, enables you to remove blemishes more quickly than does the Healing Brush, because it only involves clicking and/or dragging on an imperfection to smooth it. The Healing Brush can be customized, and requires that you Alt-click to establish a source reference area.

4 The Dust & Scratches filter smooths out pixels in an image by blurring them slightly, effectively putting detail slightly out of focus. It was necessary to create a selection so that only the background was blurred, preserving sharpness and detail in the subjects.

5   A mask is simply the opposite of a selection. A selection is an active area to which adjustments can be applied; everything outside the selection is unaffected by any changes that are made. A mask protects an area from changes. Another difference between a mask and a selection is the way Photoshop Elements presents them visually. A selection marquee is indicated by a flashing border of black and white dashes, whereas a mask appears as a colored, semi-transparent overlay on the image. You can change the color and opacity of the mask overlay using the Overlay Color options that appear in the tool options bar when the Selection Brush tool is set to operate in Mask mode.

11 WORKING WITH TEXT

Lesson Overview

Adding text messages to your photos is another way to make your images and compositions even more memorable and personal.

Whether you want to add straightforward classic typography, or use effects, masks, and transparencies to make your text a striking design element in its own right, Photoshop Elements has all the right tools to make the job easy.

In this lesson you'll learn the skills and techniques you need to work with text in Photoshop Elements:

- Working with the canvas

- Adding a border to an image

- Formatting and editing text

- Overlaying text on an image

- Applying effects and Layer Styles

- Hiding, revealing, merging and deleting layers

- Copying a text layer from one image to another

- Working with multiple image windows

- Warping text

- Creating a type mask

 You'll probably need between one and two hours to complete this lesson.

Photoshop Elements provides you with the tools you'll need to add crisp, flexible, and editable type to your pictures. Whether you want classic typography or wild effects and wacky colors, it's all possible in Photoshop Elements. Apply effects and layer styles to make your text really stand out or blend it into your image using transparency. Create a type mask and fill your text with any image you can imagine.

Getting started

Before you start working on the exercises in this lesson, make sure that you have installed the software on your computer from the application CD (see the Photoshop Elements 8 documentation) and that you have correctly copied the Lessons folder from the CD in the back of this book onto your computer's hard disk. (See "Copying the Classroom in a Book files" on page 2.)

This lesson assumes that you are already familiar with the main features of the Photoshop Elements workspace. Should you need to brush up on the basic concepts review "Getting Started" and "A Quick Tour of Photoshop Elements" at the start of this book, or refer to Photoshop Elements Help.

This lesson includes several projects, each of which builds on the skills learned in the previous exercises.

Placing text on an image

The first project involves creating a text layer, and then formatting and arranging text on a photograph. You'll also add a border and a greeting to the photo so it can be printed as a card or even mounted in a picture frame.

The original photograph and the completed project file.

Using a text search to find a file

If you've worked through the previous lessons you're already familiar with locating files by their keyword tags. The image files for this lesson are tagged "Lesson 11" but all of them also have descriptive names, which will make it easy to find just the pictures required for each exercise rather than all the files in your Lesson11 folder. With such a relatively small number of sample images in your Lessons folder these methods may seem like overkill but as your photo library grows you will appreciate having as many options as possible to help find the file you want quickly and easily.

Searching text on Windows

1   Open Photoshop Elements and click the Organize button in the Welcome screen. When the Organizer has opened, check the name of the currently loaded catalog displayed in the lower left corner of the workspace. If the CIB Catalog is not already loaded, choose File > Catalog and select it from the list in the Catalog Manager.

2   Once the CIB Catalog has loaded, type the letters **ato** in the Text Search box, at the left of the bar above the Media Browser pane.

3   The Media Browser displays a single photo: atomium_belgium.jpg—an image of a family on vacation in Europe. Select the image in the Media Browser, click the small arrow on the orange Fix tab above the Task Pane and choose Full Photo Edit. When the Editor opens you're ready for the first exercise on the next page.

● **Note:** For more detailed information on searching by text in the Organizer, see the section "Find photos using a text search" on page 111 in chapter 4.

Searching text on Mac OS

1   Start Photoshop Elements and click Browse With Adobe Bridge in the Welcome Screen. If Photoshop Elements opens without displaying the Welcome Screen, choose File > Browse With Bridge and wait until Bridge opens.

2   In Bridge, click the link to the PSE8CIB folder in the Favorites panel, or use another method to navigate to the PSE8CIB folder and select it.

3   Click the magnifying glass icon in the Search text box in the top right corner of the workspace and choose Bridge Search: Current Folder from the menu.

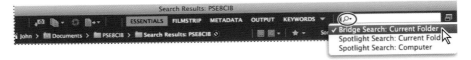

4 Type the letters **ato** in the Search box, and then press Return. The Content panel displays a single image file: atomium_belgium.jpg.

5 Right-click / Ctrl-click the file and choose Open With > Adobe Photoshop Elements 8.

Adding an asymmetrical border

In this exercise you'll enlarge the canvas without increasing the size of the image. By default, the canvas—which is the equivalent of the paper on which a photo is printed—is the same size as the image.

By increasing the size of the canvas without enlarging the image you can effectively add a border. By default, the extended canvas, and therefore the border, takes on the Background color as set in the color swatches at the bottom of the Toolbox.

You'll create the border in two stages in order to make it asymmetrical.

1 Click the double-arrow Collapse To Icons button at the top right of the Panels bin to create more space for the image window.

2 Click the Arrange button at the top of the workspace, and then click the Consolidate All button at the upper left of the Arrange menu.

3 If you don't see a reasonable amount of blank canvas surrounding the image, choose View > Zoom Out or press Ctrl+- (minus) / Command+- (minus).

4 Choose Image > Resize > Canvas Size.

5 Set up the Canvas Size dialog box as shown in the illustration:

- Activate the Relative option.

- Choose Inches from the units menus and type **1** for both the Width and Height of the border.

- Leave the default centered setting for the Anchor control.

6 Click the color swatch beside the Canvas Extension Color menu. A color picker dialog box appears.

7 The pointer becomes an eye-dropper cursor when you move it over the image. Sample a blue from the clearest part of the sky in the image.

8 This color will make a good starting-point for the new border, but we need to make it slightly deeper so that there is some contrast between the image and its frame. Deepen the color by dragging the circular indicator straight downwards a little in the color field, or type in the text box for Brightness (B) to reduce the value from 96% to 75%. You don't want to make the color too dark— below 75% it starts to lose the sunny brightness of the sky and looks a little dull.

9 Click OK to close the Color Picker and again to close the Canvas Size dialog box. The new colored border appears around the photo in the image window.

10 Now you'll extend the border below the image to create a space for the text message. Choose Image > Resize > Canvas Size. In the Canvas Size dialog box, confirm that the Relative check box is still activated.

11 Set the Width value to **0** and the Height to **1.5 inches**. In the Anchor control diagram, click the center square in the top row. Leave the Canvas Extension Color setting unchanged and click OK. If you can't see all of the border framing the image, choose View > Fit On Screen.

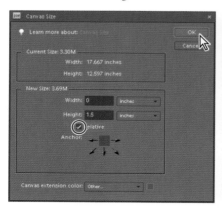 

Adding a quick border

When precision isn't an issue, you can quickly add a border to an image by using the Crop tool, rather than increasing the size of the canvas.

1 Zoom out far enough so that you can see some of the blank art-board surrounding the image in the edit window.

2 Use the crop tool to drag a cropping rectangle right around the image.

3 Drag the corner handles of the crop marquee outside the image area onto the art-board to define the size and shape of border that you wish to create.

4 When you're satisfied, click the Commit button in the lower right corner of the image. The canvas expands to fill the cropping rectangle, taking on the background color set in the color swatch at the bottom of the toolbox.

Adding a text layer

With the Type tools you can place editable type anywhere on your image.

1   In the toolbox, select the Horizontal Type tool (**T**).

2   Set up the tool options bar as shown in the illustration below. Choose Myriad Pro from the Font Family menu, Bold from the Font Style menu, and type **44** pt in the Font Size box. Choose Center Text (▤) from the paragraph alignment options and set the Leading value to 30 pt. Click the triangle beside the color swatch—not the swatch itself—and select white as the text color.

3   Click inside the extended border area below the photo to set the text input cursor, and then type **GREETINGS FROM BELGIUM!** in uppercase. Click the Commit button (✓) in the tool options bar to accept the text. Don't worry about the positioning of the text—you'll adjust that later.

4   Drag the collapsed Layers panel icon to float on top of the image, and then click the header bar to expand it. Notice that in the Layers panel the image has two layers: a locked Background layer containing the image and a text layer containing your greeting. Most of the text layer is transparent, so only the text itself interrupts your view of the Background layer.

● **Note:** Photoshop Elements includes several variants of the Type tool. Throughout the remainder of this lesson, the term Type tool will always refer to the Horizontal Type tool, which is the default variant.

● **Note:** Don't press the Enter or Return keys on the main part of your keyboard to accept text changes. When the Type tool is active, these keys add a line break in the text. Click the Commit button in the tool options bar to accept the text or press the Enter key in the numeric keypad section of your keyboard.

When you use the Type tool, Photoshop Elements automatically creates a new text layer in your image. The type you enter remains active on the text layer, like type in a word processing document—you can edit its content, scale it, reposition it, or change its color at any time.

5   Make sure the text layer is still selected in the Layers panel, and then select the Move tool ( ) in the toolbox.

6   Place the cursor inside the text box and drag to position it so that the message is aligned with the left edge of the photo and is the same distance from the lower edge of the border as it is from the left edge.

7   With the move tool, drag the handle on the upper right corner of the text box to scale the text so that the right side is aligned with the right edge of the photo. You don't need to hold down the Shift key as you drag; the text will be scaled proportionally by default.

8   If necessary, drag the text to adjust its position or use the arrow keys on your keyboard to nudge it into place; then click the Commit button on the text object bounding box.

Editing a text layer

Adding vector-based text is a nondestructive process; your original image is not overwritten by the text. If you save your file in native Photoshop (PSD) format, you can reopen it and move, edit, or delete the text layer without affecting the image.

Using the Type tool is much like typing in a word processing application. If you want to edit the message, select the text and type over it. To change the typeface, font style, size or text color, select the characters you want to change and adjust the settings in the tool options bar accordingly.

1   If necessary, choose View > Zoom In to enlarge the image until you can comfortably read the text you added in the previous exercise.

2   Confirm that the text layer GREETINGS FROM BELGIUM! is still selected in the Layers panel and that the Type tool is still active.

Now you'll change the text color for just part of the message.

3 Swipe to select just the word "GREETINGS" or simply double-click the word, and then click the Text Color swatch in the tool options bar to open the Color Picker. When you move the pointer over the image it becomes an eye-dropper cursor. Use the eye-dropper to sample the boldest color you can find on the sunlit portion of the red hat.

▶ **Tip:** If you need to correct any typing errors or make other changes to text, remember that using the Type tool is like working in a word processing application. Click once to place the insertion point within the text. Use the arrow keys to move the text cursor forward or back. Drag to select multiple characters. Type to add text or to overwrite selected characters. Press the Backspace or Delete key to erase characters. Click the Commit button in the tool options bar to accept any changes.

4 Click the radio button beside the Saturation (S) value in the Color Picker to activate the Saturation controls. The sampled color is a little *too* bold for the background blue, so you can use the slider to reduce the Saturation to 70%, and then click OK.

5 Click the Commit button (✔) in the tool options bar.

6 Swipe to select the exclamation mark (!) at the end of the message, and then click the Text Color swatch in the tool options bar to open the Color Picker. With the eyedropper cursor, sample the color from the word "GREETINGS."

7 Click OK, and then click the Commit button in the tool options bar.

Saving a work file with layers

You can save your work file complete with layers so you can return to it later. As long as you save it in the right format and enable layers, your text and adjustment layers remain "live" and editable.

1 Choose File > Save. The Save As dialog box opens. Navigate to your My CIB Work folder, name the file **atomium_card_work,** and choose Photoshop (PSD) from the Format menu.

2 Under Save Options, confirm that the option Layers is activated. On Windows activate Include In The Organizer and disable Save In Version Set With Original.

3 Review your settings and click the Save button. If the Photoshop Elements Format Options dialog box appears, keep Maximize Compatibility selected and click OK.

4 Choose File > Close.

Bravo, you've finished your first text project. In this section, you've formatted and edited text, and worked with a text layer. You've also created a photo border by increasing the canvas size without enlarging the image itself and gained experience with using the color picker.

Distinguishing between pixel-based and vector graphics

Computer graphics can be divided into two types: pixel-based images (otherwise called bit-mapped, or raster images), which are primarily created by cameras and scanners, and vector images—graphics constructed with drawing programs.

Pixel-based images such as photos are made up of pixels that you can detect when you zoom in. To produce a medium quality print of a photo, you need to make sure that the file is at least 250 ppi (pixels per inch). For viewing on screen, 72 ppi is fine.

Vector images consist of artwork formed from paths, like a technical line drawing. Vectors may form the outlines of an illustration, a logo, or type. The big advantage of vector images over pixel-based images is that they can be enlarged or reduced by any factor without losing detail. Live type on a text layer has this advantage.

Pixel-based image   Vector type   Rasterized type

Overlaying text on an image

In the last exercise, you preserved the layering of your work file by saving in a file format that supports layers. This gives you the flexibility to make changes to the images, text, and effects even after the file has been saved, without needing to rebuild the image from the beginning or modify the original. Your layers have kept the text and effects separate from the image itself.

In this project, you'll do what many professional photographers and studios sometimes do to protect proprietary images: stamp a copyright notice over the photos. You'll apply a style to a text layer so that it appears as if the type is set in clear glass overlaid on the images.

About type

A font is a collection of characters—letters, numerals, punctuation marks, and symbols—in a particular typeface, which share design characteristics such as size, weight, and style. A typeface family is a collection of similar fonts designed to be used together. One example is the Myriad typeface family, which is a collection of fonts in a number of styles including Regular, Bold, Italic, Condensed and other variations. Other typeface families might consist of different font style variations.

Font family
Myriad Pro
Font style
Regular, **Bold**, *Italic*, Condensed

Times New Roman
Regular, **Bold**, *Italic*

Traditionally, font sizes are measured in points, but can also be specified in millimeters or inches, as with large lettering on signs, for example. The most common formats for computer fonts are Type 1 PostScript, TrueType, and OpenType.

Each font conveys a feeling or mood. Some are playful or amusing, some are serious and businesslike, while others might convey an impression of elegance and sophistication. To get a feel for which typeface best suits your project, it's a good idea to try out several fonts. One way to find out more about type is to go to www.adobe.com/type. Adobe Type offers more than 2,200 fonts from the world's leading type designers, which you can browse by categories such as style, use, theme, classification, and designer. This will make it easy to find the perfect font for any assignment. You can even type in your sample copy and compare different fonts.

Creating a new document for the text

You'll start by preparing the text in its own file. In this procedure, you'll see a gray-and-white checkerboard pattern. This pattern indicates 100% transparency, where an area or complete layer acts like a pane of clear glass onto which you can place text or graphics.

1 Do one of the following:

- **On Windows** If Photoshop Elements is not already running, start it now; then open the Organizer and make sure your CIB Catalog is loaded. You should be in the Editor in Full Edit mode for this exercise.

- **On Mac OS** If Photoshop Elements is not already running, start it now; you should be in Full Edit mode for this exercise.

2 Choose Window > Reset Panels or click the Reset Panels button at the top of the workspace.

3 Choose File > New > Blank File. In the New dialog box, name the file **Overlay**. Type **600** for both the Width and Height values and choose Pixels from both units menus.

4 Set the file Resolution to **72** pixels/inch, the Color Mode to RGB Color, and the Background Contents to Transparent. Click OK.

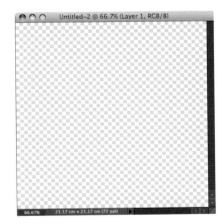

The image window should show only a checkerboard pattern. If it doesn't, choose Edit > Undo and repeat the last two steps, being careful to select Transparent from the Background Contents menu. If you still don't see a checkerboard pattern, check your preferences; choose Preferences > Transparency from the Edit menu on Windows / Photoshop Elements menu on Mac OS. The checkerboard pattern represents the background transparency you specified when creating the file.

5   Select the Type tool (**T**), and then set up the tool options bar as shown in the illustration below. Choose Arial from the Font Family menu, choose Bold from the Font Style menu, and type **120** pt in the Font Size box. Choose Centered for the paragraph alignment. Click the triangle beside the color swatch—not the swatch itself—and choose black as the text color. Make sure that Leading (to the left of the color swatch) is set to Auto.

6   Click near the center of the image window and type **copyright** ; then press Enter / Return and type **2010**. Click the green Commit button (✔) in the tool options bar to accept the text you typed.

7   Select the Move tool (▸⊕) in the toolbox and move the pointer outside a corner of the text bounding box. When the pointer changes to the curved double-arrow rotate cursor, drag the text counter-clockwise to rotate it around its center by 45°. Hold down the Shift key as you drag to constrain the rotation to 15° increments.

8   Drag the text to the lower right of the square image as shown in the illustration below, and then click the Commit button near the edge of the bounding box.

Note: You can scale or reshape the text by dragging the handles on the bounding box with the Move tool. Because Photoshop Elements treats text as vector shapes, the letter shapes remain smooth even if you enlarge the text. If you tried this with bit-mapped text, you'd see jagged, stair-step edges in the enlarged text.

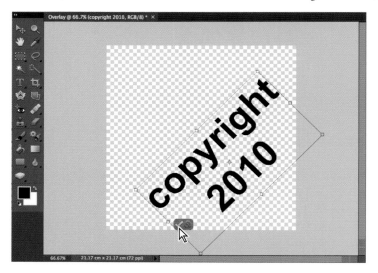

Applying a Layer Style to a text layer

Next, you'll apply an effect to your text by adding a Layer Style. Layer Styles are combinations of several adjustments that can be applied to your text layer in one easy action. Photoshop Elements gives you a wide variety of choices, from bevels and drop shadows to imaginative chrome and neon effects.

1. Make sure the text layer is still selected. At the top of the Effects panel in the Panel Bin, Click the Layer Styles button (<img>), and then choose the second to last category in the effects categories menu, Wow Plastic.

2. In the top row of the Effects panel, select the Wow Plastic Clear effect and click Apply. You could also apply the effect to the selected text layer by double-clicking the swatch, or even by dragging the effect swatch directly onto your text.

When you apply a Layer Style to a text layer, both the text and the effect remain editable. You could go back and change the year of the copyright in the text layer without affecting the layer style, or double-click the *fx* icon on the text layer and edit, replace, or remove the effect without affecting your ability to edit the text.

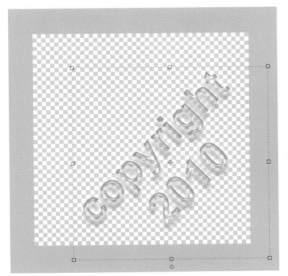

3. Choose File > Save and save the file to your My CIB Work folder in Photoshop (PSD) format, making sure you activate the Layers option. Click Save. If the Photoshop Elements Format Options dialog box appears, keep Maximize Compatibility selected, and then click OK. Keep the file open.

Note: On Windows, always disable the Save In Version Set option for the files you create in these exercises.

Now that you've prepared the copyright text, you'll place it onto a series of images.

Locating the lesson files on Windows

1 In the Organizer—with your CIB Catalog loaded—type the wort **art** in the Text Search box, at the left of the bar above the Media Browser pane.

2 The Media Browser displays four images: kat_art_1.jpg to kat_art_4.jpg photos of details from paintings. Select all four images, and then click the small arrow on the orange Fix tab and choose Full Photo Edit. When the Editor opens you're ready for the first exercise on the next page.

Locating the lesson files on Mac OS

1 Click the Launch Bridge button at the top of the workspace or choose File > Browse With Bridge.

2 In Bridge, click the link to your PSE8CIB folder in the Favorites panel, or use another method to navigate to the PSE8CIB folder and select it.

3 Click the magnifying glass icon in the search text box in the top right corner of the workspace and choose Bridge Search: Current Folder from the menu.

4 Type the word **art** in the search text box, and then press Return. The Content panel displays four images: kat_art_1.jpg to kat_art_4.jpg.

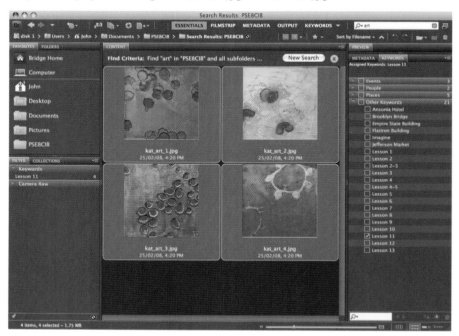

5 Select all four images, and then right-click / Control-click any one of the thumbnails and choose Open With > Adobe Photoshop Elements 8.

Adding text to multiple images

A great advantage of text layers is that they can be copied from one image to another, making it easy to add text to a number of images at the same time.

1 Make sure you have the Project Bin open. Collapse the Effects panel by clicking its header bar, and then choose Window > Images > Tile.

2 Click the title bar of the file Overlay.psd, or make it the active window by double-clicking its thumbnail in the Project Bin. Press Ctrl+- (minus sign) / Command+- (minus sign) repeatedly until you can see the entire image.

3 Choose Window > Images > Match Zoom or choose the same command from the menu on the Arrange button (⊞) at the top of the workspace. The view in all of the open image windows is matched to the active image.

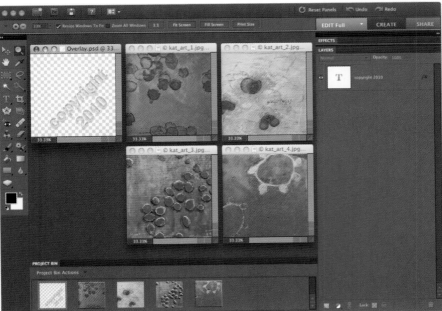

In the Layers panel, you can see that the active image, Overlay.psd, has only one layer: the text layer that you created in the last exercise.

4 In the Project Bin, double-click each of the other thumbnail images in turn; each has a single layer named "Background."

5 Make Overlay.psd the active image once more; then hold down the Shift key and drag the text layer from the Layers panel onto the image kat_art_1.jpg.

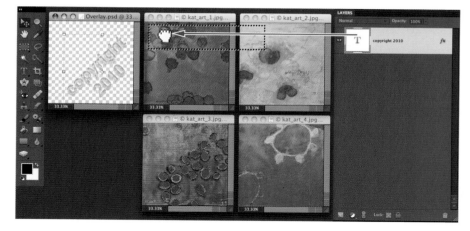

Note: Holding down the Shift key as you drag a text layer to another file ensures that the text will appear in the same position in the target file as it occupies in the source.

6 To make the new text layer more transparent, reduce its opacity to 33%, either by typing **33** into the Opacity value box, or by dragging the slider to the left.

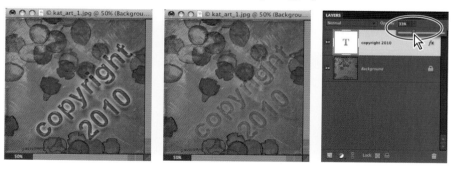

7 Make sure that the image kat_art_1.jpg is still the active file. In the Layers panel, double-click the *fx* icon on the text layer. The Style Settings dialog box appears.

8 In the Style Settings dialog box, you need to change only one setting. In the Glow options, change the size of the Outer Glow from 22 pixels to 10 pixels. Click OK to close the Style Settings dialog box.

9 Hold down the Shift key and drag the copyright 2010 text layer with its refined layer style from the image kat_art_1.jpg onto the other three images. Zoom in to each image and use the Move tool to position the message as you wish for each image independently. The text looks less visible against some of the images than it does on the first; tweak the Opacity value for the text layer on each of the other images accordingly. We set a value of 65% for the copyright message on the green painting.

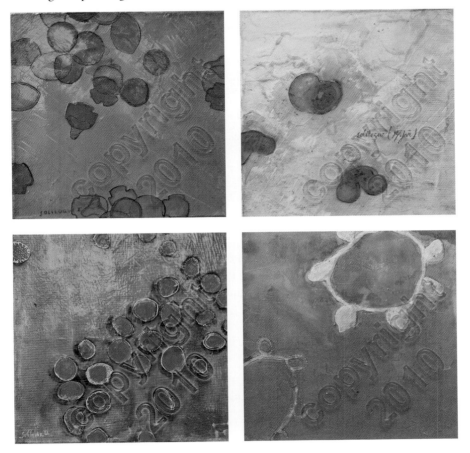

10 Choose File > Close All. If you wish, you can save your efforts to your My CIB Work folder. If you do save the files, be sure to activate the Layers option for the Photoshop (PSD) format so that the layers in the files are preserved.

Done! In this project, you've created a new Photoshop (PSD) format document without an image and added text to that document. You've used the Effects panel to apply a Layer Style to the text layer, copied the text layer to other image files, and edited the layer style and opacity.

Using Layer styles and distortions

In this exercise you'll have more fun with text. You'll distort text and apply effects, all the while keeping the text layer live and editable.

Locating the lesson image on Windows

1   In the Organizer—with your CIB Catalog loaded—type the word **any** in the Text Search box, at the left of the bar above the Media Browser pane.

The Media Browser displays a single image: anything.jpg, a cropped photograph of raindrops on a car window.

2   Click to select the image in the Media Browser, and then click the small arrow on the orange Fix tab and choose Full Photo Edit. When the Editor opens you're ready for the first exercise, which begins on the next page.

Locating the lesson image on Mac OS

1   Click the Launch Bridge button at the top of the workspace or choose File > Browse With Bridge.

2   In Bridge, click the link to your PSE8CIB folder in the Favorites panel, or use another method to navigate to the PSE8CIB folder and select it.

3   Click the magnifying glass icon in the search text box in the top right corner of the workspace and choose Bridge Search: Current Folder from the menu.

4   Type the word **any** in the search text box, and then press Return. The Content panel displays a single image: anything.jpg, a cropped photograph of raindrops on a car window.

5   Right-click / Ctrl-click the image in the Content panel and choose Open With > Adobe Photoshop Elements 8.

Adding a layer style

In the first exercise, you'll add a layer style to give your text a three-dimensional look that will lift it from the background image.

1   Click the Reset Panels button at the top of the workspace, and then choose Window > Images > Consolidate All To Tabs. Alternatively, simply drag the title bar of the image window to the top of the Edit pane and release the mouse when the image dims and a blue line appears around the Edit pane.

2   Select the Type tool (**T**) from the toolbox, and then set up the tool options bar as shown in the illustration below:

   - From the Font Family menu, choose a bold sans-serif style such as Impact (as an alternative, you could choose Arial Black).

   - Type **200** pt in the Font Size box.

   - Choose Centered from the paragraph alignment options.

   - Click the triangle beside the color swatch (not the swatch itself) to open the color panel. For the text color, choose Pastel Green Cyan.

3   Using the Horizontal Type tool, click near the center of the image and type the word **ANYTHING** in upper case.

4   Click the Commit button (✔) in the tool options bar to accept the text.

5   Choose the Move tool (▶✥) in the toolbox and drag the text to center it as shown in the illustration below.

6 Expand the Effects panel and click the Layer Styles button (⬛). Choose the category Bevels from the effects categories menu and double-click the third effect in the second row: Simple Sharp Outer.

The bevel effect, like all the Effects presets, is made up of a combination of image adjustments that are all applied to the image at once. The effect, in this case a Layer Style, remains "live" and editable. In the Layers panel you can double click the *fx* icon on the text layer and make adjustments to the depth of the effect and also change the lighting angle. For now, keep the default settings.

7 In the Layers panel, change the opacity of the text layer to 60%, either by typing the new value directly into the text box or by dragging the Opacity slider.

8 Save the file to your My CIB Work folder. Type the name **anything_text**, choose the Photoshop (PSD) format and make sure the Layers option is activated so that you can edit opacity and effects even after the file has been closed.

Warping text

It's easy to stretch and skew text into unusual shapes using the Photoshop Elements Warp Text effects; the hard part is to avoid *over*using them!

1 Make sure the Type tool is active, and then click anywhere on the text "ANYTHING" in the image window. It's not necessary to highlight the text because warp effects are automatically applied to the entire text layer.

2 In the tool options bar, click the Create Warped Text button (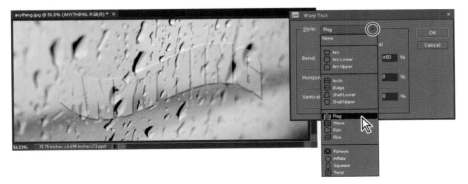) to open the Warp Text dialog box. Choose the Flag effect from the Style menu.

3 The Warp Text dialog offers a number of controls for changing the way the effect is applied. For this exercise, you need only make one adjustment: set the Bend value to **-50**% and click OK to close the Warp Text dialog box.

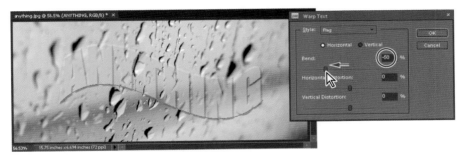

4 The text layer is still editable. You can check this out by dragging to select the word ANYTHING with the Type tool, and then typing **INTERESTING** over it.

5 Choose File > Save.

Creating an un-stylized copy of the text layer

In the next exercise, you'll experiment with an effect that requires your type layer to be simplified, meaning that the vector text will be converted to a bitmap image and will therefore no longer be editable as text. For this purpose you'll create a separate copy of the text layer.

Tip: You can also duplicate a layer by dragging it onto the New Layer button at the bottom of the Layers panel, or by selecting the layer, and then choosing Layer > Duplicate Layer. The Duplicate Layer command is also accessible from the context menu when you right-click / Control-click the layer itself.

1 In the Layers panel, select the text layer. Click the Options menu icon in the upper right corner of the panel to open the Layers panel Options menu. Choose Duplicate Layer. Click OK to accept the default name: INTERESTING copy.

2 Click the eye icon to the left of the original text layer: INTERESTING. The layer becomes invisible in the image window.

3 In the Layers panel, change the opacity of the newly copied layer to 100%. The warped text once more appears as a solid color.

4 Right-click / Control-click on the text layer INTERESTING copy and choose Clear Layer Style from the context menu.

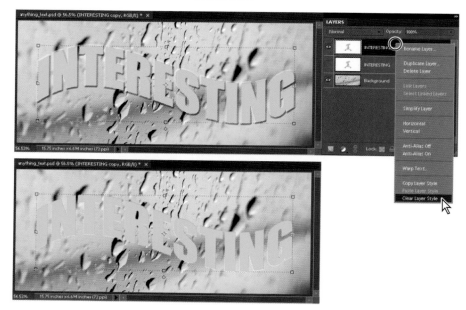

Simplifying text and applying a pattern

You can now add a different look to the copy of the text layer. In preparation, you'll lock the transparent pixels on the text layer, which will enable you to paint on the filled areas in the layer without needing to be careful about the edges.

1 Select the Pattern Stamp tool, which is grouped with the Clone Stamp tool. Set up the tool options as shown in the illustration below: brush Size: **100** px, brush Mode: Normal, Opacity: 100%. Click on the triangle beside the Pattern swatch and choose the Pink Fur pattern.

2 Make sure that the text layer INTERESTING copy is active in the Layers panel, and then click once on the text in the image window with the Pattern Stamp tool. A message appears, asking if you want to simplify the layer. Click OK.

3 In the Layers panel, click the Lock Transparent Pixels button to prevent changes being made to the transparent areas of the simplified layer. Notice that there is now a lock icon displayed on the INTERESTING copy layer.

⬤ Note: Remember that once you simplify a text layer, the text is no longer live—you can no longer edit it with the Type tool. However, you can still change the appearance of the simplified text layer by painting on it as you will do in this exercise, changing the blending mode and opacity, or adding a Layer Style such as a Bevel or Drop Shadow using the Effects panel.

4 Make sure the Pattern Stamp tool is still selected in the toolbox and paint over the text in the image window, applying the pattern as solidly or as unevenly as you like. The pattern is applied only to the simplified text; the locked transparent pixels remain unaffected.

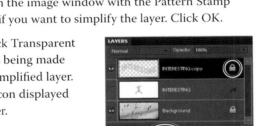

Of course, the pattern is painted only onto the selected layer (the simplified text) and does not affect the Background layer or the text layer that is currently hidden.

Hiding and revealing layers

Toggling the visibility of layers by clicking the eye icons in the Layers panel is a great way to assess different design solutions within one file.

1   In the Layers panel, click the eye icon beside the top text layer, INTERESTING copy, to hide it. The eye icon is hidden also, leaving an empty box to indicate that the layer is not visible. Note that although the layer is selected, the Blending Mode and Opacity options are dimmed and unavailable. You cannot edit a hidden layer.

2   In the Layers panel, click the empty box to the left of the text layer INTERESTING. The eye icon reappears and the warped blue text with the bevelled effect is once more visible in the document window.

Deleting layers and layer styles

You can now delete the layer with the pink fur pattern, leaving just the Background layer with the original image, and the live text layer INTERESTING just above it. Deleting layers that you no longer need reduces the size of your image file.

> **Tip:** You can use this method to delete more than one layer at the same time—just make sure all the layers are visible and selected, and then right-click / Ctrl-click any of them. You can also delete selected layers by choosing Layer > Delete Layer from the main menu bar, by choosing the same command the Layers panel Options menu, or by simply dragging them to the Trash icon at the bottom of the Layers panel.

1   To delete the layer INTERESTING copy, first make sure the layer is visible—look for the eye icon to the left of the layer's name in the Layers panel. Right-click / Ctrl-click the layer and choose Delete Layer from the context menu.

2   In the Layers panel, select the original text layer, INTERESTING. Right-click / Ctrl-click the layer and choose Clear Layer Style from the context menu. Alternatively, choose the same command from the Layer menu or the Layers panel Options menu. The type in text layer no longer has a bevelled effect, but it's still warped.

3   Select the Type tool, and then click the Create Warped Text button in the tool option bar to open the Warp Text dialog box. Choose None from the Style menu, and then click OK to close the Warp Text dialog box.

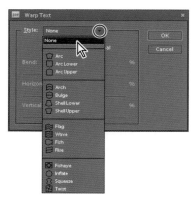

Now you're back to where you began, before applying the bevelled Layer Style and before you added the Flag text warp effect.

4 Choose File > Save, and then choose File > Close.

In this section, you've applied a Layer Style to live text, warped it, and painted it with pink fur. You should be ashamed of yourself! You learned about locking transparent pixels on a layer and how to edit or clear layer styles and text effects. You also learned how to hide, reveal or delete a layer.

Working with paragraph type

With point type, or headline type, each line of type is independent—the line expands or shrinks as you edit it, but it doesn't automatically wrap to the next line. Point type (the name derives from the fact that it is preceded by a single anchor point) is perfect for small blocks of text like headlines, logos, and headings for Web pages. Probably most of the text you add to your images will be of this type.

If you work with larger blocks of type and you want your text to reflow and wrap automatically, it's best to use the paragraph type mode. By clicking and dragging with the type tool you'll create a text bounding box on your image. The bounding box can be easily resized to fit your paragraph text perfectly.

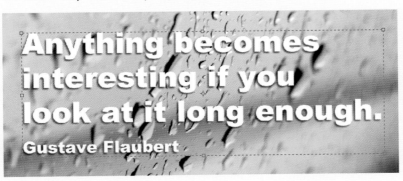

Creating a type mask

You can have a lot of fun with the Type Mask tool. Photoshop Elements offers two variants—one for horizontal type and the other for vertical type. The Type Mask tool turns text outlines into a mask through which an underlying image is visible.

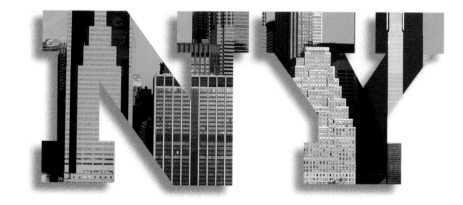

Locating the lesson image on Windows

1 In the Organizer—with your CIB Catalog loaded—type the wort **sky** in the Text Search box, at the left of the bar above the Media Browser pane.

2 The Media Browser displays a single image: ny_skyline.jpg, a photo of part of the New York City skyline. Click to select the image in the Media Browser, and then click the small arrow on the orange Fix tab and choose Full Photo Edit. When the Editor opens you're ready for the first exercise, which begins on the next page.

Locating the lesson image on Mac OS

1 Click the Launch Bridge button at the top of the workspace or choose File > Browse With Bridge.

2 In Bridge, click the link to your PSE8CIB folder in the Favorites panel, or use another method to navigate to the PSE8CIB folder and select it.

3 Click the magnifying glass icon in the search text box in the top right corner of the workspace and choose Bridge Search: Current Folder from the menu.

4 Type the word **sky** in the search text box, and then press Enter / Return. The Content panel displays a single image: ny_skyline.jpg, a photo of part of the New York City skyline.

5 Right-click / Control-click the image in the Content panel and choose Open With > Adobe Photoshop Elements 8.

Working with the Type Mask tool

The Type Mask tool (🌢) enables you to fill letter shapes with parts of an image. This can create a much more interesting graphic effect than plain text filled with a solid color.

1   Drag the title bar of the image window to the top of the Edit pane. Release the mouse button when the image dims and a blue line highlights the Edit pane. Your image is consolidated on a tab in the Edit pane.

2   Select the Horizontal Type Mask tool (🌢) which you'll find grouped with the other type tools in the tool box.

3   Set up the text attributes in the tool options bar. We chose Rockwell Extra Bold from the Font Family menu but if you don't have that font, choose another blocky typeface such as Arial Black. Type a new value of **600** pt for the font Size (you may need to adjust that for a different font). Choose Center Text from the text alignment options. You don't need to worry about the color attributes as the type will be filled with detail from our skyline image.

4   Click at a horizontally centered point near the bottom of the image and type the letters **NY**.

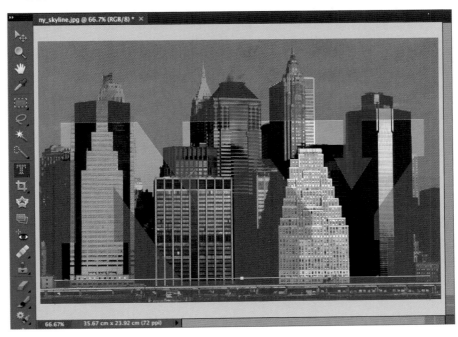

The background pattern of architectural detail shows through the shapes of the letters you typed, while the rest of the picture is masked, as indicated by the semi-transparent red overlay.

5 Hold down the Ctrl / Command key on your keyboard; the text is surrounded by a bounding box. Drag inside the bounding box to reposition the type mask. Hold down the Shift and Ctrl / Command keys together and drag a corner handle on the bounding box to scale the text proportionally.

6 When you're satisfied with the result, click the green Commit button in the tool options bar. The outline of the text becomes an active selection. If you are not happy with the placement of the text, you can use the arrow keys on your keyboard to nudge the selection into place.

7 Choose Edit > Copy, and then Edit > Paste; you'll notice that the new cutout type image has been placed onto a new layer.

8 In the Layers panel, hide the Background layer by clicking the eye icon beside the layer name.

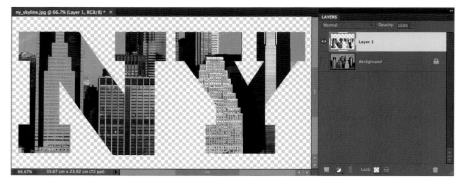

The text is no longer live—the mask was converted to a selection outline and can no longer be edited as type; however, you can still apply a layer style or an effect to enhance it or make it more prominent.

9 Select Layer 1 in the Layers panel to make it the active layer.

10 Expand the Effects panel and click the Layer Styles button (🔲). Select the effects category Drop Shadows from the menu.

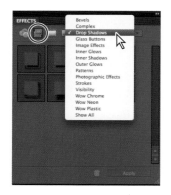

11 In the Drop Shadows panel, double-click the shadow effect named Noisy: the second drop-shadow effect in the second row. Note that on Windows you may find a slightly different set of drop shadow options—try High or Soft Edge and experiment with the effect.

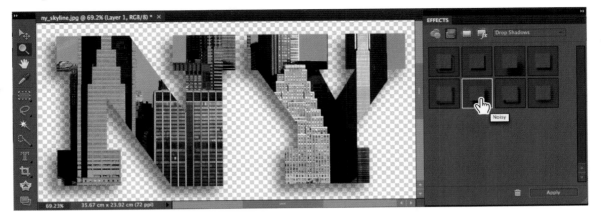

You can tweak the drop shadow effect by double-clicking the *fx* icon on Layer 1 in the Layers panel. The Style Settings dialog box appears, where you can change the angle, distance, color, and opacity of the drop shadow as you wish.

12 Since you no longer need the background layer with the photo of the city skyline, delete it by choosing Flatten Image from the Layers panel Options menu. Click OK in the dialog box that appears to ask whether you want to discard the hidden layer. Alternatively, you could choose Delete hidden Layers from the Layers panel Options menu.

13 Choose File > Save As. In the Save As dialog box, name the file **ny_mask**, choose Photoshop (PSD) as the file format, and save the file to your My CIB Work folder.

Congratulations! You've completed another lesson. You've learned how to format and edit text, and how to work with a text layer. You've created a photo border by working with the document canvas, used the Effects panel to apply Layer Styles, warped and painted text, and created a text mask. You learned about locking transparent pixels on a layer and how to edit and clear layer styles and text effects. You also learned how to hide, reveal and delete a layer. Take a few moments to work through the lesson review on the next page before you move on.

Review questions

1 What is the advantage of having your text on a separate layer?

2 How do you hide a layer without removing it?

3 In the Layers panel, what do the lock buttons do and how do they work?

4 What's the difference between point type and paragraph type?

Review answers

1 Because the text remains separate from the image, Photoshop Elements text layers remain "live"—text can be edited in later work sessions, just as it can in a word processing application.

2 You can hide a layer by clicking the eye icon to the left of the layer's name in the Layers panel. To make the layer visible again, click the empty box where the eye icon should be to restore it.

3 Lock buttons prevent changes to a layer. The Lock All button, which looks like a padlock, locks all the pixels on the selected layer so that the layer is protected from changes. Blending and Opacity options become unavailable. The Lock Transparent Pixels button, which looks like a checkerboard, locks only the transparent pixels on a layer. To remove a lock, select the locked layer and click the active lock icon to toggle it off. (This does not work for the Background layer, which can be unlocked only by renaming and converting it into an ordinary layer.)

4 Point type is ideal for headlines, logos and other small blocks of text where each line is independent and does not wrap to the next line. Paragraph text is used where you want larger amounts of text to wrap automatically to the next line. The size of the paragraph text bounding box can be easily changed to fit the text perfectly to your design.

12 COMBINING MULTIPLE IMAGES

Lesson Overview

Although you can do a lot to improve a photo with tonal adjustments, color corrections and retouching, sometimes the best way to produce the perfect image is simply to fake it!

Photoshop Elements delivers powerful tools that will enable you to do just that by combining multiple images. Merge ordinary scenic photos into stunning panoramas that truly recapture the feel of the location or combine a series of shots to produce the perfect group photo where everybody is smiling and there are no closed eyes. Deal with difficult lighting conditions by blending differently exposed pictures.

In this lesson you'll learn some of the tricks you'll need for combining multiple images to create that perfect shot that you didn't actually get:

- Merging multiple photos into a panorama
- Assembling the perfect group shot
- Removing unwanted elements
- Blending differently exposed photographs
- Combining images using layers
- Resizing and repositioning selections
- Creating a gradient clipping mask
- Defringing a selection

You'll probably need between one and two hours to complete this lesson.

If you're ready to go beyond fixing pictures in conventional ways, this lesson is for you. Why settle for that scenic photo that just doesn't capture the way it really looked? Or that group portrait where Dad's looking away and Mom's eyes are closed? Combine images to produce the perfect shot. Merge photos to make a stunning panorama, remove obstructions from the view, and even get little Jimmy to stop making faces.

Getting started

Before you start working on the exercises in this lesson, make sure that you have installed the software on your computer from the application CD (see the Photoshop Elements 8 documentation) and that you have correctly copied the Lessons folder from the CD in the back of this book onto your computer's hard disk. (See "Copying the Classroom in a Book files" on page 2.)

Locating the lesson files on Windows

While you're working on the projects in this lesson, you'll use sample images from the CIB Catalog that you created in the "Getting Started" section at the beginning of this book:

1 Start Photoshop Elements and click the Organize button in the Welcome Screen. In the Organizer, check the name of the currently active catalog, which is displayed in the lower left corner of the Organizer window. If your CIB Catalog is already open, you can go on to step 3.

2 If your CIB Catalog is not already open, choose File > Catalog; then select the CIB Catalog in the Catalog Manager dialog box and click Open. If you don't see the CIB Catalog file listed, see "Creating a catalog file" on page 3.

3 Click Show All if it's visible above the Media Browser. In the Keyword Tags panel, expand the Imported Keyword Tags category, and then click the find box beside the Lesson 12 tag to isolate the images for the projects in this lesson.

4 If you don't see the filenames below the thumbnails in the Photo Browser, choose View > Show File Names.

Locating the lesson files on Mac OS

For the projects in this lesson, you'll be working with the sample image files in the PSE8CIB > Lessons > Lesson12 folder that you copied to your hard disk in the section "Copying the Classroom in a Book files" at the beginning of this book.

1 Start Photoshop Elements and click Browse With Adobe Bridge in the Welcome Screen. If Photoshop Elements opens without displaying the Welcome Screen, choose File > Browse With Bridge. Wait until Bridge has finished launching.

Note: If you have not yet added the PSE8CIB folder to your Favorites in Bridge, locate the PSE8CIB folder inside your Documents folder and either drag it into the Favorites panel or choose File > Add To Favorites.

2 In Bridge, click your link to the PSE8CIB folder in the Favorites panel. If you don't see the Favorites panel, right-click / Control-click the header of any other panel and choose Favorites Panel from the context menu.

3 Choose Edit > Find or press Command+F on your keyboard. Under Source in the Find dialog box, your PSE8CIB folder is already selected as the Look In folder. Under Criteria, choose Keywords from the first menu, choose Equals from the second menu, and then type lesson 12 in the text box. Activate the Include All Subfolders option and click Find.

Merging photos into a panorama

The images you'll use for this first exercise are two slightly overlapping photos taken at Mont Saint Michel in France. The camera lens used for these shots did not have a wide enough angle to capture the entire scene—a common problem for many of us when taking photos at a scenic location. These pictures provide an ideal opportunity to create a panorama; in the following exercises you'll learn how to have Photoshop Elements do most of the work for you.

1 Do one of the following:

- On **Windows** In the Organizer, Ctrl-click to select the two pictures of Mont Saint Michel (12_01a.jpg and 12_01b.jpg) in the Media Browser, and then choose File > New > Photomerge Panorama.

- On **Mac OS** In Bridge, Command-click to select the two pictures of Mont Saint Michel (12_01a.jpg and 12_01b.jpg) in the Content panel; then choose Tools > Photoshop Elements > Photomerge Panorama.

Photoshop Elements opens the selected files in Full Edit mode and the Photomerge dialog box appears.

You can use more than two files to create a Photomerge Panorama composition. In the Photomerge dialog box you have the option to select individual source files or the entire contents of a specified folder and a choice of layout methods that will affect the way the source images will be stitched together to create your panorama.

2 Under Source Files in the Photomerge dialog box, select Files from the Use menu, and then click the Add Open Files button.

3 Under Layout, select Auto; then click OK.

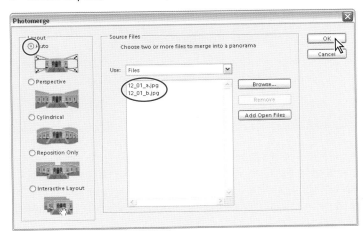

> **Tip:** To add all the photos from a specific folder on your hard disk as source images for a panorama, select Folder from the Use menu, and then click Browse. To remove photos from the selection, select them in the source file list, and then click Remove.

4 Wait while Photoshop Elements creates the panorama and opens it in a new image window.

That's really all there is to it! All that remains is to crop the image and save your work. But first, let's have a closer look at how well Photoshop Elements did merging the two images. Depending on your source files, you may at times notice small problem areas—edge artifacts along the line where the images are blended. In these cases you need to try a different layout option for the photomerge operation.

5 In the Layers panel, click the eye icon () beside the top layer to hide it.

In the edit window, you can now see which part of the image in the lower layer was used to create the panorama. The unused portion is hidden by a layer mask. You can see a black and white thumbnail of the layer mask in the Layers panel; black represents the masked area of the image and white represents the part of the image that has contributed to the panorama.

6 Choose View > Actual Pixels, or zoom in even closer if you wish, and then use the Hand tool to move the image in the edit window so that you can inspect the edge of the layer mask. Click the eye icon (👁) for the top layer repeatedly to hide and reveal that layer while you look for irregularities along the edge between the two images.

Hide the top layer to reveal the edge of the image mask.

Look for pixels along the masked edge of one image that appear misaligned with pixels in the other. Use the Hand tool to inspect the entire edge of the mask.

Show the top layer and check for irregularities along the edge between the two source images.

7 If your inspection does not reveal any problem areas, make the top layer visible and you're ready to crop the picture and save it.

If you do find problems in a merged panorama, close the file without saving it and repeat the procedure, choosing a different layout option in the Photomerge dialog box when you get to step 3.

You'll find a brief summary of the different layout options on the next page. Later in this lesson, the section "Creating a Photomerge Panorama interactively" explains the interactive layout option, which gives you the most control over the way the panorama is put together.

Choosing a Photomerge layout option

Auto Photoshop Elements analyzes the source images and applies either a Perspective or Cylindrical layout, depending on which produces a better photomerge.

Perspective Creates a consistent composition by designating one of the source images (by default, the middle image) as the reference image. The other images are then transformed (repositioned, stretched or skewed as necessary) so that overlapping content across layers is matched.

Cylindrical Reduces the "bow-tie" distortion that can occur with the Perspective layout by displaying individual images as on an unrolled cylinder. Overlapping content across layers is still matched. The reference image is placed at the center. Best suited for creating wide panoramas.

Reposition Only Aligns the layers and matches overlapping content, but does not transform (stretch or skew) any of the source layers.

Interactive Layout Opens the source images in a dialog where you position them manually for the best result (see "Creating a Photomerge Panorama interactively").

—From Photoshop Elements Help

Cropping the merged image

Now you'll use the Crop tool to give the merged image a uniform edge.

1   Choose View > Fit On Screen, and then choose Image > Crop. Drag the handles of the cropping rectangle to make it as large as possible without including any of the checkerboard areas where the image is transparent.

● **Note:** The Crop tool removes those parts of an image that fall outside the adjustable cropping rectangle. Cropping can be very useful for changing the visual focus of a photo. When you crop an image, the resolution remains unchanged.

2 When you're happy with the result, click the Commit button in the lower right corner of the cropping rectangle.

3 Choose File > Save and save the merged image to your My CIB Work folder as **12_01_Work**, in Photoshop (.PSD, .PDD) format, making sure that the Layers option is activated.

Saving your file in Photoshop format preserves the layers, so that you can always return to adjust them if necessary. If you save in JPEG format the image will be flattened and layer information will be lost.

4 Choose File > Close to close the file 12_01_Work.psd, but keep the two source files, 12_01a.jpg and 12_01b.jpg, open, ready for the next exercise.

Cropping ratio options

Though you won't need to do so for this exercise, you can set options for the Crop tool in the tool options bar.

In the Aspect Ratio menu you can choose between several options:

- **No Restriction** lets you crop the image to any proportions.
- **Use Photo Ratio** retains the aspect ratio of the original photo.
- The menu also offers a range of **preset sizes** for your cropped photo, should you want your final output to fit a particular layout or a favorite picture frame.

The Width and Height fields enable you to specify custom dimensions that are not available from the Aspect Ratio menu. Type in the Resolution value box to specify a new resolution for the cropped image in pixels per inch or per centimeter.

Creating a Photomerge Panorama interactively

The automatic layout options in the Photomerge dialog box usually do a good job, but if you need manual control over the way source images are combined to create a panorama, choose the Interactive Layout option in the Photomerge dialog box.

1 With the original images 12_01a.jpg and 12_01b.jpg still open, choose File > New > Photomerge Panorama.

2 In the Photomerge dialog box, select Files from the Use menu, and then click the Add Open Files button. Choose Interactive Layout from the Layout options; then click OK.

3 Explore the tools and controls in the Photomerge dialog box:

- Use the Zoom tool (🔍) or the Navigator controls to zoom in or out of the image. Drag the red rectangle in the Navigator to shift the view in the zoomed image.

- Switch between the Reposition Only and Perspective settings.

- With the Perspective option activated, you can click any source image in the Photomerge workspace with the Set Vanishing Point tool (✂) to set the vanishing point in that image as the reference around which the other images will be composed.

● **Note:** If the composition can't be assembled automatically, a message will appear on screen. You can then assemble the panorama manually in the Photomerge dialog box by dragging images from the photo bin into the work area, and arranging them as you wish.

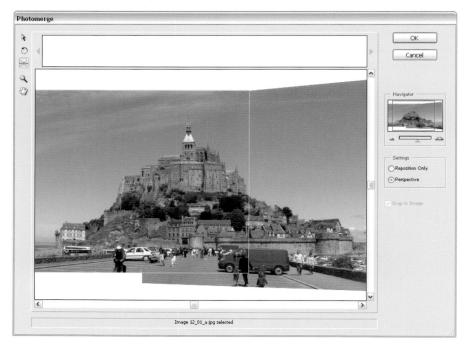

- Use the Select Image tool ( ) to select any of the photos in the work area; then drag the selected photo or use the arrow keys on the keyboard to reposition it as desired.

- To remove a photo from the composition (if you are using more than two source images), drag it from the work area into the photo bin above. To add an image to the composition, drag it from the photo bin into the work area.

- Use the Rotate Image tool ( ) to rotate a selected photo.

4 When you're satisfied with the result, click OK. The Photomerge dialog box closes, and Photoshop Elements goes to work. You'll see windows open and close as you wait for Photoshop Elements to create the panorama.

5 If you like your new composition better than the one you created in the previous exercise, crop the image and save your work in the My CIB Work folder.

6 Choose File > Close All to close all open windows. When asked whether you want to save your changes, click No.

Vanishing point

A vanishing point is the point at which receding parallel lines seem to meet when seen in perspective. For example, as a road stretches out ahead of you, it appears to grow narrower with distance, until it has almost no width at the horizon. This is the vanishing point.

You can change the perspective of the Photomerge Panorama composition by specifying a different image to be used as reference for the vanishing point. Select Perspective under Settings in the Photomerge dialog box, and then click an image with the Vanishing Point tool. Photoshop Elements analyzes the image and composes the Photomerge Panorama in reference to the vanishing point in that image.

Creating a composite group shot

Shooting the perfect group photo is a difficult task, especially if you have a large family of squirmy kids. Fortunately, Photoshop Elements offers a solution: a powerful photo blending tool called Photomerge Group Shot. The next exercise will show you how multiple photos can be blended together into one with amazing precision.

Setting up on Windows

1   If you're still in the Editor from the last exercise, switch to the Organizer now by clicking the Organizer button (⊞) at the top right of the Editor window, and then go on to step 2. If you're beginning a new session, start Photoshop Elements, click the Organize button in the Welcome screen, and then make sure your CIB Catalog is active.

2   In the Organizer, click the Find box beside the Lesson 12 tag in the Keyword Tags panel, and then Ctrl-click to select the three images of a girl in a pink dress: 12_02a.jpg, 12_02b.jpg and 12_02c.jpg.

Now you're ready to begin the exercise which starts at the bottom of the page.

Setting up on Mac OS

1   Start Photoshop Elements if it's not already running.

2   Click Browse With Adobe Bridge in the Welcome Screen or chose File > Browse With Bridge.

3   If you still have the lesson 12 files isolated in the Content panel, you can go on to step 4; otherwise, once Bridge opens choose Edit > Find or press Command+F on your keyboard. In the Find dialog box choose Browse from the Look In menu and locate your PSE8CIB folder. Under Criteria, choose Keywords from the first menu, choose Equals from the second menu, and then type **lesson 12** in the text box. Activate the Include All Subfolders option and click Find.

4   In the Bridge Content panel, Command-click to select the three images of a girl in a pink dress: 12_02a.jpg, 12_02b.jpg and 12_02c.jpg.

Working with Photomerge Group Shot

No longer do you need to put up with family photos where someone has their eyes closed, someone else has looked away at the wrong moment, and you-know-who has just made an even odder facial expression than usual.

Photomerge Group Shot lets you merge the best parts of several images into the perfect group photo.

Typically, you would use the Photomerge Group Shot feature to create a merged image from a series of very similar source images such as you might capture with your camera's burst mode, as was the case with the photos in this illustration.

Tip: The Photomerge Faces tool works similarly to the Photomerge Group Shot tool, except that it's specialized for working with faces. You can have a lot of fun merging different faces into one. Try merging parts of a picture of your own face with one of your spouse to predict the possible appearance of future offspring. Choose File > New > Photomerge Faces, or click the Faces button in the Photomerge panel In Guided Edit mode to create your own Frankenface.

For this exercise however, you'll work with just three distinctly different images to make it easier for you to learn the technique.

1   Make sure you have all three images selected in the Media Browser / Bridge Content panel, and then do one of the following:

* On Windows, choose File > New > Photomerge Group Shot.

* On Mac OS, choose Tools > Photoshop Elements > Photomerge Group Shot.

2 Photoshop Elements has automatically placed the first image (12_02a.jpg) as the source image. Drag the yellow framed image (12_02b.jpg) from the Project Bin and drop it into the Final image pane on the right.

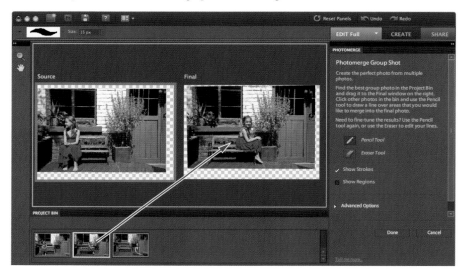

3 Use the Zoom tool to zoom in on the image so you can see all of the girl in the Source image and at least part of the girl in the Final image. Use the Hand tool to reposition the view if necessary.

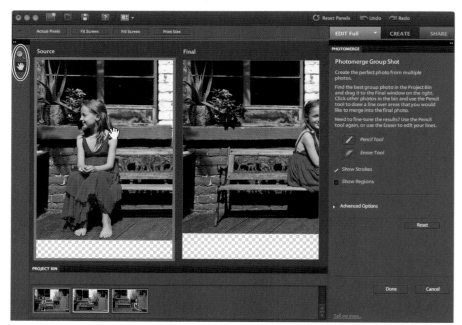

4 In the Photomerge Group Shot panel at the right of the workspace, select the Pencil Tool.

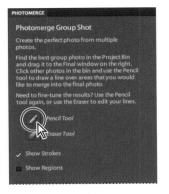

5 With the Pencil tool (...), draw one stroke from head to toe of the girl in the source image, as shown in the illustration below. Be sure to cover her toes and a little of the flooring, as the Source image includes foreground detail not included in the Final—or target—image.

When you release the pointer, Photoshop Elements will merge the girl from the Source image into the Final image—including her shadow below the seat! Seeing the magic of this tool in action will probably cause you some healthy mistrust whenever you come across an unlikely photo in the future.

● **Note:** Sometimes it can be a little tricky to make the perfect selection—especially when you're working with a more complex source image than our example. You may find you are copying more of the source image than you want. If you've switched several times between the Pencil and Eraser tools and you still can't get the selection right, it's better to undo the operation and start again. Try modifying the shape that you're drawing with the Pencil tool and making shorter strokes.

If necessary, use the Pencil tool to add additional image areas from the source. Use the Eraser tool ( ) to delete a stroke—or parts of a stroke—drawn with the Pencil tool. The image copied to the Final image will be adjusted accordingly.

6 Double-click the green framed image (12_02c.jpg) in the Project Bin to make it the Source image. Use the Zoom and Hand tools to move the Source image in its frame so you can see the girl and the floor in front of her; then use the Pencil tool to add her to the Final image. Be sure to include the edges of her dress on the floor and the foreground at the lower right.

7 Use the Hand tool to drag the Source image to the right in its frame so that you can see the parts of the foreground that are missing from the Final image.

8 Use the pencil tool to add the extra foreground detail from the Source image.

9 To see which part of each of the three source images was used for the merged composition, first click the Fit Screen button above the Edit pane so that you can see the entire image, and then activate the Show Regions option in the Photomerge Group Shot panel. The regions in the Final image are color coded.

▶ **Tip:** If you don't see the Fit Screen button and other zoom presets in the bar above the Edit pane, click either tool in the toolbox. Alternatively, double-click the Hand tool to see the entire image.

10 Click the Actual Pixels button above the edit pane, or zoom in even closer, and then use the Hand tool to position the image at a region boundary in the Final image. Toggle Show Regions off and on while you look for imperfections along the region boundaries in the merged image. If necessary, you can use the Pencil and Eraser tools to add to or subtract from the portions of the source images that are being merged to the Final image. When you are satisfied with the result, click Done in the Photomerge Group Shot panel.

11 The merged image needs to be cropped slightly. Do one of the following:

- In Full Edit mode, choose Image > Crop to place a cropping rectangle on the image, and then hold the Shift key as you drag the handles of the cropping rectangle to constrain the aspect ratio to that of the original photo.

- In Guided Edit mode, click Crop Photo in the Basic Photo Edits panel, and then choose Use Photo Ratio from the Crop Box Size menu to maintain the original proportions.

12 Click the Commit button at the bottom right of the cropping rectangle.

● **Note:** The menu command File > Close All is available only in the Full Edit mode. In the Quick Fix and Guided Edit modes you can close only one file at a time using the File > Close command.

13 Choose File > Save and save the merged image to your My CIB Work folder as **12_02_Work**, in Photoshop (.PSD, .PDD) format, making sure that the Layers option is activated. If you are not in Full Edit mode, switch back to it now, and then choose File > Close All.

Removing unwanted intruders

The Photomerge Scene Cleaner helps you improve a photo by removing passing cars, tourists, and other unwanted elements.

This feature works best when you have several shots of the same scene, so that you can combine the unobstructed areas from each source picture to produce a traffic and tourist free photograph.

In fact, when you're sightseeing you should deliberately take a few extra shots of any busy scene so that later you can use the Photomerge Scene Cleaner to put together an unobstructed view.

Setting up on Windows

1   If you're still in the Editor from the last exercise, switch to the Organizer now by clicking the Organizer button (▦) at the top right of the Editor window, and then go on to step 2. If you're beginning a new session, start Photoshop Elements, click the Organize button in the Welcome screen, and then make sure your CIB Catalog is active.

2   In the Organizer, click the Find box beside the Lesson 12 tag in the Keyword Tags panel, and then Ctrl-click to select the images 12_03a.jpg and 12_03b.jpg.

3   Click the small arrow on the orange Fix tab above the Task Pane and choose Full Photo Edit.

Now you're ready to begin the exercise which starts on the next page.

Setting up on Mac OS

1   Start Photoshop Elements if it's not already running.

2   Click Browse With Adobe Bridge in the Welcome Screen or chose File > Browse With Bridge.

3   If you still have the lesson 12 files isolated in the Content panel, you can go on to step 4; otherwise, once Bridge opens choose Edit > Find or press Command+F on your keyboard. In the Find dialog box choose Browse from the Look In menu and locate your PSE8CIB folder. Under Criteria, choose Keywords from the first menu, choose Equals from the second menu, and then type **lesson 12** in the text box. Activate the Include All Subfolders option and click Find.

4   In the Bridge Content panel, Command-click to select the images 12_03a.jpg and 12_03b.jpg.

5   Right-click / Control-click one of the selected images and choose Open With > Adobe Photoshop Elements 8.

Using the Scene Cleaner tool

In this exercise, you'll politely remove a tourist who walked into shot at just the wrong moment.

● **Note:** You can use up to ten images in a single Scene Cleaner operation; the more images you use, the more chance that you'll produce a perfect result.

1 Ctrl-click / Command-click to select both photos in the Photo Bin, and then choose File > New > Photomerge Scene Cleaner.

2 The first image in the Photo Bin, 12_03a.jpg (framed in blue), has been loaded as the Source image. Drag the image framed in yellow, 12_03b.jpg, into the Final pane. This is the image we will clean: the base image for your composite.

3 Zoom in and use the Hand tool to position the images so that you can see the lower right corner. Scroll down in the Photomerge Scene Cleaner panel so that you can see the tools at the bottom.

4 Select the Pencil tool (✎) in the Photomerge Scene Cleaner panel and drag a line through the man's head in the foreground of the Final image.

5 Move the pointer away from the image window and wait a moment while information is copied from the source photo to cover the unwanted area in the Final image.

6 Click the Fit Screen button above the edit window.

You can see that the Source image has some information across the top and down the right hand side of the photo that is missing from the Final image.

7 Make sure the Pencil tool is selected, and then drag a line through those areas in either image.

Tip: You can hold down the Shift key as you drag with the Pencil tool to constrain the movement to a straight line.

8 Working with only two images, there's not a lot more we can do. Click Done in the Photomerge Scene Cleaner panel, and then choose View > Fit On Screen.

9 You can see that there are small empty patches in both the top left corner and the bottom right corner of the photo. You can crop the image to remedy that. Choose Image > Crop and drag the corner handles of the cropping rectangle to maximize the image while avoiding the empty areas. When you're satisfied, click the Commit button in the corner of the bounding box.

10 Choose File > Save. Name the file **12_03_Work** and save it to your My CIB Work folder, in Photoshop (.PSD, .PDD) format with the Layers option activated.

11 Choose File > Close All.

Blending differently exposed photos

There are many common situations where we (or our cameras in automatic mode) are forced to choose between properly exposing the foreground or background. Interior shots often feature overexposed window views where interesting content outside is lost. Subjects posing in front of a brightly lit scene or backlit by a window are often underexposed and appear dark and dull. The classic example is a person posing in front of a city skyline at night; we need a flash to make the most of our foreground subject, but the background is better exposed without it.

The new addition to the Photomerge tools, Photomerge Exposure provides a great new way to deal with photos captured in difficult lighting conditions, enabling you to combine the best-lit areas from two or more images to make the perfect shot.

Setting up on Windows

1 If you're still in the Editor from the last exercise, switch to the Organizer now by clicking the Organizer button (▦) at the top right of the Editor window, and then go on to step 2. If you're beginning a new session, start Photoshop Elements, click the Organize button in the Welcome screen, and then make sure your CIB Catalog is active.

2 In the Organizer, click the Find box beside the Lesson 12 tag in the Keyword Tags panel, and then Ctrl-click to select the images 12_04a.jpg and 12_04b.jpg, two different exposures of a stained-glass window.

3 Click the small arrow on the orange Fix tab above the Task Pane and choose Full Photo Edit.

Now you're ready to begin the exercise which starts on the next page.

Setting up on Mac OS

1 Start Photoshop Elements if it's not already running.

2 Click Browse With Adobe Bridge in the Welcome Screen or chose File > Browse With Bridge.

3 If you still have the lesson 12 files isolated in the Content panel, you can go on to step 4; otherwise, once Bridge opens choose Edit > Find or press Command+F on your keyboard. In the Find dialog box choose Browse from the Look In menu and locate your PSE8CIB folder. Under Criteria, choose Keywords from the first menu, choose Equals from the second menu, and then type **lesson 12** in the text box. Activate the Include All Subfolders option and click Find.

4 In the Bridge Content panel, Command-click to select the images 12_04a.jpg and 12_04b.jpg, two different exposures of a stained-glass window.

5 Right-click / Control-click either of the selected images, and then choose Open With > Adobe Photoshop Elements 8.

Using the Photomerge Exposure tool

When you're faced with difficult lighting conditions, simply take two or more shots with different exposures and let the Photomerge Exposure tool blend them together. Photomerge Exposure has two modes: Automatic and Manual; Photoshop Elements can detect if a set of images was taken with the exposure bracketing feature on your camera or with and without flash, and will default to either Automatic or Manual mode respectively.

Merging exposures automatically

For this exercise you'll work with two interior shots of a stained-glass window captured with exposure bracketing. One shot is exposed correctly for the dimly lit interior but the window shows no color or detail; the other captures the stained glass well, but has none of the detail of the church walls and vaulted ceiling.

1 Ctrl-click / Command-click to select both photos in the Photo Bin, and then choose File > New > Photomerge Exposure. Wait while Photoshop Elements aligns the content in the source photos and creates the composite image.

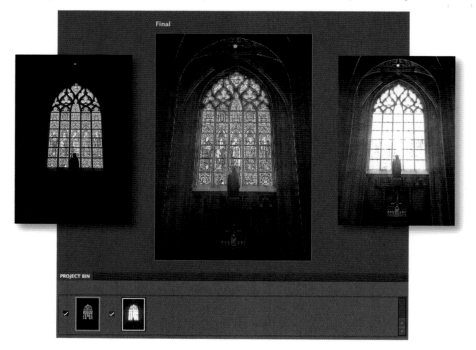

Photomerge Exposure has defaulted to Automatic mode for these exposure brack-eted shots, and has successfully combined the differently exposed areas to produce an image that looks like what we actually saw but couldn't capture in a single shot.

2 Use the Zoom and Hand tools to inspect the merged image.

Adjusting the automatically merged image

Even in Automatic mode, Photomerge Exposure provides you with controls to fine-tune the way the source images are combined.

1   If necessary, click the Fit Screen button above the Edit pane or double-click the Hand tool so that you can see the entire image.

2   To increase the contrast in the blended image, drag the Shadows slider in the Photomerge Exposure panel to the left to set a Shadows value of -50. Alternatively, you can type the new value in the associated text box.

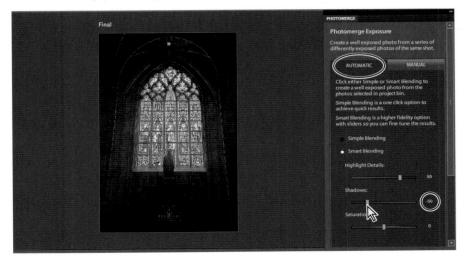

3   Use the Zoom tool to zoom in on the stained-glass window. Increase the Highlight Details value to 100 and the Saturation value to 10.

4   Click Done, and then wait while the merged image file is generated.

5   Choose File > Save. Name the file **12_04_Work** and save it to your My CIB Work folder, in the default Photoshop (.PSD, .PDD) format with the Layers option activated.

6   Choose File > Close All.

Merging exposures manually

Photomerge Exposure does a great job of merging your exposure bracketed shots automatically, producing good results in Automatic mode for most backlit situations. When Photoshop Elements detects shots taken with Flash / No Flash, Photomerge Exposure defaults to Manual mode.

Select two or more images in the Photo Bin, and then choose File > New > Photomerge Exposure. Depending on your photos, Photomerge Exposure may open in Manual or Automatic mode.

You can easily switch modes by clicking the Manual and Automatic tabs in the Photomerge Exposure panel.

On the Manual tab you'll find basic instructions together with the Selection (Pencil) tool—for identifying the areas you wish to copy from the Foreground (source) image—and the Eraser tool for modifying your selection.

There are also controls for showing or hiding Selection tool strokes and the color-coded regions indicating the areas being contributed to the blend by each source image.

Activating the Edge Blending option will smooth the edges between merged regions and the Transparency slider lets you fine tune the way each source photo is blended into the final composite image.

For more detail on using the Photomerge Exposure feature, please refer to Photoshop Elements Help.

Combining multiple photographs in one file

In this project, you'll combine three photos into one—yet another way to use the power of Photoshop Elements to produce that great image that you never actually captured.

You'll apply a clipping mask to one image in order to blend it smoothly into the background picture; then, you'll add a selection from another photo and learn how to remove the colored fringe that is often visible surrounding such a selection.

Your final work file will retain the original pixel information from all three source images, so you can go back and make adjustments to your composition at any time.

Setting up on Windows

1 If you're still in the Editor from the last exercise, switch to the Organizer now by clicking the Organizer button (▦) at the top right of the Editor window, and then go on to step 2. If you're beginning a new session, start Photoshop Elements, click the Organize button in the Welcome screen, and then make sure your CIB Catalog is active.

2 In the Organizer, click the Find box beside the Lesson 12 tag in the Keyword Tags panel, and then Ctrl-click to select the images 12_05a.jpg and 12_05b.jpg, images of a European castle and an airplane.

3 Click the small arrow on the orange Fix tab above the Task Pane and choose Full Photo Edit.

Now you're ready to begin the exercise which starts on the next page.

Setting up on Mac OS

1 Start Photoshop Elements if it's not already running.

2 Click Browse With Adobe Bridge in the Welcome Screen or chose File > Browse With Bridge.

3 If you still have the lesson 12 files isolated in the Content panel, you can go on to step 4; otherwise, once Bridge opens choose Edit > Find or press Command+F on your keyboard. In the Find dialog box choose Browse from the Look In menu and locate your PSE8CIB folder. Under Criteria, choose Keywords from the first menu, choose Equals from the second menu, and then type **lesson 12** in the text box. Activate the Include All Subfolders option and click Find.

4 In the Bridge Content panel, Command-click to select the images 12_05a.jpg and 12_05b.jpg, images of a European castle and an airplane.

5 Right-click / Control-click one of the selected images and choose Open With > Adobe Photoshop Elements 8.

Arranging the image layers

In this exercise, you'll combine two images to make a background to which you'll later add foreground figures. You'll blend an image of a flying airplane into a scenic photograph of King Ludwig's castle in Bavaria—the masterpiece that inspired Disney's Sleeping Beauty castle.

1   Click the Arrange button (⊞) at the top of the workspace and choose Tile All Horizontally, the option at the right of the top row of layout icons in the menu.

2   Click the title tab of the image 12_05b.jpg (the airplane) to make it the active window. Select the Move tool (⊹) and hold down the Shift key as you drag the airplane onto the image of the castle. When a highlight outline appears around the castle photo, release the mouse button and then release the Shift key.

3   Close the image 12_05b.jpg (the one you just copied from).

4   In the Layers panel, select Layer 1 (the airplane). Choose Image > Resize > Scale. In the tool options bar, make sure Constrain Proportions is activated, and then type **50%** in the W (width) field. The image is scaled proportionally. Click the Commit button in the lower right corner of the bounding box.

5 With the Move tool, drag the airplane on Layer 1 right into the upper right corner of the image. Drag the lower left handle of the bounding box to reduce the size of the airplane image further, as shown in the illustration below.

6 Release the mouse button, and then click the Commit button in the corner of the bounding box to accept the changes.

Creating a gradient clipping mask

A clipping mask allows part of an image to show while hiding the rest by making it transparent. In the next steps you'll create a gradient that fades from fully opaque to fully transparent, and then use this gradient as a clipping mask to blend the castle and aircraft layers together.

1 Click the New Layer button ( ) at the bottom of the Layers panel to create a new blank layer, named Layer 2.

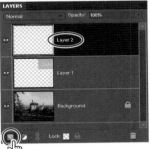

2 In the toolbox, select the Gradient tool ( ) and click the Default Foreground And Background Colors button beside the foreground and background color swatches, or press the D key on your keyboard.

3 In the tool options bar, click the arrow to open the gradient selection menu. Locate the Foreground To Transparent thumbnail (the name of the swatch appears in a tooltip when you roll the cursor over it). Double-click the Foreground To Transparent gradient swatch.

4 Set up the other settings in the tool options bar as you see in the illustration. Click the Radial Gradient (▣) button. Set the Mode to Normal, the Opacity to 100%, disable Reverse, and activate Transparency.

5 Make sure that Layer 2 is still selected in the Layers panel. Drag a short line downwards from the center of the airplane with the Gradient tool, and then release the mouse button.

The circular gradient appears on layer 2, fading from opaque black in the center and gradually becoming transparent at the edges.

You'll use this gradient as a clipping mask for the image of the airplane in Layer 1, leaving the airplane visible while the sky surrounding it blends smoothly into the sky in the background image.

Applying the clipping mask to a layer

Now that you have your gradient layer, it's time to put it to work.

1 In the Layers panel, drag Layer 2—the layer with the new gradient—to reposition it below Layer 1.

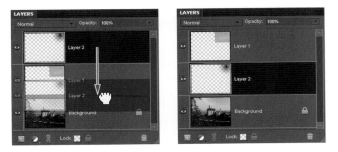

2 In the Layers panel, select Layer 1, now the top layer, and then choose Layer > Create Clipping Mask.

This action defines Layer 2 as the clipping mask for Layer 1. In the Layers panel, Layer 1 is now indented and shows a tiny arrow beside its thumbnail, pointing down to Layer 2. In the image window, the image of the airplane image now blends nicely with the sky in the castle photo.

3 Choose File > Save As. In the Save As dialog box, name the file **12_05_Work** and save it to your My CIB Work folder, in Photoshop (.PSD, .PDD) format with the Layers option activated. On Windows, disable Save In Version Set With Original. Click Save. If the Photoshop Elements Format Options dialog box appears, keep Maximize Compatibility selected and click OK. Keep the merged image open for the next exercise.

Creating a clean edge with defringing

Defringing removes the annoying halo of color that often surrounds a selection pasted into another image. In this exercise you'll composite an image of a family so that they appear to be standing in front of the fence in the castle picture by selecting and deleting the background and using the Defringe feature to blend the selection halo into the background.

1   Do one of the following:

   • On Windows, switch to the Organizer, select the file 12_05c.jpg—the picture of the family—and open it in Full Edit mode.

   • On Mas OS, click the Launch Bridge button at the top of the workspace. In the Bridge Content panel, right-click / Control-click the file 12_05c.jpg (a picture of a family) and choose Open With > Adobe Photoshop Elements 8.

2   With the image 12_05c.jpg selected as the active window in the Edit pane, choose Select > All. Choose Edit > Copy, and then File > Close. Select the Background layer of the image 12_05_Work.psd, and then choose Edit > Paste. The image of the family is placed on a new layer, named Layer 3, just above the background layer.

3   With Layer 3 still selected in the Layers panel, choose Image > Resize > Scale.

4   In the tool options bar, make sure Constrain Proportions is activated, and then type **80** in the W (width) field. Click the Commit button near the lower right corner of the bounding box to accept the changes.

5 If necessary, scroll to see the lower left corner of the image in the document window. Select the Move tool and drag the image in Layer 3 to position it flush with the lower left corner of the castle image.

6 Select the Magic Wand tool (✦). In the tool options bar, set the Tolerance to **25**, activate Anti-alias, and disable Contiguous and Sample All Layers. Click on the pink-colored background of the family image with the Magic Wand tool. If necessary, hold down the Shift key and click to select any unselected pink areas in the background.

7 Press the Delete key to delete the pink background, and then press Ctrl+D / Command+D, or choose Select > Deselect to clear the selection.

8 Zoom in to the area between the man's right hand and his sweater in the lower left corner of the image. A pinkish fringe or halo is clearly visible here.

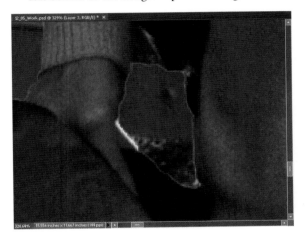

9 Choose Enhance > Adjust Color > Defringe Layer. In the Defringe dialog box, enter **1** pixel for the width and click OK. The fringe is eliminated.

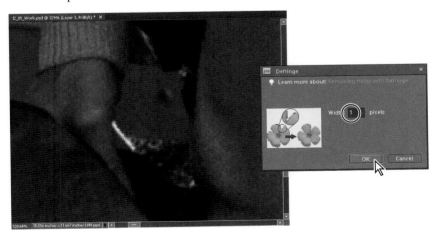

10 Double-click the Hand tool in the toolbox, or choose View > Fit On Screen to fit the whole image in the edit window.

11 Make sure that Layer 3 is still selected in the Layers panel. Select the Move tool in the toolbox and drag the top right handle of the selection rectangle to enlarge the image of the family so that they become more the focus of the composition. Click the Commit button near the lower right corner of the selection rectangle to accept the changes.

12 Choose File > Save, and then close the document.

Congratulations, you've completed the last exercise in this lesson. You've learned how to create a stunning composite panorama, how to merge multiple photos into the perfect group shot, how to remove obstructions from a view, and how to compose several photos into a single image by arranging layers and using a gradient layer as a clipping mask. You've also gained some experience with solving difficult lighting problems by combining shots taken at different exposures.

Take a moment to work through the lesson review on the next page before you move on to the next chapter, "Advanced Editing Techniques."

Review questions

1 In the Photomerge dialog box, which tools can be used to fine-tune a panorama created from multiple images, and how do they work?

2 What does the Photomerge Group Shot tool do?

3 Why is it that sometimes when you think you're finished with a transformation in Photoshop Elements you cannot select another tool or perform other actions?

4 Why does Photomerge Exposure open sometimes in Automatic mode and at others in Manual mode?

5 What is a fringe and how can you remove it?

Review answers

1 The Select Image tool is used to select a specific image from within the merged panorama. This tool can also be used to drag an image so that it lines up more closely with the other images in the panorama. The Rotate Image tool is used to rotate merged images so that their content aligns seamlessly. The Set Vanishing Point tool is used to specify the vanishing point for the perspective in the panorama. Setting the vanishing point in a different photo changes the point around which the other photos will be stretched and skewed to match the perspective.

2 With the Photomerge Group Shot tool you can pick and choose the best parts of several pictures taken successively, and merge them together to form one perfect picture.

3 Photoshop Elements is waiting for you to confirm the transformation by clicking the Commit button, or by double-clicking inside the transformation boundary.

4 Photomerge Exposure detects whether your source photos were taken with exposure bracketing or with and without flash and defaults to Automatic or Manual mode accordingly. Manual mode works better for source files taken with flash/no flash.

5 A fringe is the annoying halo of color that often surrounds a selection pasted into another image. When the copied area is pasted onto another background color, or the selected background is deleted, pixels of the original background color show around the edges of your selection. The Defringe Layer command (Enhance > Adjust Color > Defringe Layer) blends the halo away so you won't see an artificial-looking edge.

13 ADVANCED EDITING TECHNIQUES

Lesson Overview

In this final chapter you'll learn some advanced editing techniques and try some of the innovative tools that Adobe Photoshop Elements delivers to help you improve the quality and clarity of your images.

Discover the benefits of working with raw image files and how the power and simplicity of the Camera Raw plug-in makes it easy for you to achieve professional-looking results with color correction and tonal adjustment. Save your raw files in the versatile DNG format and take advantage of Camera Raw's non-destructive editing.

Enjoy the creative possibilities of combining and calibrating multiple filters, creating your own special effects to turn your photos into art.

This lesson will introduce some essential concepts and skills for making the most of your photos:

- Working with raw images
- Converting files to DNG format
- Using the histogram to assess a photo
- Improving the quality of highlights and shadows
- Resizing and sharpening an image
- Creating custom effects in the filter gallery
- Using the Cookie Cutter tool

 You'll probably need between one and two hours to complete this lesson.

Discover the advantages of working with raw images in the Camera Raw window, where the easy-to-use controls make it simple to correct and adjust your photos like a professional. Learn how to use the Histogram panel to help you understand what a less-than-perfect picture needs and to give you visual feedback on the solutions you apply. Finally, have some fun putting together your own filter effects.

Getting started

Before you start working on the exercises in this lesson, make sure that you have installed the software on your computer from the application CD (see the Photoshop Elements 8 documentation) and that you have correctly copied the Lessons folder from the CD in the back of this book onto your computer's hard disk. (See "Copying the Classroom in a Book files" on page 2.)

This lesson builds on the skills and concepts covered in the earlier chapters and assumes that you are already familiar with the main features of the Photoshop Elements workspace. Should you need to brush up on the basic concepts, see Lesson 1, "A Quick Tour of Photoshop Elements" and Photoshop Elements Help.

Working with camera raw images

In this first exercise you'll be working with a raw image from a Nikon camera as you explore the correction and adjustment controls in the Camera Raw window.

Locating the lesson file by text on Windows

1   Open Photoshop Elements and click the Organize button in the Welcome screen. When the Organizer has opened, check the name of the currently loaded catalog displayed in the lower left corner of the workspace. If your CIB Catalog is not already loaded, choose File > Catalog and select it from the list in the Catalog Manager.

2   Once the CIB Catalog has loaded, type the word **greek** in the Text Search box, at the left of the bar above the Media Browser pane.

● **Note:** For more detailed information on searching by text in the Organizer (Windows), see the section "Find photos using a text search" in Lesson 4.

3   The Media Browser displays a single photo: 13_01_GreekRelief.NEF—a detail of a classical sculpture. Select the image in the Media Browser, click the small arrow on the orange Fix tab above the Task Pane and choose Full Photo Edit.

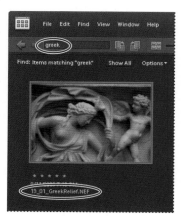

4   When the image opens in the Camera Raw window, make sure that the Preview checkbox above the image pane is activated. Now you're ready for the first exercise which begins on the next page.

Locating the lesson file by text on Mac OS

1   Start Photoshop Elements and click Browse With Adobe Bridge in the Welcome Screen. If Photoshop Elements opens without displaying the Welcome Screen, choose File > Browse With Bridge and wait until Bridge opens.

2   In Bridge, click the link to your PSE8CIB folder in the Favorites panel, or use another method to navigate to the PSE8CIB folder and select it.

3   Click the magnifying glass icon in the Search text box at the top right of the workspace and choose Bridge Search: Current Folder. Type the word **greek** in the text box; then press Return.

● **Note:** For more detailed information on searching by text in Bridge, see the section "Find photos using a text search" in Lesson 5

4   The Content panel displays a single photo: 13_01_GreekRelief.NEF—a detail of a classical sculpture. Right-click / Control-click the file and choose Open With > Adobe Photoshop Elements 8. When the Camera Raw window opens, make sure that the Preview checkbox above the image pane is activated.

Improving a camera raw image

On the right side of the Camera Raw window is a control panel with three tabs: Basic, Detail, and Camera Calibration. For this exercise you'll use the Basic tab which provides controls for image correction that allow you to make adjustments that are not possible with the standard editing tools in Photoshop Elements.

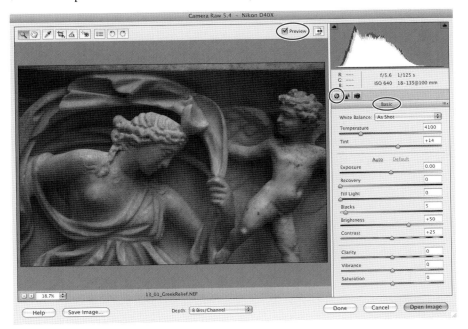

When you open a camera raw file, Photoshop Elements reads information in the file to ascertain which model of camera created it and applies the appropriate camera settings to the image data. In the control panel Options menu you can save your own settings as the default for the camera that created the image by choosing Save New Camera Raw Defaults, or have Photoshop Elements use the default settings for your camera by choosing Reset Camera Raw Defaults.

Note: Adjustments made to a raw file are actually only applied when saving to an output format—the raw image data remains unchanged. For other image formats, each adjustment-save cycle degrades the image data quality.

Any kind of edit or adjustment you make to a digital photograph will result in some loss of image data. However, because a RAW file contains much more information to begin with, any changes made to settings such as exposure and white balance will have less impact in terms of data loss than the same adjustments would have if made to a .PSD, Tiff or JPEG file.

Workflow overview for raw images

To make use of the raw image editing capabilities in Photoshop Elements, you'll first need to set your camera to save images in its own raw format.

After processing the raw file in the Camera Raw window, you can then open the image in Photoshop Elements, where you can work with it in the same way as you would with any other photo. You can save the results in any format supported by Photoshop Elements.

Photoshop Elements can open raw files only from supported cameras. To see an up-to-date list of the currently supported camera models and file formats, visit: www.adobe.com/products/photoshop/cameraraw.html.

Note: The RAW plug-in, used to open raw files from a digital camera, is updated over time as new cameras are added to the list of those supported. You can check for updates and download the latest version of the plug-in at www.adobe.com.

What is a raw image?

Raw files are referred to as such because, unlike many of the more common image file formats that you may recognize, such as JPEG or GIF, they are unprocessed by the digital camera or image scanner. In other words, a raw file contains all the unprocessed image data captured for every pixel by the camera's sensors, without any software instructions about how that data is to be interpreted and displayed as an image on any particular device.

A limited but basically effective analogy or model for understanding the distinction is the difference between sending a film off for automatic processing by a commercial machine and using your own darkroom where you can control everything from the development of the negative to the way the image is exposed and printed onto paper.

The benefits of working with a raw image

Raw images are high-quality image files that contain the maximum amount of original image data in a relatively small file size. Though larger than a compressed image such as a JPEG file, a raw image contains more data than a TIFF image and uses less space.

Many types of image processing result in loss of data, effectively degrading the quality of the image. If a camera produces compressed files for instance, some data deemed superfluous is discarded. If a camera maps the whole range of captured image data to a defined color space, the spread of the image data can be narrowed. Processes such as sharpening and white balance correction will also alter the original captured data.

Whether you are an amateur photographer or a professional, it can be difficult to understand all the process settings on your digital camera and just what they mean in terms of data loss and image degradation. One solution is to use the camera's raw setting. Raw images are derived directly from the camera's sensors, prior to any camera data processing. Not all digital cameras have the capability to capture raw images, but many of the newer and more advanced cameras do offer this option.

Capturing your photos in a raw format means you have more flexibility when it comes to producing the image you want. Many of the camera settings such as sharpening, white balance, levels, and color adjustments can be undone when you're working with your image in Photoshop Elements. For instance, automatic adjustments to exposure can be undone and recalculated based on the raw data.

Another advantage is that, with 12 bits of data per pixel, it's possible to extract shadow and highlight detail from a raw image that would have been lost in the 8 bits/channel JPEG or TIFF formats.

Raw files provide an archival image format, much like a digital negative. In much the same way that you could produce a range of vastly different prints from the same film negative in a darkroom, you can reprocess a raw file repeatedly to achieve whatever results you want. Photoshop Elements doesn't save your changes to the original raw file; rather, it saves the settings you used to process it.

Note: Raw filenames have different extensions, depending on the camera used to capture the image. Examples are Canon's CRW and CR2, Epson's ERF, Fuji's RAF, Kodak's KDE and DER, Minolta's MRW, Olympus' ORF, Pentax's PTX and PEF, Panasonic's RAW, and the various flavors of Nikon's NEF.

Adjusting the white balance

The Camera Raw white balance presets can be helpful when you need to compensate for a color cast caused by incorrect camera settings or poor lighting conditions when an image was captured. For example, if your camera was not correctly set up to deal with overcast conditions, you could correct your image by choosing the Cloudy preset from the White Balance menu.

In the case of our lesson image the subject is virtually monochromatic; there is no outside reference by which to set a naturalistic color balance or make a judgement about a color cast without knowledge of the subject and the lighting conditions in which it was captured.

If we knew, for instance, that in reality the stone had a bluish appearance, we could make adjustments accordingly. If we knew that the photo was taken under incandescent or fluorescent lighting, we could use the appropriate white balance preset, either "as is" or as a starting point for manual fine-tuning. Even without such reference, the white balance settings can help to improve the tonal range and can also be used creatively to achieve atmospheric and dramatic color effects.

1 Experiment with some of the presets available in the White Balance menu. Compare the Auto, Daylight, and Tungsten settings. In the following pages you'll discover why setting the appropriate white balance is so important to the overall look of the image.

| Auto | Daylight | Tungsten |

2 For now, choose As Shot from the White Balance presets menu.

3 Zoom into the image by choosing 100% from the Zoom Level menu in the lower left corner of the preview window.

4 Select the Hand tool (🖐) from the tools above the preview window and drag the image so that you can see the braided hair above the woman's face.

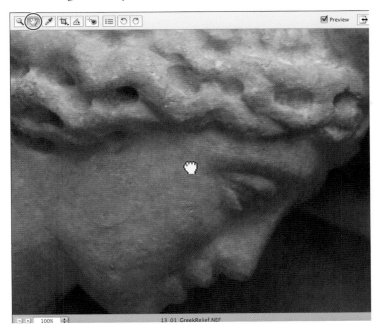

5 Select the White Balance tool (✐), right beside the Hand tool in the tool bar.

To correct a color cast in an image, use the White Balance eyedropper to sample a neutral color—the ideal choice is a mid-light gray that is neither too warm or cool.

6 In the absence of a real reference for a neutral tone in our lesson image, sample the pale chipped area on the braid, which we can assume to be relatively free of discoloration due to aging. If you see little effect, click a slightly different point.

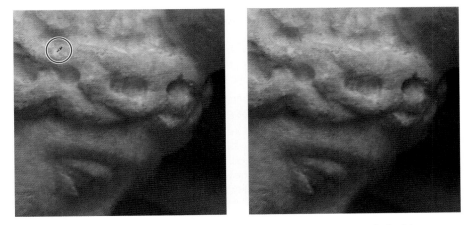

The White Balance is now set to Custom and the image has lost its slight blue cast.

7 Zoom out by choosing Fit In View from the Zoom Level menu in the lower left corner of the preview window.

8 Use the White Balance menu to alternate between your custom settings and the As Shot preset, noting the differences in the settings for Temperature and Tint.

9 Repeat step 8 for each of the other white balance presets, comparing the position of the sliders and look of the image to your custom adjustment. When you're done, return the white balance to your custom setting.

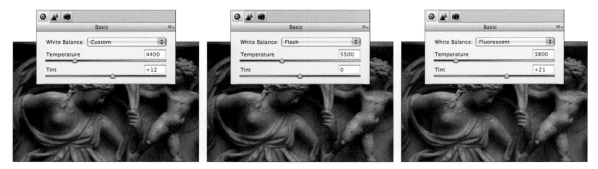

Camera Raw white balance settings

A digital camera records the white balance at the time of exposure as metadata, which you can see when you open the file in the Camera Raw dialog box. This setting usually yields the correct color temperature. You can adjust it if the white balance is not quite right. The Basic tab in the Photoshop Camera Raw dialog box includes three controls for correcting a color cast in your image:

White Balance Sets the color balance of the image to reflect the lighting conditions under which the photo was taken. A white balance preset may produce satisfactory results or you may want to customize the Temperature and Tint settings.

Temperature Fine-tunes the white balance to a custom color temperature. Move the slider to the left to correct a photo taken in light of a lower color temperature; the plug-in makes the image colors bluer to compensate for the lower color temperature of yellowish ambient light. Move the slider to the right to correct a photo taken in light of higher color temperature; the plug-in makes the image colors warmer to compensate for the higher color temperature of bluish ambient light.

Tint Fine-tunes the white balance to compensate for a green or magenta tint. Move the slider to the left to add green to the photo; move it to the right to add magenta.

To adjust the white balance quickly, click an area in the preview image that should be a neutral gray or white with the White Balance tool. The Temperature and Tint sliders automatically adjust to make the selected color as close to neutral as possible. If you're using a white area to set the white balance, choose a highlight area that contains significant white detail rather than a specular highlight.

—From Photoshop Elements Help

Working with the Temperature and Tint settings

The White Balance tool can accurately remove any color cast or tint from an image but you may still want to tweak the Temperature and Tint settings. Depending on the subject matter and the effect you wish to achieve, you might actually want a slight, controlled color tint. In this instance, the color temperature seems fine, but you can fine-tune the green/magenta balance of the image using the Tint control.

1 If you don't see the entire image in the Camera Raw preview zoom out by double-clicking the Hand tool or by choosing Fit In View from the Zoom Level menu in the lower left corner of the preview window.

2 Test the Temperature slider in the Basic tab by dragging it from one end of its range to the other. You'll see that the colors of the image become cooler or warmer as you move the slider. In this case, the corrected temperature of the image seemed fine but this slider could help you on other occasions—for toning down the overly warm tones resulting from tungsten lighting, for example.

3 Reset the Temperature control to the corrected value of 4400 either by dragging the slider or typing the value **4400** into the Temperature text box.

4 Experiment with the extremes of the Tint slider. The corrected value was +12. Change the setting to +8 with the slider or type **+8** in the Tint text box.

Using the tone controls on a raw image

The settings for tonal adjustments are located below the White Balance controls on the Basic tab. In this exercise, you'll use these controls to correct exposure, check highlights and shadows, and adjust brightness, contrast, and saturation. Before you adjust any of the settings, you should understand what each of the controls does:

Exposure adjusts the lightness or darkness of an image. Underexposed images are too dark and look dull and murky; overexposed images are too light and look washed out. Use the Exposure control to lighten an underexposed image or correct the faded look of an overexposed image.

Recovery attempts to recover details from burned-out highlights. The Recovery control can reconstruct some detail in areas where one or two color channels have been clipped to white. Clipping occurs when a pixel's color values are higher or lower than the range that can be represented in the image; over-bright values are clipped to output white, and over-dark values are clipped to output black.

Fill Light recovers details from shadows, without brightening blacks. The Fill Light control does something close to the inverse of the Recovery control, reconstructing detail in areas where one or two of the color channels have been clipped to black.

Blacks specifies which input levels are mapped to black in the final image. Raising the Blacks value expands the areas that are mapped to black.

Brightness adjusts the brightness of the image, much as the Exposure slider does. However, instead of clipping the image in the highlights (areas that are completely white, with no detail) or shadows (areas that are completely black, with no detail), Brightness compresses the highlights and expands the shadows when you move the slider to the right. In general, it's best to use the Brightness slider to adjust the overall brightness after you have set the white and black clipping points with the Exposure and Blacks sliders.

Contrast is the amount of difference in brightness between light and dark areas of an image. The Contrast control determines the number of shades in the image, and has the most noticeable effect in the midtones. An image without enough contrast can appear flat or washed out. Use the Contrast slider to adjust the midtone contrast after setting the Exposure, Blacks, and Brightness values.

Clarity sharpens the definition of edges in the image. This process helps restore detail and sharpness that tonal adjustments may reduce.

Vibrance adjusts the saturation so that clipping is minimized as colors approach full saturation, acting on all lower saturated colors but having less impact on higher saturated colors. Vibrance also prevents skin tones from becoming oversaturated.

Saturation is the purity, or strength, of a color. A fully saturated color contains no gray. The Saturation control makes colors more vivid (containing less black or white) or more muted (containing more black or white).

First you'll adjust the Exposure setting, checking for clipping in the brighter areas.

1 Hold down the Alt / Option key as you drag the Exposure slider to see which parts of the image will be forced towards white as the highlights are clipped. Set the Exposure to +2.25. You can clearly see the clipping indicated the histogram.

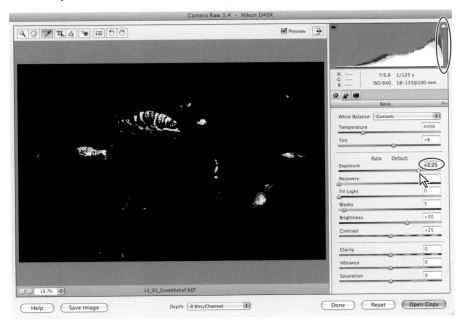

2 Now hold down Alt / Option as you drag the Recovery slider to 15. Most of the clipping is corrected, as you can see in both the preview and the histogram. However, we do not really expect to find any true whites in this image, so without changing the Recovery setting you can reduce the Exposure to 1.25, noting the effect on the image and the movement of the histogram curve.

3 Hold down the Alt / Option key and drag the Blacks slider to the right. Areas that appear in the clipping preview will be forced to a solid black. Release the mouse button when only the deepest shadows register as black. We set the Blacks value to 18.

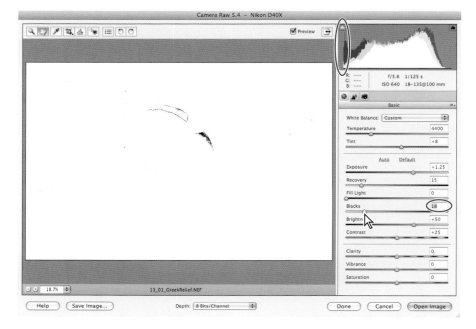

4 Click the Brightness slider and press the up arrow on the keyboard to increase the value to 65. Click the Contrast slider and press the up arrow key on the keyboard to increase the value to 35. Drag the Clarity slider to 30.

The image, which was actually shot in a very poorly lit interior, looked dull, a little indistinct, and far too dark. It now shows a broader range of detail and is more vivid; the color is warmer and the tones are much closer to what we would expect of aged white marble.

Saving the image

By saving this raw file in the DNG format you can reprocess it repeatedly to achieve a different result as many times as you want. Photoshop Elements doesn't save your changes to the original raw file—it simply saves a separate record of all your adjustments and settings; the original image data remains intact.

About the DNG format

Raw file formats are becoming common in digital photography. However, each camera manufacturer has its own proprietary raw format. This means that not every raw file can be read by software other than that provided with the camera. This may make it difficult to use these images in the future, as the manufacturers might not support every format indefinitely. Proprietary formats are also a problem if you want to use software other than that supplied by the camera manufacturers.

To help alleviate these problems, you can save raw images in Photoshop Elements in the DNG format, a publicly available archival format for raw files generated by digital cameras. The DNG format provides an open standard for files created by different camera models, and helps to ensure that you will be able to access your files in the future.

1   To convert and save the image, click the Save Image button at the lower left of the Camera Raw dialog box. The Save Options dialog box appears.

2   Under Destination, click Select Folder. In the Select Destination Folder dialog box, navigate to and open your Lessons folder; then click to highlight your My CIB Work folder and click Select.

3   Under File Naming, leave Document Name selected in the menu on the left. Click the menu on the right and select 1 Digit Serial Number. This will add the number 1 to the end of the file name.

4 Click Save. The file, together with all your current settings, will be saved in DNG format, which you can reprocess repeatedly without losing the original data.

5 Click the Open Image button in the right lower corner of the Camera Raw dialog box. Your image will open in a regular image window in Photoshop Elements.

6 Choose File > Save. Navigate to your My CIB Work folder, name the file 13_01_GreekRelief_Work.psd, and choose the Photoshop format.

7 Click Save, and then choose File > Close.

You've now experienced some of the advantages of using a camera raw format. Even though this format gives you more control and allows you to edit your image in a non-destructive way, a lot of professionals choose not to use raw images. Raw files are usually considerably bigger than high-quality JPEGs and take much longer to be saved in your camera—quite a disadvantage for action shots or when you're taking a lot of pictures.

About histograms

For your images in JPEG, TIFF, and PSD formats, you'll do most of your serious editing in Full Edit mode.

In this part of the lesson, you'll learn how to use the histogram in Full Edit mode as a tool both to help you understand an image's deficiencies and to give you feedback as you make changes to improve its quality.

In the following exercises, you'll work on an image that was shot in poor lighting and also has a slight magenta cast. This is quite a common problem—many digital cameras introduce a slight color cast into images.

Using the histogram

A histogram is a graph that maps the spread of tonal ranges present in an image. The Histogram panel in Full Edit mode (Window > Histogram), indicates whether an image contains enough tonal detail in the shadows (at the left end of the curve), in the midtones, and in the highlights (at the right end of the curve). The histogram can help you recognize where changes need to be made in the image, and to see which adjustments are effective.

In the histogram below it's very apparent that there is not a good spread of tonal information in this image. You can see clearly that the image is deficient in the midtones, which is why it has a flat appearance, lacking in midtone contrast.

Tonal corrections such as lightening an image remove information. Excessive correction causes posterization, or color-banding in the image. The histogram in the illustration below reveals that this image is already lacking detail; you can see gaps, bands, and anomalous spikes in the curve. Any further adjustments made to the image will only degrade it more.

Understanding highlights and shadows

In the next part of this lesson, you'll adjust the highlights and shadows and make additional tonal corrections to this photo while keeping an eye on the Histogram.

1 Make sure you are in Full Edit mode. Choose File > Open, navigate to your Lesson13 folder, select the file 13_02.psd and click Open.

2 Choose File > Save As. Name the image **13_02_Work** and save it to your My CIB Work folder in Photoshop (.PSD, .PDD) format.

3   If the Histogram panel is not already visible, choose Window > Histogram. From the Channel menu at the top of the Histogram panel, choose RGB.

4   In order to see the effects of your adjustments more directly, you can drag the Histogram panel and position it beside the face of the girl. You'll notice that the face is a little dark.

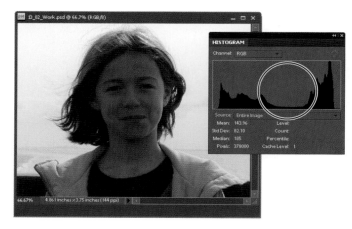

According to the histogram, there is a lack of data in the midtone range for this image—it needs more pixels with values in the midtones and less clustered in the shadows and highlights at either end of the distribution curve. You'll adjust the tonal range of this image using the Levels controls.

Adjusting levels

1   Choose Enhance > Adjust Lighting > Levels. The Levels dialog box appears. Make sure that Preview is activated.

You'll use the shadows, midtone, and highlights sliders (left, middle, and right respectively) below the histogram graph in the Levels panel as well as the Set Black Point, Set Gray Point, and Set White Point eyedroppers (left, middle, and right respectively).

Although the midtones range is the most problematic area of this image, it is important to first adjust the highlights and shadows correctly.

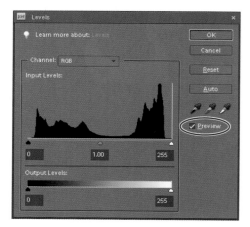

We'll look at two slightly different methods for setting the white and black points in the image using the Levels controls.

2 In the Levels dialog box, hold down the Alt / Option key as you drag the highlights slider to the left to a value of 242—just inside the right-hand end of the tonal curve. The clipping preview shows you where the brightest parts of the image are: a few highlights in the girl's hair and a portion of the sky near the upper right corner of the image.

3 Watch the histogram as you release first the Alt / Option key, and then the mouse button. The curve in the histogram shifts—possibly a bit far—to the right. You can see that the right-hand end of the curve has become truncated. Move the highlights slider in the Levels dialog box to a value of 245. The curve in the histogram is adjusted accordingly.

4 In the Levels dialog box, click Reset and we'll try another method for adjusting the highlights. Select the Set White Point Eyedropper tool and watch the histogram as you click in the brightest part of the sky.

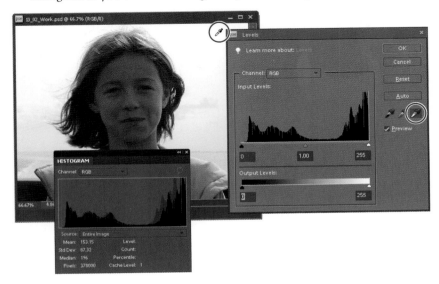

▶ **Tip:** If your image has an easily identified neutral tone, you can remove a color cast quickly using the Set White Point Eyedropper tool. Neutrals are areas in the image that contain only a gray tone mixed with as little color as possible.

The result is very similar to the previous method, but it won't be as easy to fine-tune the clipping at the right end of the curve. Now you'll correct the shadows.

5 Hold down the Alt / Option key and drag the shadow slider to a value of 16. The area below the girl's right ear shows as a dark patch in the clipping preview. Watch the histogram as you release the mouse button and the Alt / Option key.

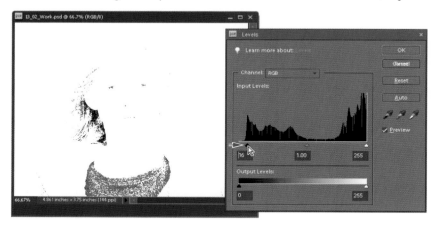

6 In the Levels controls, drag the midtone slider (the gray triangle below the center of the graph) to the left to set the midtone value to 1.50.

7 Notice the change in the Histogram. Compare the original data (displayed in gray) to the data for the corrections that you have made (displayed in black). Some gaps have been created. You want to avoid creating large gaps—even if the image still looks fine on screen, large gaps may cause a loss of data that will be visible as color banding when printed.

8 Click OK to close the Levels dialog box. If an Adobe Photoshop Elements alert dialog box appears, click Yes.

9 Select Edit > Undo Levels, or press Ctrl+Z / Command+Z to see how the image looked prior to redistributing the tonal values. Choose Edit > Redo Levels, or Press Ctrl+Y / Command+Y to reinstate your corrections. Leave this image open for the next part of this lesson.

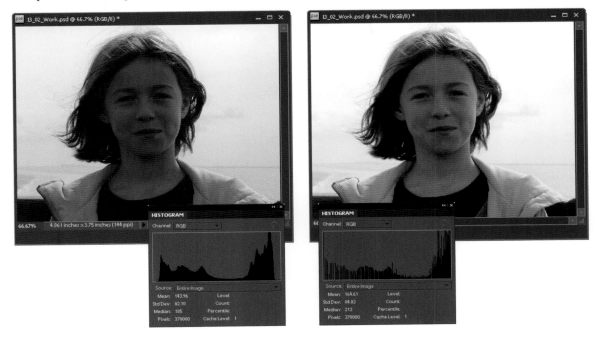

About Unsharp Mask

Now you can add some crispness to the image, which will make it look much better when printed. Using the sharpening tools correctly can improve an image's clarity and impact significantly.

In this exercise you'll use the Unsharp Mask feature in Photoshop Elements. How can something be *un*sharp and yet sharpen an image? The term unsharp mask has it roots in the print production industry: the technique was implemented by making an out-of-focus negative film—the unsharp mask—and then printing the original in a sandwich with this unsharp mask. This produced a halo around the edges of objects—optically giving them more definition.

If you are planning to resize an image, do it before you apply the Unsharp mask filter. The halo effect mentioned above can appear as an obvious artefact if it is scaled with the image.

1 With the file 13_02_Work.psd still open in the Full Edit mode, choose
Image > Resize > Image Size.

This image needs to be made smaller, but with a higher resolution (pixels per inch).

2 If necessary, disable the Resample Image check box at the bottom of the dialog
box, and then type **300** in the Resolution text field. Notice that the width and
height values adjust. This method increases the resolution in the image without
loss of information.

Resolution refers to the fineness of detail you can see in an image, measured in
pixels per inch (ppi): the more pixels per inch, the greater the resolution. Generally,
the higher the resolution of your image, the better the printed result.

3 Now select Resample Image, to reduce the height and width of the image
without affecting the resolution. Click OK.

4 Choose File > Save. Keep the file open for the next part of this lesson.

Applying the Unsharp Mask filter

Before you apply any filter in Adobe Photoshop Elements, it is best to set the zoom
level to 100%.

1 With the file 13_02_Work.psd still open in the Full Edit mode, choose View >
Actual Pixels.

2 Choose Enhance > Unsharp Mask. The Unsharp Mask dialog box appears.

The amount of unsharp masking that you apply is determined by the subject matter. A portrait, such as this image, should be softer than an image of an object
such as an automobile. The adjustments range from 1 to 500, with 500 being the
sharpest.

3 Drag the Amount slider or type **150** in the Amount text field. Leave the Radius
at 1 pixel.

4 Increase the Threshold only slightly to 2 levels. Threshold is a key control in this dialog box, as it tells the filter what not to sharpen. In this case the value 2 means that a pixel will not be sharpened if it is within 2 shades of the pixel beside it (on a scale of 255).

**Tip:** Disable the preview in the Unsharp Mask window by clicking on the preview pane and holding down the mouse button. When you release the mouse button, the preview is enabled again. To see another part of the image, drag the image in the preview pane.

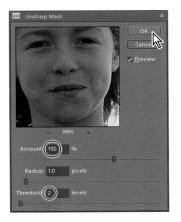

5 Click OK to close the Unsharp Mask dialog box.

6 Choose File > Save, and then File > Close.

Without sharpening.

Unsharp mask applied.

As you've seen, the Unsharp Mask filter can't mysteriously correct the focus of your image. It only gives the impression of crispness by increasing the contrast between adjacent pixels. As a rule of thumb, the Unsharp Mask filter should be applied to an image only once, as a final step in your processing. If you use Unsharp Mask too much, you'll run the risk of over sharpening your image producing artifacts that will give it a flaky, grainy look.

Note: There are other ways to adjust the sharpness of your photos: Choose Enhance > Auto Sharpen or, if you want more control over the sharpening process, choose Enhance > Adjust Sharpness.

Using the filter gallery

▶ **Tip:** Not all filters are available from the Filter Gallery—some are available only individually as Filter menu commands. The Filter Gallery does not offer effects and layer styles as does the Effects panel.

You can have a lot of fun experimenting with filter effects using the Filter Gallery, where you can apply multiple filters to your image and tweak the way they work together, effectively creating new custom effects. Each filter has its own sliders and settings, giving you a great deal of control over the effect on your photo. The possibilities are endless—it's up to you! Have a look at "About Filters" in Photoshop Elements Help to find out more about the different filters.

Setting up on Windows

1   If you're still in the Editor from the last exercise, switch to the Organizer now, and then go on to step 2. If you're beginning a new session, start Photoshop Elements, open the Organizer, and then make sure your CIB Catalog is active.

2   In the Organizer, click the Find box beside the Lesson 13 tag in the Keyword Tags panel, and then select the image 13_03.jpg in the Media Browser.

3   Click the small arrow on the orange Fix tab above the Task Pane and choose Full Photo Edit.

Now you're ready to begin the exercise which starts at the bottom of this page.

Setting up on Mac OS

1   Start Photoshop Elements if it's not already running. Either click Browse With Adobe Bridge in the Welcome Screen or chose File > Browse With Bridge.

2   In Bridge, choose Edit > Find or press Command+F. In the Find dialog box, choose Browse from the Look In menu and locate your PSE8CIB folder. Under Criteria, choose Keywords from the first menu, choose Equals from the second menu, and then type **lesson 13** in the text box. Activate the Include All Subfolders option and click Find.

3   In the Bridge Content panel, right-click / Control-click the image 13_03.jpg and choose Open With > Adobe Photoshop Elements 8.

Creating effects with filters

Many filters use the foreground and background colors currently active in the toolbar to create effects, so you should take a moment to set them now.

▶ **Tip:** It's a good idea to apply filters to a duplicate layer in your image—you can't undo filters after you've saved your file. to duplicate a selected layer, press Ctrl+J / Command+J.

1   Click the Default Foreground And Background Colors button beside the color swatches at the bottom of the toolbar. This resets the default colors: black in the foreground and white for the background.

2   Choose File > Save As. Navigate to your My CIB Work folder, name the file 13_03_Work, choose the Photoshop (.PSD, .PDD) format, and then click Save.

3 Choose Filter > Filter Gallery. If necessary, use the menu in the lower left corner of the Filter Gallery window to set the magnification level to 100%.

4 When you move the pointer over the image in the preview pane, the cursor changes into the hand tool (🖑). If you can't see the entire photo, drag the image in the preview pane so that you can see at least two of the three faces.

▶ **Tip:** When you're working with filters, setting the zoom level to 100% is the best way to judge the effects of the filters you apply.

The center pane in the Filter Gallery window lists the available filters by category.

5 Expand the Brush Strokes category by clicking the arrow to the left of the category name, and then choose the Spatter filter.

6 Experiment with the entire range of the control sliders. You can see the effect of the filter in the preview pane. Set the sliders as shown in the illustration below.

7 Click the New Effect layer button () at the lower right of the Filter Gallery dialog box, expand the Artistic filters category, and choose the Watercolor filter. The Spatter and Watercolor filters are applied simultaneously.

8 Experiment with the full range of the sliders, and then set the Brush Detail to 8, Shadow Intensity to 0, and Texture to 2. Collapse the Artistic filters category.

9 Click the New Effect Layer button () again. Expand the Texture category and select the Grain filter. Experiment with the sliders; then set Intensity to 50, Contrast to 75 and choose Clumped from the Grain Type menu. Once again, the image has changed totally.

Experimenting with filters in the gallery

The possibilities are endless for the effects that you might create in your image by combining different filters at varied settings.

1 Click the button at the top right of the filters pane to hide the filters menu. Choose Fit In View from the zoom menu at the bottom left of the Preview pane.

2 Experiment with the three filters that you've applied, turning them off or on by clicking the eye icon to the left of each filter name.

3 The order of the filters in the list will alter the way they interact. Experiment by dragging the filters to rearrange their order.

4 There is no need to apply the changes to the image; click Cancel to close the Filter Gallery dialog box, keeping the file open for the next exercise.

Using the Cookie Cutter tool

The Cookie Cutter tool enables you to crop an image with one of a library of Cookie Cutter shapes. In this exercise, you'll crop the image with a heart-shaped cutter.

1 Select the Cookie Cutter tool from the toolbox.

▶ **Tip:** There are many more cutout shapes available; click the double arrow in the upper right corner of the shapes panel to see a menu of over 20 different categories.

2 Click the Shapes menu in the tool options bar to view the default selection of shapes. Double-click to select the shape named Heart Card. The name of each shape appears as a tool tip when you move the pointer over its swatch.

3 From the Shape Options menu in the tool options bar, choose From Center.

Set Shape Options

Unconstrained Draws the shape to any size or proportion you'd like.

Defined Proportions Keeps the height and width of the cropping shape in proportion.

Defined Size Crops the photo to the exact size of the shape you choose.

Fixed Size Lets you specify exact measurements for the finished shape.

From Center Draws the shape from the center.

Enter a value for **Feather** to soften the edges of the finished shape.

Note: Feathering softens the edges of the cropped image so that the edges fade out and blend in with the background.

—From Adobe Photoshop Elements Help

4 Drag in the image to create the cutter shape. Press the Shift key as you drag to maintain the original proportions of the shape, or press the Space key to reposition the shape. After releasing the pointer, you can still use the handles on the bounding box to scale the shape. Click inside the bounding box and drag the shape to reposition it.

5 Click the Commit button at the lower right corner of the bounding box, or press Enter / Return to crop the image. To cancel the cropping operation, click the Cancel button or press the Esc key.

6 Choose File > Save, and then File > Close.

Congratulations, you've finished this lesson on advanced editing techniques in Adobe Photoshop Elements. You discovered how to take advantage of the Camera Raw plug-in and learned how to correct images using the Histogram panel as both a diagnostic tool and a feedback reference. You also found out how to create custom effects using the Filter Gallery and had a little fun with the Cookie Cutter tool.

Learning more

We hope you've gained confidence in using Photoshop Elements to bring out the best in your photographs. You've picked up some great tricks and techniques, but this book is just the start. You can learn even more by using the Photoshop Elements Help system, which is built into the application. Also, don't forget to look for tutorials, tips, and expert advice on the Adobe website, www.adobe.com.

Review questions

1 What is a camera raw image, and what are some of its advantages?

2 What are the different methods for adjusting the white balance in the Camera Raw window?

3 How do you use the Levels controls to correct highlights and shadows?

4 What is the Cookie Cutter tool used for?

Review answers

1 A raw file is one that is unprocessed by a digital camera, though not all cameras create raw files. One of the advantages of raw images is the flexibility of having detailed control over settings that are usually pre-applied by the camera. Image quality is another plus—because raw formats have 12 bits of available data, it's possible to extract shadow and highlight detail that would have been lost in an 8 bits/channel JPEG or TIFF file. Finally, raw files provide an archival image format, much like a digital negative: you can reprocess the file whenever you want to produce different results, while your original image data remains unchanged.

2 In the Camera Raw window you can set the white balance in an image automatically by using the White Balance eyedropper. Clicking on a neutral color with the White Balance eyedropper automatically adjusts the Temperature and Tint sliders. Alternatively, you can choose a preset from the White Balance menu. The options include corrections based on a range of common lighting conditions. It's also possible to correct the white balance manually with the Temperature and Tint sliders.

3 In the Levels dialog box, you can adjust the shadows and highlights in your image by using either the slider controls below the Levels histogram, or the Set Black Point and Set White Point eyedroppers. You can hold down the Alt key as you drag a slider to see a clipping preview, which gives you visual feedback on the location of the darkest and lightest areas of your image. With the Set Black Point and Set White Point eyedroppers you can click directly in the image to define the white and black points, or double-click the eyedroppers to call up the color picker where you can define the values precisely.

4 The Cookie Cutter tool is used to crop an image into a variety of shapes. Use the default shapes set, or select a shape from an extensive library.

INDEX

Production Notes

The *Adobe Photoshop Elements 8 Classroom in a Book* was created electronically using Adobe InDesign CS3. Art was produced using Adobe InDesign, Adobe Illustrator, and Adobe Photoshop.

References to company names in the lessons are for demonstration purposes only and are not intended to refer to any actual organization or person.

Team credits

The following individuals contributed to the development of this edition of the *Adobe Photoshop Elements Classroom in a Book*:

Project coordinators, technical writers: John Evans & Katrin Straub

Production: Manneken Pis Productions (www.manneken.be)

Copyediting & Proofreading: John Evans & Katrin Straub

Designer: Katrin Straub

Special thanks to Torsten Buck, Tracey Croom, Victor Gavenda, Connie Jeung-Mills, Petra Laux, and Christine Yarrow.

Typefaces used

Adobe Myriad Pro and Adobe Warnock Pro are used throughout the lessons. For more information about OpenType and Adobe fonts, visit www.adobe.com/type/opentype/.

Photo Credits

Photographic images and illustrations supplied by Torsten Buck, Han Buck, John Evans, Yanin Jotisuta, Rémy Level, Katrin Straub, Rich Willis, and Adobe Systems Incorporated. Photos are for use only with the lessons in the book.

Contributors

 John Evans has worked in computer graphics and design for more than 20 years—initially as a graphic designer, and then since 1993 as a multimedia author, software interface designer, and technical writer. His multimedia and digital illustration work associated with Japanese type attracted an award from Apple Computer Australia. His other projects range from music education software for children to interface design for innovative Japanese font design software. As a technical writer his work includes software design specifications, user manuals, and more recently copyediting for *Adobe Photoshop Elements 7 Classroom in a Book*, *Adobe Photoshop Lightroom 2 Classroom in a Book*, and *Adobe Creative Suite 4 Classroom in a Book*.

 Katrin Straub is an artist, a graphic designer, and author. Her award-winning print, painting, and multimedia work has been exhibited worldwide. With more than 15 years experience in design, Katrin has worked as Design Director for companies such as Landor Associates and Fontworks in the United States, Hong Kong, and Japan. Her work includes packaging, promotional campaigns, multimedia, website design, and internationally recognized corporate and retail identities. She holds degrees from the FH Augsburg, ISIA Urbino, and The New School University in New York. Katrin has authored many books, from the *Adobe Creative Suite Idea Kit* to Classroom in a Book titles for Adobe Photoshop Lightroom 2, Adobe Creative Suite 4, Adobe Soundbooth, and several versions of *Adobe Photoshop Elements Classroom in a Book* and *Adobe Premiere Elements Classroom in a Book*.

 Tao Buck and her sisters have been volunteering as photomodels for the last four editions of the Photoshop Elements Classroom in a Book. When she is not riding her unicycle, Tao wants to become a top model or at least as famous as Audrey Hepburn.

 Zoë Buck loves to juggle with numbers, play chess, do gymnastics, and at this very moment is considering becoming a biologist.

 Han Buck would like to become a rock singer, an architect, a painter (actually, she is one already), or else "work from home and do nothing like her parents."

 Mia Buck strives to become a ballerina and great pianist (although she does not believe in practicing).